TRANZLATY

Language is for everyone

اللغة للجميع

The Call of the Wild

نداء البرية

Jack London

English / العربية

Into the Primitive
إلى البدائية

Buck did not read the newspapers.

لم يقرأ باك الصحف.

Had he read the newspapers he would have known trouble was brewing.

لو كان قد قرأ الصحف لكان قد عرف أن المشاكل كانت تلوح في الأفق.

There was trouble not alone for himself, but for every tidewater dog.

لم تكن هناك مشكلة بالنسبة له وحده، بل بالنسبة لكل كلب من كلاب المد والجزر.

Every dog strong of muscle and with warm, long hair was going to be in trouble.

كل كلب قوي العضلات وذو شعر طويل ودافئ سيكون في ورطة.

From Puget Bay to San Diego no dog could escape what was coming.

من خليج بوغيت إلى سان دييغو لم يتمكن أي كلب من الهروب مما كان قادمًا.

Men, groping in the Arctic darkness, had found a yellow metal.

كان الرجال يبحثون في ظلام القطب الشمالي عن معدن أصفر.

Steamship and transportation companies were chasing the discovery.

وكانت شركات السفن البخارية والنقل تلاحق الاكتشاف.

Thousands of men were rushing into the Northland.

كان الآلاف من الرجال يتدفقون إلى الشمال.

These men wanted dogs, and the dogs they wanted were heavy dogs.

أراد هؤلاء الرجال كلابًا، وكانت الكلاب التي أرادوها كلابًا ثقيلة.

Dogs with strong muscles by which to toil.

الكلاب ذات العضلات القوية التي يمكنها العمل بها.

Dogs with furry coats to protect them from the frost.

كلاب ذات معاطف فروية لحمايتها من الصقيع.

Buck lived at a big house in the sun-kissed Santa Clara Valley.

عاش باك في منزل كبير في وادي سانتا كلارا المشمس.

Judge Miller's place, his house was called.

مكان القاضي ميلر، كان يسمى منزله.

His house stood back from the road, half hidden among the trees.

كان منزله بعيدًا عن الطريق، مخفيًا جزئيًا بين الأشجار.

One could get glimpses of the wide veranda running around the house.

كان من الممكن إلقاء نظرة خاطفة على الشرفة الواسعة التي تحيط بالمنزل.

The house was approached by graveled driveways.

تم الوصول إلى المنزل عبر ممرات مرصوفة بالحصى.

The paths wound about through wide-spreading lawns.

تتعرج المسارات عبر المروج الواسعة.

Overhead were the interlacing boughs of tall poplars.

في الأعلى كانت هناك أغصان متشابكة من أشجار الحور الطويلة.

At the rear of the house things were on even more spacious.

في الجزء الخلفي من المنزل كانت الأمور أكثر اتساعًا.

There were great stables, where a dozen grooms were chatting

كانت هناك اسطبلات رائعة، حيث كان هناك عشرة من العرسان يتحادثون

There were rows of vine-clad servants' cottages

كانت هناك صفوف من أكواخ الخدم المغطاة بالكروم

And there was an endless and orderly array of outhouses

وكان هناك مجموعة لا نهاية لها ومنظمة من المراحيض الخارجية

Long grape arbors, green pastures, orchards, and berry patches.

شرفات العنب الطويلة، والمراعي الخضراء، والبساتين، وبقع التوت.

Then there was the pumping plant for the artesian well.

وبعد ذلك كانت هناك محطة الضخ للبئر الارتوازي.

And there was the big cement tank filled with water.

وكان هناك خزان الأسمنت الكبير المملوء بالماء.

Here Judge Miller's boys took their morning plunge.

هنا أخذ أولاد القاضي ميلر غطستهم الصباحية.

And they cooled down there in the hot afternoon too.

وتبردوا هناك في فترة ما بعد الظهر الحارة أيضًا.

And over this great domain, Buck was the one who ruled all of it.

وعلى هذا النطاق العظيم، كان باك هو الذي يحكم كل ذلك.

Buck was born on this land and lived here all his four years.

وُلِد باك على هذه الأرض وعاش هنا طوال سنواته الأربع.

There were indeed other dogs, but they did not truly matter.

لقد كانت هناك بالفعل كلاب أخرى، لكنها لم تكن ذات أهمية حقيقية.

Other dogs were expected in a place as vast as this one.

كان من المتوقع وجود كلاب أخرى في مكان واسع مثل هذا.

These dogs came and went, or lived inside the busy kennels.

جاءت هذه الكلاب وذهبت، أو عاشت داخل بيوت الكلاب المزدحمة.

Some dogs lived hidden in the house, like Toots and Ysabel did.

بعض الكلاب عاشت مختبئة في المنزل، مثل توتس وإيزابيل.

Toots was a Japanese pug, Ysabel a Mexican hairless dog.

كان توتس كلبًا من فصيلة البج اليابانية، بينما كانت إيزابيل كلبة مكسيكية أصلع.

These strange creatures rarely stepped outside the house.

نادرًا ما كانت هذه المخلوقات الغريبة تخرج من المنزل.

They did not touch the ground, nor sniff the open air outside.

لم يلمسوا الأرض، ولم يشتموا الهواء الطلق في الخارج.

There were also the fox terriers, at least twenty in number.

وكان هناك أيضًا كلاب فوكس تيرير، وكان عددها عشرين على الأقل.

These terriers barked fiercely at Toots and Ysabel indoors.

نبح هؤلاء الكلاب بشدة على توتس وإيزابيل في الداخل.

Toots and Ysabel stayed behind windows, safe from harm.

بقيت توتس وإيزابيل خلف النوافذ، في مأمن من الأذى.

They were guarded by housemaids with brooms and mops.

وكانوا تحت حراسة الخادمات بالمكانس والمماسح.

But Buck was no house-dog, and he was no kennel-dog either.

لكن باك لم يكن كلبًا منزليًا، ولم يكن كلبًا بيتيًا أيضًا.

The entire property belonged to Buck as his rightful realm.

كانت الممتلكات بأكملها مملوكة لباك باعتبارها مملكته الشرعية.

Buck swam in the tank or went hunting with the Judge's sons.

كان الغزال يسبح في الخزان أو يذهب للصيد مع أبناء القاضي.

He walked with Mollie and Alice in the early or late hours.

كان يمشي مع مولي وأليس في الساعات الأولى أو المتأخرة.

On cold nights he lay before the library fire with the Judge.

وفي الليالي الباردة كان يرقد أمام نار المكتبة مع القاضي.

Buck gave rides to the Judge's grandsons on his strong back.

قام باك بنقل أحفاد القاضي على ظهره القوي.

He rolled in the grass with the boys, guarding them closely.

كان يتدحرج في العشب مع الأولاد، ويحرسهم عن كثب.

They ventured to the fountain and even past the berry fields.

لقد ذهبوا إلى النافورة وحتى حقول التوت.

Among the fox terriers, Buck walked with royal pride always.

بين كلاب فوكس تيرير، كان باك يمشي بفخر ملكي دائمًا.

He ignored Toots and Ysabel, treating them like they were air.

لقد تجاهل توتس وإيزابيل، وعاملهما كما لو كانا هواءً.

Buck ruled over all living creatures on Judge Miller's land.

كان باك يحكم كل الكائنات الحية على أرض القاضي ميلر.

He ruled over animals, insects, birds, and even humans.

لقد حكم الحيوانات والحشرات والطيور وحتى البشر.

Buck's father Elmo had been a huge and loyal St. Bernard.

كان والد باك إلمو كلبًا كبيرًا من نوع سانت برنارد ومخلصًا.

Elmo never left the Judge's side, and served him faithfully.

لم يترك إلمو جانب القاضي أبدًا، وخدمه بإخلاص.

Buck seemed ready to follow his father's noble example.

وبدا باك مستعدًا لاتباع مثال والده النبيل.

Buck was not quite as large, weighing one hundred and forty pounds.

لم يكن باك كبيرًا تمامًا، إذ كان وزنه مائة وأربعين رطلاً.

His mother, Shep, had been a fine Scotch shepherd dog.

كانت والدته، شيب، كلبة راعية اسكتلندية رائعة.

But even at that weight, Buck walked with regal presence.

ولكن حتى مع هذا الوزن، كان باك يمشي بحضور ملكي.

This came from good food and the respect he always received.

جاء هذا من خلال الطعام الجيد والاحترام الذي كان يحظى به دائمًا.

For four years, Buck had lived like a spoiled nobleman.

لقد عاش باك لمدة أربع سنوات مثل النبيل المدلل.

He was proud of himself, and even slightly egotistical.

لقد كان فخوراً بنفسه، وحتى أنانياً بعض الشيء.

That kind of pride was common in remote country lords.

كان هذا النوع من الفخر شائعًا بين أمراء المناطق النائية.

But Buck saved himself from becoming pampered house-dog.

لكن باك أنقذ نفسه من أن يصبح كلبًا مدللًا في المنزل.

He stayed lean and strong through hunting and exercise.

لقد ظل نحيفًا وقويًا من خلال الصيد وممارسة الرياضة.

He loved water deeply, like people who bathe in cold lakes.

كان يحب الماء بشدة، مثل الأشخاص الذين يستحمون في البحيرات الباردة.

This love for water kept Buck strong, and very healthy.

لقد ساعد هذا الحب للماء باك على البقاء قويًا وصحيًا للغاية.

This was the dog Buck had become in the fall of 1897.

كان هذا هو الكلب الذي أصبح عليه باك في خريف عام 1897.

When the Klondike strike pulled men to the frozen North.

عندما دفعت ضربة كلوندايك الرجال إلى الشمال المتجمد.

People rushed from all over the world into the cold land.

هرع الناس من جميع أنحاء العالم إلى الأرض الباردة.

Buck, however, did not read the papers, nor understand news.

لكن باك لم يقرأ الصحف ولم يفهم الأخبار.

He did not know Manuel was a bad man to be around.

لم يكن يعلم أن مانويل رجل سيء للتعامل معه.

Manuel, who helped in the garden, had a deep problem.

مانويل، الذي كان يساعد في الحديقة، كان يعاني من مشكلة عميقة.

Manuel was addicted to gambling in the Chinese lottery.

كان مانويل مدمنًا على القمار في اليانصيب الصيني.

He also believed strongly in a fixed system for winning.

وكان يؤمن أيضًا بشدة بوجود نظام ثابت للفوز.

That belief made his failure certain and unavoidable.

وهذا الاعتقاد جعل فشله مؤكدا ولا مفر منه.

Playing a system demands money, which Manuel lacked.

يتطلب اللعب بنظام ما المال، وهو ما كان يفتقر إليه مانويل.

His pay barely supported his wife and many children.

كان راتبه بالكاد يكفي زوجته وأطفاله الكثيرين.

On the night Manuel betrayed Buck, things were normal.

في الليلة التي خان فيها مانويل باك، كانت الأمور طبيعية.

The Judge was at a Raisin Growers' Association meeting.

وكان القاضي حاضرا في اجتماع جمعية مزارعي الزبيب.

The Judge's sons were busy forming an athletic club then.

وكان أبناء القاضي منشغلين آنذاك بتأسيس نادي رياضي.

No one saw Manuel and Buck leaving through the orchard.

لم يشاهد أحد مانويل وبوك يغادران البستان.

Buck thought this walk was just a simple nighttime stroll.

اعتقد باك أن هذه الرحلة كانت مجرد نزهة ليلية بسيطة.

They met only one man at the flag station, in College Park.

لقد التقوا برجل واحد فقط في محطة العلم، في كوليدج بارك.

That man spoke to Manuel, and they exchanged money.

وتحدث ذلك الرجل مع مانويل، وتبادلا الأموال.

"Wrap up the goods before you deliver them," he suggested.

"قم بتغليف البضائع قبل تسليمها"، اقترح.

The man's voice was rough and impatient as he spoke.

كان صوت الرجل خشنًا وغير صبور أثناء حديثه.

Manuel carefully tied a thick rope around Buck's neck.

قام مانويل بربط حبل سميك حول رقبة باك بعناية.

"Twist the rope, and you'll choke him plenty"

"لف الحبل، وسوف تخنقه كثيرًا"

The stranger gave a grunt, showing he understood well.

أطلق الغريب أنينًا، مما يدل على أنه فهم جيدًا.

Buck accepted the rope with calm and quiet dignity that day.

لقد تقبل باك الحبل بهدوء وكرامة في ذلك اليوم.

It was an unusual act, but Buck trusted the men he knew.

لقد كان هذا تصرفًا غير عادي، لكن باك كان يثق بالرجال الذين يعرفهم.

He believed their wisdom went far beyond his own
thinking.

كان يعتقد أن حكمتهم كانت أبعد بكثير من تفكيره.

But then the rope was handed to the hands of the stranger.

ولكن بعد ذلك تم تسليم الحبل إلى يد الغريب.

Buck gave a low growl that warned with quiet menace.

أطلق باك هديرًا منخفضًا حذر من خلال التهديد الهادئ.

He was proud and commanding, and meant to show his
displeasure.

لقد كان فخوراً ومتسلطاً، وكان ينوي أن يُظهر استياءه.

Buck believed his warning would be understood as an order.

اعتقد باك أن تحذيره سوف يُفهم على أنه أمر.

To his shock, the rope tightened fast around his thick neck.

لقد صدم عندما شدّ الحبل بسرعة حول رقبته السميكة.

His air was cut off and he began to fight in a sudden rage.

انقطع عنه الهواء وبدأ بالقتال في غضب مفاجئ.

He sprang at the man, who quickly met Buck in mid-air.

اندفع نحو الرجل، الذي التقى بسرعة بباك في الهواء.

The man grabbed Buck's throat and skillfully twisted him in the air.

أمسك الرجل بحلق باك وقام بلفه في الهواء بمهارة.

Buck was thrown down hard, landing flat on his back.

تم إلقاء باك بقوة، وهبط على ظهره.

The rope now choked him cruelly while he kicked wildly.

الآن خنقه الحبل بقسوة بينما كان يركل بعنف.

His tongue fell out, his chest heaved, but gained no breath.

سقط لسانه، وارتفع صدره، لكنه لم يلتقط أنفاسه.

He had never been treated with such violence in his life.

لم يتم التعامل معه بمثل هذا العنف في حياته.

He had also never been filled with such deep fury before.

ولم يسبق له أن امتلأ بمثل هذا الغضب العميق من قبل.

But Buck's power faded, and his eyes turned glassy.

لكن قوة باك تلاشت، وتحولت عيناه إلى زجاجيتين.

He passed out just as a train was flagged down nearby.

لقد أغمي عليه عندما تم إيقاف القطار بالقرب منه.

Then the two men tossed him into the baggage car quickly.

ثم ألقاه الرجلان بسرعة في عربة الأمتعة.

The next thing Buck felt was pain in his swollen tongue.

الشيء التالي الذي شعر به باك هو الألم في لسانه المتورم.

He was moving in a shaking cart, only dimly conscious.

كان يتحرك في عربة تهتز، ولم يكن واعيًا إلا بشكل خافت.

The sharp scream of a train whistle told Buck his location.

أخبر صراخ صافرة القطار الحاد باك بمكانه.

He had often ridden with the Judge and knew the feeling.

لقد ركب مع القاضي عدة مرات وكان يعرف هذا الشعور.

It was the unique jolt of traveling in a baggage car again.

لقد كانت الصدمة الفريدة من نوعها هي السفر في عربة الأمتعة مرة أخرى.

Buck opened his eyes, and his gaze burned with rage.

فتح باك عينيه، وكانت نظراته مليئة بالغضب.

This was the anger of a proud king taken from his throne.

كان هذا غضب الملك الفخور الذي تم نزعه عن عرشه.

A man reached to grab him, but Buck struck first instead.

حاول رجل أن يمسك به، لكن باك ضربه أولاً بدلاً من ذلك.

He sank his teeth into the man's hand and held tightly.

غرس أسنانه في يد الرجل وأمسك بها بقوة.

He did not let go until he blacked out a second time.

لم يتركه حتى فقد وعيه للمرة الثانية.

"Yep, has fits," the man muttered to the baggageman.

"نعم، يصاب بنوبات"، تمتم الرجل لحامل الأمتعة.

The baggageman had heard the struggle and come near.

سمع حامل الأمتعة الصراع وجاء بالقرب.

"I'm taking him to 'Frisco for the boss," the man explained.

"سآخذه إلى فريسكو من أجل الرئيس"، أوضح الرجل.

"There's a fine dog-doctor there who says he can cure them."

"يوجد طبيب كلاب جيد هناك يقول أنه يستطيع علاجهم."

Later that night the man gave his own full account.

وفي وقت لاحق من تلك الليلة، قدم الرجل روايته الكاملة.

He spoke from a shed behind a saloon on the docks.

كان يتحدث من سقيفة خلف صالون على الأرصفة.

"All I was given was fifty dollars," he complained to the saloon man.

"كل ما أعطوني هو خمسون دولارًا"، اشتكى إلى صاحب الصالون.

"I wouldn't do it again, not even for a thousand in cold cash."

"لن أفعل ذلك مرة أخرى، حتى ولو مقابل ألف نقدًا."

His right hand was tightly wrapped in a bloody cloth.

كانت يده اليمنى ملفوفة بإحكام بقطعة قماش ملطخة بالدماء.

His trouser leg was torn wide open from knee to foot.

كانت ساق بنطاله ممزقة على نطاق واسع من الركبة إلى القدم.

"How much did the other mug get paid?" asked the saloon man.

"كم حصل صاحب الصالون على أجر؟" سأل صاحب الصالون.

"A hundred," the man replied, "he wouldn't take a cent less."

"مائة"، أجاب الرجل، "لن يقبل بسنتين أقل".

"That comes to a hundred and fifty," the saloon man said.

"هذا يعادل مائة وخمسين"، قال صاحب الصالون.

"And he's worth it all, or I'm no better than a blockhead."

"وهو يستحق كل هذا العناء، وإلا فلن أكون أفضل من أحمق."

The man opened the wrappings to examine his hand.

فتح الرجل الغلافات لفحص يده.

The hand was badly torn and crusted in dried blood.

كانت اليد ممزقة بشدة ومغطاة بالدماء الجافة.

"If I don't get the hydrophobia…" he began to say.

"إذا لم أحصل على رهاب الماء …" بدأ يقول.

"It'll be because you were born to hang," came a laugh.

"سيكون ذلك لأنك ولدت لتشنق"، جاء ضحك.

"Come help me out before you get going," he was asked.

"تعال ساعدني قبل أن تذهب"، طلب منه.

Buck was in a daze from the pain in his tongue and throat.

كان باك في حالة ذهول من الألم في لسانه وحلقه.

He was half-strangled, and could barely stand upright.

لقد كان مخنوقًا جزئيًا، وبالكاد كان قادرًا على الوقوف منتصبًا.

Still, Buck tried to face the men who had hurt him so.

ومع ذلك، حاول باك مواجهة الرجال الذين أذوه كثيرًا.

But they threw him down and choked him once again.

لكنهم ألقوه أرضًا وخنقوه مرة أخرى.

Only then could they saw off his heavy brass collar.

حينها فقط استطاعوا أن يخلعوا طوقه النحاسي الثقيل.

They removed the rope and shoved him into a crate.

قاموا بإزالة الحبل ووضعوه في صندوق.

The crate was small and shaped like a rough iron cage.

كان الصندوق صغيرًا وشكله يشبه قفصًا حديديًا خشنًا.

Buck lay there all night, filled with wrath and wounded pride.

ظل باك ملقى هناك طوال الليل، ممتلئًا بالغضب والكبرياء الجريح.

He could not begin to understand what was happening to him.

لم يكن يستطيع أن يفهم ما كان يحدث له.

Why were these strange men keeping him in this small crate?

لماذا كان هؤلاء الرجال الغريبون يحتجزونه في هذا الصندوق الصغير؟

What did they want with him, and why this cruel captivity?

ماذا يريدون منه ولماذا هذا الأسر القاسي؟

He felt a dark pressure; a sense of disaster drawing closer.

لقد شعر بضغط مظلم، وإحساس بالكارثة تقترب.

It was a vague fear, but it settled heavily on his spirit.

لقد كان خوفًا غامضًا، لكنه استقر بشكل كبير على روحه.

Several times he jumped up when the shed door rattled.

قفز عدة مرات عندما اهتز باب السقيفة.

He expected the Judge or the boys to appear and rescue him.

كان يتوقع أن يظهر القاضي أو الأولاد وينقذوه.

But only the saloon-keeper's fat face peeked inside each time.

لكن في كل مرة كان وجه صاحب الصالون السمين فقط هو الذي يظهر إلى الداخل.

The man's face was lit by the dim glow of a tallow candle.

كان وجه الرجل مضاءً بضوء خافت من شمعة الشحم.

Each time, Buck's joyful bark changed to a low, angry growl.

في كل مرة، كان نباح باك المبهج يتغير إلى هدير منخفض وغاضب.

The saloon-keeper left him alone for the night in the crate

تركه صاحب الصالون بمفرده طوال الليل في الصندوق

But when he awoke in the morning more men were coming.

ولكن عندما استيقظ في الصباح كان هناك المزيد من الرجال قادمين.

Four men came and gingerly picked up the crate without a word.

جاء أربعة رجال وأخذوا الصندوق بحذر دون أن يقولوا كلمة.

Buck knew at once the situation he found himself in.

أدرك باك على الفور الوضع الذي وجد نفسه فيه.

They were further tormentors that he had to fight and fear.

وكانوا معذبين آخرين كان عليه أن يقاتلهم ويخاف منهم.

These men looked wicked, ragged, and very badly groomed.

بدا هؤلاء الرجال أشرارًا، رثِّين، ومهندمين للغاية.

Buck snarled and lunged at them fiercely through the bars.

هدر باك وانقض عليهم بشراسة عبر القضبان.

They just laughed and jabbed at him with long wooden sticks.

لقد ضحكوا فقط وضربوه بالعصي الخشبية الطويلة.

Buck bit at the sticks, then realized that was what they liked.

عض باك العصي، ثم أدرك أن هذا هو ما يحبونه.

So he lay down quietly, sullen and burning with quiet rage.

لذلك استلقى بهدوء، متجهمًا ومشتعلًا بالغضب الهادئ.

They lifted the crate into a wagon and drove away with him.

رفعوا الصندوق إلى عربة وسافروا به.

The crate, with Buck locked inside, changed hands often.

كان الصندوق، الذي كان باك محبوسًا بداخله، يتغير من يد إلى أخرى كثيرًا.

Express office clerks took charge and handled him briefly.

تولى موظفو مكتب البريد السريع المسؤولية وتعاملوا معه لفترة وجيزة.

Then another wagon carried Buck across the noisy town.

ثم حملت عربة أخرى باك عبر المدينة الصاخبة.

A truck took him with boxes and parcels onto a ferry boat.

أخذته شاحنة مع الصناديق والطرود إلى عبارة.

After crossing, the truck unloaded him at a rail depot.

بعد العبور، أنزلته الشاحنة في مستودع للسكك الحديدية.

At last, Buck was placed inside a waiting express car.

وأخيرًا، تم وضع باك داخل سيارة سريعة كانت في انتظاره.

For two days and nights, trains pulled the express car away.

لمدة يومين وليلتين، سحبت القطارات عربة القطار بعيدًا.

Buck neither ate nor drank during the whole painful journey.

لم يأكل باك ولم يشرب طيلة الرحلة المؤلمة.

When the express messengers tried to approach him, he growled.

وعندما حاول الرسل الوصول إليه، أطلق صوتا غاضبا.

They responded by mocking him and teasing him cruelly.

فاستجابوا له بالسخرية والاستهزاء الشديد.

Buck threw himself at the bars, foaming and shaking

ألقى باك نفسه على القضبان، وهو يرغي ويرتجف

they laughed loudly, and taunted him like schoolyard bullies.

لقد ضحكوا بصوت عالي، وسخروا منه مثل المتنمرين في ساحة المدرسة.

They barked like fake dogs and flapped their arms.

لقد نبحوا مثل الكلاب المزيفة ولوحوا بأذرعهم.

They even crowed like roosters just to upset him more.

حتى أنهم صاحوا مثل الديكة فقط لإزعاجه أكثر.

It was foolish behavior, and Buck knew it was ridiculous.

لقد كان هذا سلوكًا أحمقًا، وكان باك يعلم أنه سخيف.

But that only deepened his sense of outrage and shame.

ولكن هذا فقط زاد من شعوره بالغضب والعار.

He was not bothered much by hunger during the trip.

لم يزعجه الجوع كثيرًا أثناء الرحلة.

But thirst brought sharp pain and unbearable suffering.

لكن العطش جلب الألم الحاد والمعاناة التي لا تطاق.

His dry, inflamed throat and tongue burned with heat.

كان حلقه ولسانه الجافان الملتهبان يحترقان من الحرارة.

This pain fed the fever rising within his proud body.

لقد أدى هذا الألم إلى تغذية الحمى المتصاعدة داخل جسده الفخور.

Buck was thankful for one single thing during this trial.

كان باك شاكراً لشيء واحد فقط خلال هذه المحنة.

The rope had been removed from around his thick neck.

لقد تم إزالة الحبل من حول رقبته السميكة.

The rope had given those men an unfair and cruel advantage.

لقد أعطى الحبل لهؤلاء الرجال ميزة غير عادلة وقاسية.

Now the rope was gone, and Buck swore it would never return.

والآن ذهب الحبل، وأقسم باك أنه لن يعود أبدًا.

He resolved no rope would ever go around his neck again.

لقد قرر أن لا يلف الحبل حول رقبته مرة أخرى.

For two long days and nights, he suffered without food.

لمدة يومين وليلتين طويلتين، عانى من عدم تناول الطعام.

And in those hours, he built up an enormous rage inside.

وفي تلك الساعات، تراكم غضب هائل في داخله.

His eyes turned bloodshot and wild from constant anger.

تحولت عيناه إلى اللون الأحمر والأحمر بسبب الغضب المستمر.

He was no longer Buck, but a demon with snapping jaws.

لم يعد باك، بل أصبح شيطانًا ذو فكين متقطعين.

Even the Judge would not have known this mad creature.

حتى القاضي لن يعرف هذا المخلوق المجنون.

The express messengers sighed in relief when they reached Seattle

تنهد الرسل السريعون بارتياح عندما وصلوا إلى سياتل

Four men lifted the crate and brought it to a back yard.

قام أربعة رجال برفع الصندوق وحملوه إلى الفناء الخلفي.

The yard was small, surrounded by high and solid walls.

كانت الساحة صغيرة، محاطة بأسوار عالية ومتينة.

A big man stepped out in a sagging red sweater shirt.

خرج رجل كبير يرتدي قميصًا أحمر مترهلًا.

He signed the delivery book with a thick and bold hand.

وقّع على دفتر التسليم بخط سميك وجريء.

Buck sensed at once that this man was his next tormentor.

أحس باك على الفور أن هذا الرجل سيكون معذبه التالي.

He lunged violently at the bars, eyes red with fury.

انقض بعنف على القضبان، وكانت عيناه حمراء من الغضب.

The man just smiled darkly and went to fetch a hatchet.

ابتسم الرجل ابتسامة سوداء وذهب ليحضر فأسًا.

He also brought a club in his thick and strong right hand.

كما أحضر معه هراوة في يده اليمنى السميكة والقوية.

"You going to take him out now?" the driver asked, concerned.

"هل ستخرج به الآن؟" سأل السائق بقلق.

"Sure," said the man, jamming the hatchet into the crate as a lever.

"بالتأكيد،" قال الرجل وهو يدفع الفأس في الصندوق كرافعة.

The four men scattered instantly, jumping up onto the yard wall.

تفرق الرجال الأربعة على الفور، وقفزوا على جدار الفناء.

From their safe spots above, they waited to watch the spectacle.

ومن أماكنهم الآمنة في الأعلى، انتظروا لمشاهدة هذا المنظر.

Buck lunged at the splintered wood, biting and shaking fiercely.

انقض باك على الخشب المكسور، يعض ويهتز بشدة.

Each time the hatchet hit the cage), Buck was there to attack it.

في كل مرة ضربت فيها الفأس القفص، كان باك هناك لمهاجمته.

He growled and snapped with wild rage, eager to be set free.

لقد هدّر وأطلق العنان لغضبه الشديد، راغبًا في التحرر.

The man outside was calm and steady, intent on his task.

كان الرجل بالخارج هادئًا وثابتًا، يركز على مهمته.

"Right then, you red-eyed devil," he said when the hole was large.

"حسنًا، أيها الشيطان ذو العيون الحمراء"، قال ذلك عندما أصبح الثقب كبيرًا.

He dropped the hatchet and took the club in his right hand.

ألقى الفأس وأخذ النادي بيده اليمنى.

Buck truly looked like a devil; eyes bloodshot and blazing.

لقد بدا باك حقا مثل الشيطان؛ عيناه حمراء ومشتعلة.

His coat bristled, foam frothed at his mouth, eyes glinting.

كان معطفه منتفخًا، وكانت الرغوة تزبد على فمه، وكانت عيناه تلمعان.

He bunched his muscles and sprang straight at the red sweater.

لقد جمع عضلاته وقفز مباشرة نحو السترة الحمراء.

One hundred and forty pounds of fury flew at the calm man.

مائة وأربعون رطلاً من الغضب طارت نحو الرجل الهادئ.

Just before his jaws clamped shut, a terrible blow struck him.

قبل أن يغلق فكيه، ضربته ضربة رهيبة.

His teeth snapped together on nothing but air

اصطدمت أسنانه ببعضها البعض على الهواء فقط

a jolt of pain reverberated through his body

تردد صدى الألم في جسده

He flipped midair and crashed down on his back and side.

انقلب في الهواء وسقط على ظهره وجانبه.

He had never before felt a club's blow and could not grasp it.

لم يسبق له أن شعر بضربة مضرب ولم يستطع استيعابها.

With a shrieking snarl, part bark, part scream, he leaped again.

مع صرخة قوية، جزء منها نباح، وجزء منها صراخ، قفز مرة أخرى.

Another brutal strike hit him and hurled him to the ground.

ضربة وحشية أخرى أصابته وألقته على الأرض.

This time Buck understood—it was the man's heavy club.

هذه المرة فهم باك ـ كانت هذه هي الهراوة الثقيلة التي يحملها الرجل.

But rage blinded him, and he had no thought of retreat.

لكن الغضب أعماه، ولم يفكر في التراجع.

Twelve times he launched himself, and twelve times he fell.

لقد ألقى بنفسه اثنتي عشرة مرة، وسقط اثنتي عشرة مرة.

The wooden club smashed him each time with ruthless, crushing force.

كانت الهراوة الخشبية تضربه في كل مرة بقوة ساحقة لا هوادة فيها.

After one fierce blow, he staggered to his feet, dazed and slow.

وبعد ضربة عنيفة واحدة، تعثر على قدميه، مذهولاً وبطيئًا.

Blood ran from his mouth, his nose, and even his ears.

كان الدم يسيل من فمه، ومن أنفه، وحتى من أذنيه.

His once-beautiful coat was smeared with bloody foam.

كان معطفه الجميل في السابق ملطخًا برغوة دموية.

Then the man stepped up and struck a wicked blow to the nose.

ثم تقدم الرجل وضرب ضربة شريرة على الأنف.

The agony was sharper than anything Buck had ever felt.

كان الألم أشد من أي شيء شعر به باك على الإطلاق.

With a roar more beast than dog, he leaped again to attack.

مع زئير أكثر وحشية من الكلب، قفز مرة أخرى للهجوم.

But the man caught his lower jaw and twisted it backward.

لكن الرجل أمسك بفكه السفلي وأداره إلى الخلف.

Buck flipped head over heels, crashing down hard again.

انقلب باك على رأسه فوق الكعب، وسقط بقوة مرة أخرى.

One final time, Buck charged at him, now barely able to stand.

في المرة الأخيرة، انقض عليه باك، وهو الآن بالكاد قادر على الوقوف.

The man struck with expert timing, delivering the final blow.

لقد ضرب الرجل بمهارة عالية، ووجه الضربة النهائية.

Buck collapsed in a heap, unconscious and unmoving.

انهار باك في كومة، فاقدًا للوعي وغير قادر على الحركة.

"He's no slouch at dog-breaking, that's what I say," a man yelled.

"إنه ليس سيئًا في تدريب الكلاب، هذا ما أقوله"، صرخ أحد الرجال.

"Druther can break the will of a hound any day of the week."

"يستطيع درثر أن يكسر إرادة كلب الصيد في أي يوم من أيام الأسبوع."

"And twice on a Sunday!" added the driver.

"ومرتين يوم الأحد!" أضاف السائق.

He climbed into the wagon and cracked the reins to leave.

صعد إلى العربة وفتح اللجام ليغادر.

Buck slowly regained control of his consciousness

استعاد باك السيطرة على وعيه ببطء

but his body was still too weak and broken to move.

لكن جسده كان لا يزال ضعيفًا جدًا ومكسورًا لدرجة أنه لم يتمكن من الحركة.

He lay where he had fallen, watching the red-sweatered man.

كان مستلقيا حيث سقط، وهو يراقب الرجل ذو السترة الحمراء.

"He answers to the name of Buck," the man said, reading aloud.

"إنه يجيب على اسم باك"، قال الرجل وهو يقرأ بصوت عالٍ.

He quoted from the note sent with Buck's crate and details.

واقتبس من المذكرة المرسلة مع صندوق باك والتفاصيل.

"Well, Buck, my boy," the man continued with a friendly tone,

"حسنًا، باك، يا بني،" تابع الرجل بنبرة ودية،

"we've had our little fight, and now it's over between us."

"لقد كان لدينا قتالنا الصغير، والآن انتهى الأمر بيننا."

"You've learned your place, and I've learned mine," he added.

"لقد تعلمت مكانك، وتعلمت مكاني"، أضاف.

"Be good, and all will go well, and life will be pleasant."

"كن جيدًا، وسوف يكون كل شيء على ما يرام، وستكون الحياة ممتعة."

"But be bad, and I'll beat the stuffing out of you, understand?"

"لكن كن سيئًا، وسأضربك حتى الموت، هل فهمت؟"

As he spoke, he reached out and patted Buck's sore head.

وبينما كان يتحدث، مد يده وربّت على رأس باك المؤلم.

Buck's hair rose at the man's touch, but he didn't resist.

ارتفع شعر باك عند لمسة الرجل، لكنه لم يقاوم.

The man brought him water, which Buck drank in great gulps.

أحضر الرجل له الماء، فشربه باك في دفعات كبيرة.

Then came raw meat, which Buck devoured chunk by chunk.

ثم جاء اللحم النيء، الذي التهمه باك قطعة قطعة.

He knew he was beaten, but he also knew he wasn't broken.

لقد عرف أنه تعرض للضرب، لكنه عرف أيضًا أنه لم ينكسر.

He had no chance against a man armed with a club.

لم تكن لديه أي فرصة ضد رجل مسلح بهراوة.

He had learned the truth, and he never forgot that lesson.

لقد تعلم الحقيقة، ولم ينس هذا الدرس أبدًا.

That weapon was the beginning of law in Buck's new world.

كان هذا السلاح بمثابة بداية القانون في عالم باك الجديد.

It was the start of a harsh, primitive order he could not deny.

لقد كانت بداية نظام قاسٍ وبدائي لا يستطيع إنكاره.

He accepted the truth; his wild instincts were now awake.

لقد تقبل الحقيقة، وأصبحت غرائزه الجامحة مستيقظة الآن.

The world had grown harsher, but Buck faced it bravely.

لقد أصبح العالم أكثر قسوة، لكن باك واجهه بشجاعة.

He met life with new caution, cunning, and quiet strength.

لقد واجه الحياة بحذر جديد، ومكر، وقوة هادئة.

More dogs arrived, tied in ropes or crates like Buck had been.

وصل المزيد من الكلاب، مربوطة بالحبال أو الصناديق مثلما كان باك.

Some dogs came calmly, others raged and fought like wild beasts.

بعض الكلاب جاءت بهدوء، والبعض الآخر ثار وقاتل مثل الوحوش البرية.

All of them were brought under the rule of the red-sweatered man.

لقد أصبحوا جميعهم تحت حكم الرجل ذو السترة الحمراء.

Each time, Buck watched and saw the same lesson unfold.

في كل مرة، كان باك يراقب ويرى نفس الدرس يتكشف.

The man with the club was law; a master to be obeyed.

كان الرجل الذي يحمل النادي هو القانون، وهو سيد يجب طاعته.

He did not need to be liked, but he had to be obeyed.

لم يكن بحاجة إلى أن يكون محبوبًا، لكن كان لا بد من طاعته.

Buck never fawned or wagged like the weaker dogs did.

لم يتملق باك أو يهز جسده أبدًا كما تفعل الكلاب الأضعف.

He saw dogs that were beaten and still licked the man's hand.

فرأى الكلاب مضروبة ولا تزال تلعق يد الرجل.

He saw one dog who would not obey or submit at all.

لقد رأى كلبًا واحدًا لا يطيع ولا يخضع على الإطلاق.

That dog fought until he was killed in the battle for control.

لقد حارب هذا الكلب حتى قُتل في معركة السيطرة.

Strangers would sometimes come to see the red-sweatered man.

في بعض الأحيان كان يأتي الغرباء لرؤية الرجل ذو السترة الحمراء.

They spoke in strange tones, pleading, bargaining, and laughing.

لقد تحدثوا بنبرة غريبة، متوسلين، ومساومين، وضاحكين.

When money was exchanged, they left with one or more dogs.

وعندما تم تبادل الأموال، غادروا مع كلب واحد أو أكثر.

Buck wondered where these dogs went, for none ever returned.

وتساءل باك عن المكان الذي ذهبت إليه هذه الكلاب، لأنه لم يعد أي منها أبدًا.

fear of the unknown filled Buck every time a strange man came

كان الخوف من المجهول يملأ باك في كل مرة يأتي فيها رجل غريب

he was glad each time another dog was taken, rather than himself.

كان سعيدًا في كل مرة يتم فيها أخذ كلب آخر، بدلاً من نفسه.

But finally, Buck's turn came with the arrival of a strange man.

ولكن في النهاية جاء دور باك مع وصول رجل غريب.

He was small, wiry, and spoke in broken English and curses.

كان قصيرًا، نحيلًا، ويتحدث الإنجليزية المكسورة ويلعن.

"Sacredam!" he yelled when he laid eyes on Buck's frame.

"يا إلهي!" صرخ عندما رأى جسد باك.

"That's one damn bully dog! Eh? How much?" he asked aloud.

"يا له من كلبٍ شرس! هاه؟ كم ثمنه؟" سأل بصوتٍ عالٍ.

"Three hundred, and he's a present at that price,"

"ثلاثمائة، وهو هدية بهذا السعر"

"Since it's government money, you shouldn't complain, Perrault."

"بما أن هذه أموال حكومية، فلا ينبغي لك أن تشتكي، بيرولت."

Perrault grinned at the deal he had just made with the man.

ابتسم بيرولت بسبب الصفقة التي أبرمها للتو مع الرجل.

The price of dogs had soared due to the sudden demand.

ارتفعت أسعار الكلاب بسبب الطلب المفاجئ.

Three hundred dollars wasn't unfair for such a fine beast.

ثلاثمائة دولار لم تكن مبلغًا غير عادل بالنسبة لحيوان جميل كهذا.

The Canadian Government would not lose anything in the deal

لن تخسر الحكومة الكندية أي شيء في هذه الصفقة

Nor would their official dispatches be delayed in transit.

ولن تتأخر إرسالياتهم الرسمية أثناء النقل.

Perrault knew dogs well, and could see Buck was something rare.

كان بيرولت يعرف الكلاب جيدًا، وكان بإمكانه أن يرى أن باك كان شيئًا نادرًا.

"One in ten ten-thousand," he thought, as he studied Buck's build.

"واحد من عشرة آلاف،" فكر، بينما كان يدرس بنية باك.

Buck saw the money change hands, but showed no surprise.

رأى باك أن الأموال تنتقل من يد إلى أخرى، لكنه لم يظهر أي مفاجأة.

Soon he and Curly, a gentle Newfoundland, were led away.

وبعد قليل تم اقتياده هو وكيرلي، وهو كلب نيوفاوندلاند لطيف، بعيدًا.

They followed the little man from the red sweater's yard.

لقد تبعوا الرجل الصغير من ساحة السترة الحمراء.

That was the last Buck ever saw of the man with the wooden club.

كانت تلك آخر مرة رأى فيها باك الرجل الذي يحمل الهراوة الخشبية.

From the Narwhal's deck he watched Seattle fade into the distance.

من سطح السفينة النروال ، شاهد سياتل تتلاشى في المسافة.

It was also the last time he ever saw the warm Southland.

وكانت هذه أيضًا المرة الأخيرة التي رأى فيها منطقة الجنوب الدافئة.

Perrault took them below deck, and left them with François.

أخذهم بيرولت إلى أسفل سطح السفينة، وتركهم مع فرانسوا.

François was a black-faced giant with rough, calloused hands.

كان فرانسوا عملاقًا أسود الوجه وذو يدين خشنتين ومتصلبتين.

He was dark and swarthy; a half-breed French-Canadian.

كان داكن البشرة وبشرته سمراء، وهو من أصول مختلطة فرنسية كندية.

To Buck, these men were of a kind he had never seen before.

بالنسبة لباك، هؤلاء الرجال كانوا من النوع الذي لم يره من قبل.

He would come to know many such men in the days ahead.

وسوف يتعرف على العديد من هؤلاء الرجال في الأيام القادمة.

He did not grow fond of them, but he came to respect them.

لم يكن يحبهم، لكنه أصبح يحترمهم.

They were fair and wise, and not easily fooled by any dog.

لقد كانوا عادلين وحكماء، ولم يخدعهم أي كلب بسهولة.

They judged dogs calmly, and punished only when deserved.

لقد حكموا على الكلاب بهدوء، وعاقبوها فقط عندما تستحق العقاب.

In the Narwhal's lower deck, Buck and Curly met two dogs.

في الطابق السفلي من سفينة النروال ، التقى باكو كيرلي بكلبين.

One was a large white dog from far-off, icy Spitzbergen.

كان أحدهما كلبًا أبيضًا كبيرًا من مكان بعيد، من جزيرة سفالبارد الجليدية.

He'd once sailed with a whaler and joined a survey group.

لقد أبحر ذات مرة مع سفينة صيد الحيتان وانضم إلى مجموعة مسح.

He was friendly in a sly, underhanded and crafty fashion.

لقد كان ودودًا بطريقة ماكرة ومخادعة وماكرة.

At their first meal, he stole a piece of meat from Buck's pan.

في وجبتهم الأولى، سرق قطعة لحم من مقلاة باك.

Buck jumped to punish him, but François's whip struck first.

قفز باك لمعاقبته، لكن سوط فرانسوا ضربه أولاً.

The white thief yelped, and Buck reclaimed the stolen bone.

صرخ اللص الأبيض، واستعاد باك العظمة المسروقة.

That fairness impressed Buck, and François earned his respect.

لقد أثار هذا الإنصاف إعجاب باك، وكسب فرانسوا احترامه.

The other dog gave no greeting, and wanted none in return.

أما الكلب الآخر فلم يقدم أي تحية، ولم يرغب في أي تحية في المقابل.

He didn't steal food, nor sniff at the new arrivals with interest.

لم يسرق الطعام، ولم ينظر إلى الوافدين الجدد باهتمام.

This dog was grim and quiet, gloomy and slow-moving.

كان هذا الكلب متجهمًا وهادئًا، كئيبًا وبطيئ الحركة.

He warned Curly to stay away by simply glaring at her.

حذر كيرلي من الابتعاد عنها بمجرد التحديق فيها.

His message was clear; leave me alone or there'll be trouble.

كانت رسالته واضحة: اتركوني وحدي وإلا ستكون هناك مشكلة.

He was called Dave, and he barely noticed his surroundings.

كان اسمه ديف، وكان بالكاد يلاحظ ما يحيط به.

He slept often, ate quietly, and yawned now and again.

كان ينام كثيرًا، ويأكل بهدوء، ويتثاءب بين الحين والآخر.

The ship hummed constantly with the beating propeller below.

كانت السفينة تطن باستمرار بسبب نبض المروحة في الأسفل.

Days passed with little change, but the weather got colder.

مرت الأيام دون تغيير يذكر، لكن الطقس أصبح أكثر برودة.

Buck could feel it in his bones, and noticed the others did too.

كان باك يشعر بذلك في عظامه، ولاحظ أن الآخرين فعلوا ذلك أيضًا.

Then one morning, the propeller stopped and all was still.

ثم في صباح أحد الأيام، توقفت المروحة وظل كل شيء ساكنًا.

An energy swept through the ship; something had changed.

انتشرت طاقة عبر السفينة؛ لقد تغير شيء ما.

François came down, clipped them on leashes, and brought them up.

نزل فرانسوا، وربطهم بالمقود، ورفعهم.

Buck stepped out and found the ground soft, white, and cold.

خرج باك ليجد الأرض ناعمة، بيضاء، وباردة.

He jumped back in alarm and snorted in total confusion.

قفز إلى الوراء في حالة من الذعر وشخر في ارتباك تام.

Strange white stuff was falling from the gray sky.

كانت هناك أشياء بيضاء غريبة تتساقط من السماء الرمادية.

He shook himself, but the white flakes kept landing on him.

لقد هز نفسه، لكن الرقاقات البيضاء استمرت في الهبوط عليه.

He sniffed the white stuff carefully and licked at a few icy bits.

استنشق المادة البيضاء بعناية ولعق بعض القطع الجليدية.

The powder burned like fire, then vanished right off his tongue.

أحرق المسحوق مثل النار، ثم اختفى مباشرة من على لسانه.

Buck tried again, puzzled by the odd vanishing coldness.

حاول باك مرة أخرى، في حيرة من البرودة المتلاشيه الغريبة.

The men around him laughed, and Buck felt embarrassed.

ضحك الرجال من حوله، وشعر باك بالحرج.

He didn't know why, but he was ashamed of his reaction.

لم يكن يعرف السبب، لكنه كان يخجل من رد فعله.

It was his first experience with snow, and it confused him.

لقد كانت هذه تجربته الأولى مع الثلج، وقد أربكته.

The Law of Club and Fang
قانون النادي والناب

Buck's first day on the Dyea beach felt like a terrible nightmare.

كان اليوم الأول لباك على شاطئ دايا أشبه بكابوس رهيب.

Each hour brought new shocks and unexpected changes for Buck.

كل ساعة جلبت صدمات جديدة وتغييرات غير متوقعة لباك.

He had been pulled from civilization and thrown into wild chaos.

لقد تم سحبه من الحضارة وإلقائه في حالة من الفوضى العارمة.

This was no sunny, lazy life with boredom and rest.

لم تكن هذه حياة مشمسة وكسولة مليئة بالملل والراحة.

There was no peace, no rest, and no moment without danger.

لم يكن هناك سلام، ولا راحة، ولا لحظة خالية من الخطر.

Confusion ruled everything, and danger was always close.

كان الارتباك يسيطر على كل شيء، وكان الخطر دائمًا قريبًا.

Buck had to stay alert because these men and dogs were different.

كان على باك أن يبقى متيقظًا لأن هؤلاء الرجال والكلاب كانوا مختلفين.

They were not from towns; they were wild and without mercy.

لم يكونوا من المدن، بل كانوا متوحشين وبلا رحمة.

These men and dogs only knew the law of club and fang.

هؤلاء الرجال والكلاب لم يعرفوا إلا قانون الهراوة والأنياب.

Buck had never seen dogs fight like these savage huskies.

لم يسبق لباك أن رأى كلابًا تقاتل مثل هذه الكلاب الهاسكي المتوحشة.

His first experience taught him a lesson he would never forget.

لقد علمته تجربته الأولى درسًا لن ينساه أبدًا.

He was lucky it was not him, or he would have died too.

لقد كان محظوظا أنه لم يكن هو، وإلا لكان قد مات أيضا.

Curly was the one who suffered while Buck watched and learned.

كان كيرلي هو الشخص الذي عانى بينما كان باك يشاهد ويتعلم.

They had made camp near a store built from logs.

لقد أقاموا مخيمًا بالقرب من متجر مبني من جذوع الأشجار.

Curly tried to be friendly to a large, wolf-like husky.

حاول كيرلي أن يكون ودودًا مع كلب الهاسكي الكبير الذي يشبه الذئب.

The husky was smaller than Curly, but looked wild and mean.

كان الهاسكي أصغر من كيرلي، لكنه بدا متوحشًا وخبيثًا.

Without warning, he jumped and slashed her face open.

بدون سابق إنذار، قفز وفتح وجهها.

His teeth cut from her eye down to her jaw in one move.

قطعت أسنانه من عينها إلى فكها بحركة واحدة.

This was how wolves fought—hit fast and jump away.

هكذا كانت الذئاب تقاتل ـ تضرب بسرعة وتقفز بعيدًا.

But there was more to learn than from that one attack.

ولكن كان هناك المزيد لنتعلمه من ذلك الهجوم الواحد.

Dozens of huskies rushed in and made a silent circle.

اندفعت العشرات من كلاب الهاسكي وشكلوا دائرة صامتة.

They watched closely and licked their lips with hunger.

لقد راقبوا عن كثب ولحسوا شفاههم من الجوع.

Buck didn't understand their silence or their eager eyes.

لم يفهم باك صمتهم أو عيونهم المتلهفة.

Curly rushed to attack the husky a second time.

هرع كيرلي لمهاجمة الهاسكي للمرة الثانية.

He used his chest to knock her over with a strong move.

استخدم صدره ليطرحها أرضًا بحركة قوية.

She fell on her side and could not get back up.

سقطت على جانبها ولم تتمكن من النهوض مرة أخرى.

That was what the others had been waiting for all along.

وهذا ما كان ينتظره الآخرون طوال الوقت.

The huskies jumped on her, yelping and snarling in a frenzy.

قفز عليها الهاسكي، وهم ينبحون ويزمجرون في حالة من الهياج.

She screamed as they buried her under a pile of dogs.

صرخت عندما دفنوها تحت كومة من الكلاب.

The attack was so fast that Buck froze in place with shock.

كان الهجوم سريعًا جدًا لدرجة أن باك تجمد في مكانه من الصدمة.

He saw Spitz stick out his tongue in a way that looked like a laugh.

لقد رأى سبيتز يخرج لسانه بطريقة تبدو وكأنها ضحكة.

François grabbed an axe and ran straight into the group of
dogs.

أمسك فرانسوا بفأس وركض مباشرة نحو مجموعة الكلاب.

Three other men used clubs to help beat the huskies away.

ثلاثة رجال آخرين استخدموا الهراوات لمساعدتهم في ضرب الكلاب
الهاسكي.

In just two minutes, the fight was over and the dogs were
gone.

في دقيقتين فقط، انتهى القتال واختفت الكلاب.

Curly lay dead in the red, trampled snow, her body torn
apart.

كانت كيرلي ملقاة ميتة في الثلج الأحمر المدوس، وكان جسدها ممزقًا.

A dark-skinned man stood over her, cursing the brutal
scene.

كان هناك رجل ذو بشرة داكنة يقف فوقها، وهو يلعن المشهد الوحشي.

The memory stayed with Buck and haunted his dreams at
night.

ظلت الذكرى عالقة في ذهن باك وطاردته في أحلامه ليلاً.

That was the way here; no fairness, no second chance.

كانت هذه هي الطريقة هنا؛ لا عدالة، ولا فرصة ثانية.

Once a dog fell, the others would kill without mercy.

عندما يسقط كلب، فإن الآخرين سوف يقتلونه بلا رحمة.

Buck decided then that he would never allow himself to fall.

قرر باك حينها أنه لن يسمح لنفسه بالسقوط أبدًا.

Spitz stuck out his tongue again and laughed at the blood.

أخرج سبيتز لسانه مرة أخرى وضحك على الدم.

From that moment on, Buck hated Spitz with all his heart.

منذ تلك اللحظة، أصبح باك يكره سبيتز من كل قلبه.

Before Buck could recover from Curly's death, something
new happened.

قبل أن يتمكن باك من التعافي من وفاة كيرلي، حدث شيء جديد.

François came over and strapped something around Buck's
body.

جاء فرانسوا وربط شيئًا حول جسد باك.

It was a harness like the ones used on horses at the ranch.

كان عبارة عن حزام مثل الذي يستخدم على الخيول في المزرعة.

As Buck had seen horses work, now he was made to work too.

كما رأى باك الخيول تعمل، فقد أُجبر الآن على العمل أيضًا.

He had to pull François on a sled into the forest nearby.

كان عليه أن يسحب فرانسوا على مزلجة إلى الغابة القريبة.

Then he had to pull back a load of heavy firewood.

ثم كان عليه أن يسحب حمولة من الحطب الثقيل.

Buck was proud, so it hurt him to be treated like a work animal.

كان باك فخوراً، لذلك كان يؤلمه أن يتم التعامل معه كحيوان عمل.

But he was wise and didn't try to fight the new situation.

ولكنه كان حكيما ولم يحاول محاربة الوضع الجديد.

He accepted his new life and gave his best in every task.

تقبل حياته الجديدة وأعطى أفضل ما لديه في كل مهمة.

Everything about the work was strange and unfamiliar to him.

كان كل شيء في العمل غريبًا وغير مألوف بالنسبة له.

François was strict and demanded obedience without delay.

كان فرانسوا صارمًا ويطالب بالطاعة دون تأخير.

His whip made sure that every command was followed at once.

كان سوطه يضمن تنفيذ كل الأوامر على الفور.

Dave was the wheeler, the dog nearest the sled behind Buck.

كان ديف هو سائق الزلاجة، وكان الكلب الأقرب إلى الزلاجة خلف باك.

Dave bit Buck on the back legs if he made a mistake.

ديف يعض باك على رجليه الخلفيتين إذا ارتكب خطأ.

Spitz was the lead dog, skilled and experienced in the role.

كان سبيتز هو الكلب الرائد، وكان ماهرًا وذو خبرة في الدور.

Spitz could not reach Buck easily, but still corrected him.

لم يتمكن سبيتز من الوصول إلى باك بسهولة، لكنه مع ذلك قام بتصحيحه.

He growled harshly or pulled the sled in ways that taught Buck.

كان يزأر بشدة أو يسحب الزلاجة بطرق علمت باك.

Under this training, Buck learned faster than any of them expected.

بفضل هذا التدريب، تعلم باك أسرع مما توقعه أي منهم.

He worked hard and learned from both François and the other dogs.

لقد عمل بجد وتعلم من فرانسوا والكلاب الأخرى.

By the time they returned, Buck already knew the key commands.

بحلول الوقت الذي عادوا فيه، كان باك يعرف بالفعل الأوامر الرئيسية.

He learned to stop at the sound of "ho" from François.

لقد تعلم التوقف عند صوت "هو" من فرانسوا.

He learned when he had to pull the sled and run.

لقد تعلم عندما كان عليه سحب الزلاجة والركض.

He learned to turn wide at bends in the trail without trouble.

لقد تعلم كيفية الانعطاف بشكل واسع عند المنعطفات في الطريق دون مشكلة.

He also learned to avoid Dave when the sled went downhill fast.

وتعلم أيضًا كيفية تجنب ديف عندما تنحدر الزلاجة بسرعة.

"They're very good dogs," François proudly told Perrault.

"إنهم كلاب جيدة جدًا"، قال فرانسوا بفخر لبيرولت.

"That Buck pulls like hell—I teach him quick as anything."

"هذا باك يسحب مثل الجحيم ـ أعلمه بسرعة مثل أي شيء."

Later that day, Perrault came back with two more husky dogs.

وفي وقت لاحق من ذلك اليوم، عاد بيرولت مع اثنين آخرين من كلاب الهاسكي.

Their names were Billee and Joe, and they were brothers.

كان اسمهم بيلي وجو، وكانوا أخوة.

They came from the same mother, but were not alike at all.

لقد جاءوا من نفس الأم، ولكن لم يكونوا متشابهين على الإطلاق.

Billee was sweet-natured and too friendly with everyone.

كان بيلي لطيفًا جدًا وودودًا مع الجميع.

Joe was the opposite—quiet, angry, and always snarling.

كان جو على العكس تمامًا ـ هادئًا، غاضبًا، ودائمًا ما يزأر.

Buck greeted them in a friendly way and was calm with both.

استقبلهم باك بطريقة ودية وكان هادئًا مع كليهما.

Dave paid no attention to them and stayed silent as usual.

لم يهتم ديف بهم وظل صامتًا كعادته.

Spitz attacked first Billee, then Joe, to show his dominance.

هاجم سبيتز بيلي أولاً، ثم جو، لإظهار سيطرته.

Billee wagged his tail and tried to be friendly to Spitz.

حرك بيلي ذيله وحاول أن يكون ودودًا مع سبيتز.

When that didn't work, he tried to run away instead.

وعندما لم ينجح ذلك، حاول الهرب بدلاً من ذلك.

He cried sadly when Spitz bit him hard on the side.

لقد بكى بحزن عندما عضه سبيتز بقوة على جانبه.

But Joe was very different and refused to be bullied.

لكن جو كان مختلفًا جدًا ورفض أن يتعرض للتنمر.

Every time Spitz came near, Joe spun to face him fast.

في كل مرة كان سبيتز يقترب، كان جو يستدير لمواجهته بسرعة.

His fur bristled, his lips curled, and his teeth snapped wildly.

كان فراءه منتصبًا، وشفتاه ملتفة، وأسنانه تكسر بعنف.

Joe's eyes gleamed with fear and rage, daring Spitz to strike.

كانت عينا جو تلمعان بالخوف والغضب، متحديًا سبيتز بالضرب.

Spitz gave up the fight and turned away, humiliated and angry.

استسلم سبيتز للقتال واستدار بعيدًا، مهانًا وغاضبًا.

He took out his frustration on poor Billee and chased him away.

أخرج إحباطه على بيلي المسكين وطارده بعيدًا.

That evening, Perrault added one more dog to the team.

وفي ذلك المساء، أضاف بيرولت كلبًا آخر إلى الفريق.

This dog was old, lean, and covered in battle scars.

كان هذا الكلب عجوزًا ونحيفًا ومغطى بندوب المعركة.

One of his eyes was missing, but the other flashed with power.

كانت إحدى عينيه مفقودة، لكن الأخرى كانت تتألق بقوة.

The new dog's name was Solleks, which meant the Angry One.

وكان اسم الكلب الجديد هو سولييكس، والذي يعني الغاضب.

Like Dave, Solleks asked nothing from others, and gave nothing back.

مثل ديف، لم يطلب سوليكس أي شيء من الآخرين، ولم يقدم أي شيء في المقابل.

When Solleks walked slowly into camp, even Spitz stayed away.

عندما دخل سوليكس المخيم ببطء، حتى سبيتز بقي بعيدًا.

He had a strange habit that Buck was unlucky to discover.

كان لديه عادة غريبة لم يكن باك محظوظًا باكتشافها.

Solleks hated being approached on the side where he was blind.

كان سولييكس يكره أن يقترب منه أحد من الجانب الذي كان أعمى فيه.

Buck did not know this and made that mistake by accident.

لم يكن باك يعلم هذا وارتكب هذا الخطأ عن طريق الصدفة.

Solleks spun around and slashed Buck's shoulder deep and fast.

استدار سولييكس وضرب كتف باك بقوة وسرعة.

From that moment on, Buck never came near Solleks' blind side.

منذ تلك اللحظة، لم يقترب باك أبدًا من الجانب الأعمى لسوليكس.

They never had trouble again for the rest of their time together.

لم يواجهوا أي مشاكل مرة أخرى طوال الفترة التي قضوها معًا.

Solleks wanted only to be left alone, like quiet Dave.

أراد سولييكس فقط أن يُترك وحيدًا، مثل ديف الهادئ.

But Buck would later learn they each had another secret goal.

لكن باك علم لاحقًا أن كل واحد منهما كان لديه هدف سري آخر.

That night Buck faced a new and troubling challenge—how to sleep.

في تلك الليلة واجه باك تحديًا جديدًا ومزعجًا - كيفية النوم.

The tent glowed warmly with candlelight in the snowy field.

أضاءت الخيمة بدفء على ضوء الشموع في الحقل الثلجي.

Buck walked inside, thinking he could rest there like before.

دخل باك إلى الداخل، معتقدًا أنه يستطيع الراحة هناك كما كان من قبل.

But Perrault and François yelled at him and threw pans.

لكن بيرولت وفرانسوا صرخوا عليه وألقوا عليه الأواني.

Shocked and confused, Buck ran out into the freezing cold.

صُدم باك وارتبك، فركض إلى البرد القارس.

A bitter wind stung his wounded shoulder and froze his paws.

لسعته ريح مريرة في كتفه المجروح وجمدت كفوفه.

He lay down in the snow and tried to sleep out in the open.

استلقى في الثلج وحاول النوم في العراء.

But the cold soon forced him to get back up, shaking badly.

لكن البرد سرعان ما أجبره على النهوض مرة أخرى، وكان يرتجف بشدة.

He wandered through the camp, trying to find a warmer spot.

تجول في المخيم، محاولاً العثور على مكان أكثر دفئًا.

But every corner was just as cold as the one before.

لكن كل زاوية كانت باردة تمامًا مثل الزاوية التي قبلها.

Sometimes savage dogs jumped at him from the darkness.

في بعض الأحيان كانت الكلاب المتوحشة تقفز عليه من الظلام.

Buck bristled his fur, bared his teeth, and snarled with warning.

انتفض باك من شدة الغضب، وكشف عن أسنانه، وزأر محذرا.

He was learning fast, and the other dogs backed off quickly.

لقد كان يتعلم بسرعة، والكلاب الأخرى تراجعت بسرعة.

Still, he had no place to sleep, and no idea what to do.

ومع ذلك، لم يكن لديه مكان للنوم، ولم تكن لديه أي فكرة عما يجب فعله.

At last, a thought came to him — check on his team-mates.

وأخيرًا، خطرت في ذهنه فكرة وهي الاطمئنان على زملائه في الفريق.

He returned to their area and was surprised to find them gone.

عاد إلى منطقتهم وفوجئ باختفائهم.

Again he searched the camp, but still could not find them.

فبحث مرة أخرى في المخيم، لكنه لم يتمكن من العثور عليهم.

He knew they could not be in the tent, or he would be too.

لقد علم أنه لا يمكنهما التواجد في الخيمة، وإلا فإنه سيكون هناك أيضًا.

So where had all the dogs gone in this frozen camp?

إذن، أين ذهبت كل الكلاب في هذا المخيم المتجمد؟

Buck, cold and miserable, slowly circled around the tent.

كان باك باردًا وبائسًا، وكان يدور ببطء حول الخيمة.

Suddenly, his front legs sank into soft snow and startled him.

وفجأة، غرقت ساقيه الأماميتان في الثلج الناعم، مما أثار دهشته.

Something wriggled under his feet, and he jumped back in fear.

كان هناك شيء يتحرك تحت قدميه، فقفز إلى الوراء خوفًا.

He growled and snarled, not knowing what lay beneath the snow.

لقد هدَر وهدر، وهو لا يعرف ما الذي يكمن تحت الثلج.

Then he heard a friendly little bark that eased his fear.

ثم سمع نباحًا صغيرًا ودودًا خفف من خوفه.

He sniffed the air and came closer to see what was hidden.

استنشق الهواء واقترب ليرى ما كان مخفيًا.

Under the snow, curled into a warm ball, was little Billee.

تحت الثلج، كانت بيلي الصغيرة ملتفة على شكل كرة دافئة.

Billee wagged his tail and licked Buck's face to greet him.

حرك بيلي ذيله ولعق وجه باك للترحيب به.

Buck saw how Billee had made a sleeping place in the snow.

رأى باك كيف صنع بيلي مكانًا للنوم في الثلج.

He had dug down and used his own heat to stay warm.

لقد حفر بعمق واستخدم حرارته الخاصة ليبقى دافئًا.

Buck had learned another lesson—this was how the dogs slept.

لقد تعلم باك درسًا آخر ـ هكذا تنام الكلاب.

He picked a spot and started digging his own hole in the snow.

اختار مكانًا وبدأ بحفر حفرة خاصة به في الثلج.

At first, he moved around too much and wasted energy.

في البداية، كان يتحرك كثيرًا ويهدر طاقته.

But soon his body warmed the space, and he felt safe.

ولكن سرعان ما أصبح جسده دافئًا في المكان، وشعر بالأمان.

He curled up tightly, and before long he was fast asleep.

لقد التفت بإحكام، وبعد فترة وجيزة كان نائماً بسرعة.

The day had been long and hard, and Buck was exhausted.

لقد كان اليوم طويلاً وشاقًا، وكان باك مرهقًا.

He slept deeply and comfortably, though his dreams were wild.

لقد نام بعمق وبشكل مريح، على الرغم من أن أحلامه كانت جامحة.

He growled and barked in his sleep, twisting as he dreamed.

كان يزأر وينبح أثناء نومه، ويتلوى أثناء حلمه.

Buck didn't wake up until the camp was already coming to life.

لم يستيقظ باك إلا عندما بدأ المخيم ينبض بالحياة بالفعل.

At first, he didn't know where he was or what had happened.

في البداية، لم يكن يعرف أين هو أو ماذا حدث.

Snow had fallen overnight and completely buried his body.

تساقطت الثلوج طوال الليل ودفنت جسده بالكامل.

The snow pressed in around him, tight on all sides.

كان الثلج يضغط عليه من جميع الجوانب.

Suddenly a wave of fear rushed through Buck's entire body.

فجأة، موجة من الخوف اجتاح جسد باك بأكمله.

It was the fear of being trapped, a fear from deep instincts.

كان الخوف من الوقوع في الفخ، خوفًا من الغرائز العميقة.

Though he had never seen a trap, the fear lived inside him.

رغم أنه لم يرى فخًا قط، إلا أن الخوف عاش بداخله.

He was a tame dog, but now his old wild instincts were waking.

لقد كان كلبًا أليفًا، لكن غرائزه البرية القديمة كانت تستيقظ الآن.

Buck's muscles tensed, and his fur stood up all over his back.

توترت عضلات باك، ووقف فروه على ظهره بالكامل.

He snarled fiercely and sprang straight up through the snow.

لقد هدر بشدة وقفز مباشرة عبر الثلج.

Snow flew in every direction as he burst into the daylight.

تطايرت الثلوج في كل اتجاه عندما انفجر في ضوء النهار.

Even before landing, Buck saw the camp spread out before him.

حتى قبل الهبوط، رأى باك المخيم منتشرًا أمامه.

He remembered everything from the day before, all at once.

لقد تذكر كل شيء من اليوم السابق، دفعة واحدة.

He remembered strolling with Manuel and ending up in this place.

تذكر أنه كان يتجول مع مانويل وينتهي به الأمر في هذا المكان.

He remembered digging the hole and falling asleep in the cold.

تذكر أنه حفر الحفرة ونام في البرد.

Now he was awake, and the wild world around him was clear.

والآن أصبح مستيقظًا، والعالم البري من حوله أصبح واضحًا.

A shout from François hailed Buck's sudden appearance.

صرخة من فرانسوا ترحب بظهور باك المفاجئ.

"What did I say?" the dog-driver cried loudly to Perrault.

"ماذا قلت؟" صرخ سائق الكلب بصوت عالٍ إلى بيرولت.

"That Buck for sure learns quick as anything," François added.

وأضاف فرانسوا "من المؤكد أن باك يتعلم بسرعة أكبر من أي شيء آخر".

Perrault nodded gravely, clearly pleased with the result.

أومأ بيرولت برأسه بجدية، وكان سعيدًا بوضوح بالنتيجة.

As a courier for the Canadian Government, he carried dispatches.

وباعتباره رسولًا للحكومة الكندية، فقد كان يحمل الإرساليات.

He was eager to find the best dogs for his important mission.

وكان حريصًا على العثور على أفضل الكلاب لمهمته المهمة.

He felt especially pleased now that Buck was part of the team.

لقد شعر بسعادة خاصة الآن لأن باك أصبح جزءًا من الفريق.

Three more huskies were added to the team within an hour.

تمت إضافة ثلاثة كلاب هاسكي أخرى إلى الفريق خلال ساعة.

That brought the total number of dogs on the team to nine.

وبذلك أصبح العدد الإجمالي للكلاب في الفريق تسعة.

Within fifteen minutes all the dogs were in their harnesses.

في غضون خمسة عشر دقيقة كانت جميع الكلاب في أحزمتهم.

The sled team was swinging up the trail toward Dyea Cañon.

كان فريق الزلاجات يتأرجح على طول الطريق نحو ديا كانون.

Buck felt glad to be leaving, even if the work ahead was hard.

شعر باك بالسعادة لمغادرته، حتى لو كان العمل الذي ينتظره صعبًا.

He found he did not particularly despise the labor or the cold.

لقد اكتشف أنه لا يحتقر العمل أو البرد بشكل خاص.

He was surprised by the eagerness that filled the whole team.

لقد تفاجأ بالحماس الذي ملأ الفريق بأكمله.

Even more surprising was the change that had come over Dave and Solleks.

وكان الأمر الأكثر إثارة للدهشة هو التغيير الذي طرأ على ديف وسوليكس.

These two dogs were entirely different when they were harnessed.

كان هذان الكلبان مختلفين تمامًا عندما تم تسخيرهما.

Their passiveness and lack of concern had completely disappeared.

لقد اختفى سلبيتهم وعدم اهتمامهم تمامًا.

They were alert and active, and eager to do their work well.

وكانوا متيقظين ونشيطين ومتحمسين للقيام بعملهم على أكمل وجه.

They grew fiercely irritated at anything that caused delay or confusion.

لقد أصبحوا منزعجين بشدة من أي شيء يسبب التأخير أو الارتباك.

The hard work on the reins was the center of their entire being.

كان العمل الشاق على اللجام هو مركز وجودهم بأكمله.

Sled pulling seemed to be the only thing they truly enjoyed.

يبدو أن سحب الزلاجات كان الشيء الوحيد الذي يستمتعون به حقًا.

Dave was at the back of the group, closest to the sled itself.

وكان ديف في مؤخرة المجموعة، الأقرب إلى الزلاجة نفسها.

Buck was placed in front of Dave, and Solleks pulled ahead of Buck.

تم وضع باك أمام ديف، وسوليكس متقدمًا على باك.

The rest of the dogs were strung out ahead in a single file.

تم تجميع بقية الكلاب في صف واحد في المقدمة.

The lead position at the front was filled by Spitz.

شغل سبيتز منصب القائد في المقدمة.

Buck had been placed between Dave and Solleks for instruction.

تم وضع باك بين ديف وسوليكس للحصول على التعليمات.

He was a quick learner, and they were firm and capable teachers.

لقد كان سريع التعلم، وكانوا معلمين حازمين وقادرين.

They never allowed Buck to remain in error for long.

لم يسمحوا لباك أبدًا بالبقاء في الخطأ لفترة طويلة.

They taught their lessons with sharp teeth when needed.

لقد قاموا بتدريس دروسهم بأسنان حادة عندما كان ذلك ضروريا.

Dave was fair and showed a quiet, serious kind of wisdom.

كان ديف عادلاً وأظهر نوعًا من الحكمة الهادئة والجادة.

He never bit Buck without a good reason to do so.

لم يعض باك أبدًا دون سبب وجيه للقيام بذلك.

But he never failed to bite when Buck needed correction.

ولكنه لم يفشل أبدًا في العض عندما كان باك بحاجة إلى التصحيح.

François's whip was always ready and backed up their authority.

وكان سوط فرانسوا جاهزًا دائمًا ويدعم سلطتهم.

Buck soon found it was better to obey than to fight back.

سرعان ما أدرك باك أنه من الأفضل أن يطيع بدلاً من أن يقاتل.

Once, during a short rest, Buck got tangled in the reins.

ذات مرة، أثناء فترة راحة قصيرة، تشابك باك في اللجام.

He delayed the start and confused the team's movement.

أدى إلى تأخير البداية وإرباك حركة الفريق.

Dave and Solleks flew at him and gave him a rough beating.

طار ديف وسوليكس نحوه وضربوه بشدة.

The tangle only got worse, but Buck learned his lesson well.

لقد أصبح التشابك أسوأ، لكن باك تعلم درسه جيدًا.

From then on, he kept the reins taut, and worked carefully.

ومنذ ذلك الحين، أبقى زمام الأمور مشدودة، وعمل بعناية.

Before the day ended, Buck had mastered much of his task.

قبل أن ينتهي اليوم، كان باك قد أتقن جزءًا كبيرًا من مهمته.

His teammates almost stopped correcting or biting him.

كاد زملاؤه في الفريق أن يتوقفوا عن تصحيحه أو عضه.

François's whip cracked through the air less and less often.

أصبح صوت سوط فرانسوا يتكسر في الهواء بشكل أقل وأقل.

Perrault even lifted Buck's feet and carefully examined each paw.

حتى أن بيرولت رفع قدمي باك وفحص كل مخلب بعناية.

It had been a hard day's run, long and exhausting for them all.

لقد كان يومًا شاقًا، طويلًا ومضنيًا بالنسبة لهم جميعًا.

They travelled up the Cañon, through Sheep Camp, and past the Scales.

لقد سافروا عبر الوادي، عبر معسكر الأغنام، وبعد ذلك عبر المقاييس.

They crossed the timber line, then glaciers and snowdrifts many feet deep.

لقد عبروا خط الأشجار، ثم عبروا الأنهار الجليدية والثلوج التي يصل عمقها إلى عدة أقدام.

They climbed the great cold and forbidding Chilkoot Divide.

لقد تسلقوا منحدر تشيلكوت البارد والشديد القسوة.

That high ridge stood between salt water and the frozen interior.

كانت تلك التلال المرتفعة تقع بين المياه المالحة والداخل المتجمد.

The mountains guarded the sad and lonely North with ice and steep climbs.

تحرس الجبال الشمال الحزين والوحيد بالجليد والمنحدرات الشديدة.

They made good time down a long chain of lakes below the divide.

لقد حققوا وقتًا جيدًا في النزول عبر سلسلة طويلة من البحيرات أسفل التقسيم.

Those lakes filled the ancient craters of extinct volcanoes.

كانت تلك البحيرات تملأ فوهات البراكين المنقرضة القديمة.

Late that night, they reached a large camp at Lake Bennett.

وفي وقت متأخر من تلك الليلة، وصلوا إلى معسكر كبير في بحيرة بينيت.

Thousands of gold seekers were there, building boats for spring.

كان هناك آلاف الباحثين عن الذهب، يقومون ببناء القوارب للربيع.

The ice was going break up soon, and they had to be ready.

كان الجليد على وشك أن يتكسر قريبًا، وكان عليهم أن يكونوا مستعدين.

Buck dug his hole in the snow and fell into a deep sleep.

حفر باك حفرته في الثلج وسقط في نوم عميق.

He slept like a working man, exhausted from the harsh day of toil.

لقد نام كرجل عامل، منهكًا من يوم العمل الشاق.

But too early in the darkness, he was dragged from sleep.

ولكن في وقت مبكر جدًا من الظلام، تم سحبه من النوم.

He was harnessed with his mates again and attached to the sled.

تم ربطه مع زملائه مرة أخرى وربطه بالزلاجة.

That day they made forty miles, because the snow was well trodden.

في ذلك اليوم قطعوا أربعين ميلاً، لأن الثلج كان ممطراً بشكل كبير.

The next day, and for many days after, the snow was soft.

وفي اليوم التالي، ولعدة أيام بعد ذلك، كان الثلج ناعمًا.

They had to make the path themselves, working harder and moving slower.

كان عليهم أن يصنعوا الطريق بأنفسهم، ويبذلوا جهدًا أكبر ويتحركوا ببطء.

Usually, Perrault walked ahead of the team with webbed snowshoes.

عادة، كان بيرولت يمشي أمام الفريق مرتديًا أحذية الثلج المزودة بشبكة.

His steps packed the snow, making it easier for the sled to move.

كانت خطواته تضغط على الثلج، مما يجعل من السهل على الزلاجة التحرك.

François, who steered from the gee-pole, sometimes took over.

كان فرانسوا، الذي كان يقود من اتجاه الجي، يتولى القيادة في بعض الأحيان.

But it was rare that François took the lead

ولكن كان من النادر أن يتولى فرانسوا زمام المبادرة

because Perrault was in a rush to deliver the letters and parcels.

لأن بيرولت كان في عجلة من أمره لتسليم الرسائل والطرود.

Perrault was proud of his knowledge of snow, and especially ice.

كان بيرولت فخوراً بمعرفته بالثلج، وخاصة الجليد.

That knowledge was essential, because fall ice was dangerously thin.

كانت هذه المعرفة ضرورية، لأن الجليد في الخريف كان رقيقًا بشكل خطير.

Where water flowed fast beneath the surface, there was no ice at all.

حيث كان الماء يتدفق بسرعة تحت السطح، ولم يكن هناك جليد على الإطلاق.

Day after day, the same routine repeated without end.

يوما بعد يوم، نفس الروتين يتكرر بلا نهاية.

Buck toiled endlessly in the reins from dawn until night.

كان باك يتعب بلا نهاية في قيادة الحصان من الفجر حتى الليل.

They left camp in the dark, long before the sun had risen.

غادروا المخيم في الظلام، قبل وقت طويل من شروق الشمس.

By the time daylight came, many miles were already behind them.

وبحلول ضوء النهار، كانوا قد قطعوا أميالاً عديدة بالفعل.

They pitched camp after dark, eating fish and burrowing into snow.

أقاموا المخيم بعد حلول الظلام، وأكلوا الأسماك وحفروا في الثلوج.

Buck was always hungry and never truly satisfied with his ration.

كان باك دائمًا جائعًا ولم يكن راضيًا أبدًا عن حصته.

He received a pound and a half of dried salmon each day.

كان يتلقى رطلاً ونصفًا من سمك السلمون المجفف يوميًا.

But the food seemed to vanish inside him, leaving hunger behind.

لكن الطعام بدا وكأنه يختفي بداخله، تاركا الجوع خلفه.

He suffered from constant pangs of hunger, and dreamed of more food.

كان يعاني من نوبات الجوع المستمرة، ويحلم بالمزيد من الطعام.

The other dogs got only one pound of food, but they stayed strong.

حصلت الكلاب الأخرى على رطل واحد فقط من الطعام، لكنها ظلت قوية.

They were smaller, and had been born into the northern life.

لقد كانوا أصغر حجمًا، وولدوا في الحياة الشمالية.

He swiftly lost the fastidiousness which had marked his old life.

لقد فقد بسرعة الصرامة التي ميزت حياته القديمة.

He had been a dainty eater, but now that was no longer possible.

لقد كان يأكل طعامًا لذيذًا، لكن الآن لم يعد ذلك ممكنًا.

His mates finished first and robbed him of his unfinished ration.

انتهى أصدقاؤه أولاً وسرقوا منه حصته غير المكتملة.

Once they began there was no way to defend his food from them.

بمجرد أن بدأوا لم يكن هناك طريقة للدفاع عن طعامه منهم.

While he fought off two or three dogs, the others stole the rest.

بينما كان يقاتل كلبين أو ثلاثة، قام الآخرون بسرقة الباقي.

To fix this, he began eating as fast as the others ate.

ولإصلاح ذلك، بدأ يأكل بسرعة مثل الآخرين.

Hunger pushed him so hard that he even took food not his own.

كان الجوع يدفعه بقوة إلى أن يتناول طعامًا ليس من حقه.

He watched the others and learned quickly from their actions.

لقد راقب الآخرين وتعلم بسرعة من أفعالهم.

He saw Pike, a new dog, steal a slice of bacon from Perrault.

لقد رأى بايك، وهو كلب جديد، يسرق شريحة من لحم الخنزير المقدد من بيرولت.

Pike had waited until Perrault's back was turned to steal the bacon.

انتظر بايك حتى أصبح ظهر بيرولت بعيدًا لسرقة لحم الخنزير المقدد.

The next day, Buck copied Pike and stole the whole chunk.

في اليوم التالي، قام باك بنسخ بايك وسرق القطعة بأكملها.

A great uproar followed, but Buck was not suspected.

وقد أعقب ذلك ضجة كبيرة، لكن لم يكن هناك أي شك في باك.

Dub, a clumsy dog who always got caught, was punished instead.

دب، الكلب الأخرق الذي يتم القبض عليه دائمًا، تم معاقبته بدلاً من ذلك.

That first theft marked Buck as a dog fit to survive the North.

كانت تلك السرقة الأولى بمثابة إشارة إلى أن باك هو الكلب المناسب للبقاء على قيد الحياة في الشمال.

He showed he could adapt to new conditions and learn quickly.

وأظهر أنه قادر على التكيف مع الظروف الجديدة والتعلم بسرعة.

Without such adaptability, he would have died swiftly and badly.

ولولا هذه القدرة على التكيف لكان قد مات بسرعة وبصورة سيئة.

It also marked the breakdown of his moral nature and past values.

كما أنها كانت بمثابة انهيار لطبيعته الأخلاقية وقيمه الماضية.

In the Southland, he had lived under the law of love and kindness.

لقد عاش في الجنوب تحت قانون الحب واللطف.

There it made sense to respect property and other dogs' feelings.

هناك كان من المنطقي احترام الممتلكات ومشاعر الكلاب الأخرى.

But the Northland followed the law of club and the law of fang.

لكن سكان نورثلاند اتبعوا قانون النادي وقانون الأنياب.

Whoever respected old values here was foolish and would fail.

من احترم القيم القديمة هنا كان أحمقًا وسوف يفشل.

Buck did not reason all this out in his mind.

لم يكن باك قادراً على تفسير كل هذا في ذهنه.

He was fit, and so he adjusted without needing to think.

لقد كان لائقًا، لذا فقد تكيف دون الحاجة إلى التفكير.

All his life, he had never run away from a fight.

طوال حياته، لم يهرب أبدًا من القتال.

But the wooden club of the man in the red sweater changed that rule.

لكن الهراوة الخشبية للرجل ذو السترة الحمراء غيّرت هذه القاعدة.

Now he followed a deeper, older code written into his being.

والآن أصبح يتبع قانونًا أعمق وأقدم مكتوبًا في كيانه.

He did not steal out of pleasure, but from the pain of hunger.

لم يسرق من أجل المتعة، بل من أجل ألم الجوع.

He never robbed openly, but stole with cunning and care.

لم يسرق علانيةً قط، بل سرق بمكر وحرص.

He acted out of respect for the wooden club and fear of the fang.

لقد تصرف بدافع الاحترام للنادي الخشبي والخوف من الناب.

In short, he did what was easier and safer than not doing it.

باختصار، لقد فعل ما كان أسهل وأكثر أمانًا من عدم فعله.

His development—or perhaps his return to old instincts—was fast.

وكان تطوره - أو ربما عودته إلى غرائزه القديمة - سريعًا.

His muscles hardened until they felt as strong as iron.

تصلبت عضلاته حتى أصبح شعرها قويا مثل الحديد.

He no longer cared about pain, unless it was serious.

لم يعد يهتم بالألم، إلا إذا كان خطيرًا.

He became efficient inside and out, wasting nothing at all.

لقد أصبح فعالاً من الداخل والخارج، ولم يهدر أي شيء على الإطلاق.

He could eat things that were vile, rotten, or hard to digest.

كان بإمكانه أن يأكل أشياء كريهة، أو فاسدة، أو صعبة الهضم.

Whatever he ate, his stomach used every last bit of value.

مهما كان ما يأكله، فإن معدته تستهلك كل ما فيه من قيمة.

His blood carried the nutrients far through his powerful body.

حمل دمه العناصر الغذائية إلى كل أنحاء جسده القوي.

This built strong tissues that gave him incredible endurance.

لقد أدى ذلك إلى بناء أنسجة قوية أعطته قدرة تحمل لا تصدق.

His sight and smell became much more sensitive than before.

أصبحت حاسة البصر والشم لديه أكثر حساسية من ذي قبل.

His hearing grew so sharp he could detect faint sounds in sleep.

لقد أصبح سمعه حادًا لدرجة أنه كان قادرًا على اكتشاف الأصوات الخافتة أثناء النوم.

He knew in his dreams whether the sounds meant safety or danger.

كان يعرف في أحلامه ما إذا كانت الأصوات تعني الأمان أم الخطر.

He learned to bite the ice between his toes with his teeth.

لقد تعلم كيفية قضم الجليد بين أصابع قدميه بأسنانه.

If a water hole froze over, he would break the ice with his legs.

إذا تجمدت حفرة الماء، فإنه يكسر الجليد بساقيه.

He reared up and struck the ice hard with stiff front limbs.

نهض وضرب الجليد بقوة بأطرافه الأمامية الصلبة.

His most striking ability was predicting wind changes overnight.

كانت قدرته الأبرز هي التنبؤ بتغيرات الرياح أثناء الليل.

Even when the air was still, he chose spots sheltered from wind.

حتى عندما كان الهواء ساكنًا، اختار أماكن محمية من الرياح.

Wherever he dug his nest, the next day's wind passed him by.

أينما حفر عشه، مرت به رياح اليوم التالي.

He always ended up snug and protected, to leeward of the breeze.

لقد انتهى به الأمر دائمًا إلى أن يكون مرتاحًا ومحميًا، في مأمن من النسيم.

Buck not only learned by experience — his instincts returned too.

لم يتعلم باك من خلال الخبرة فحسب، بل عادت غرائزه أيضًا.

The habits of domesticated generations began to fall away.

بدأت عادات الأجيال المستأنسة في التلاشي.

In vague ways, he remembered the ancient times of his breed.

وبطرق غامضة، تذكر العصور القديمة لسلالاته.

He thought back to when wild dogs ran in packs through forests.

لقد فكر في الوقت الذي كانت فيه الكلاب البرية تركض في مجموعات عبر الغابات.

They had chased and killed their prey while running it down.

لقد طاردوا فريستهم وقتلوها أثناء مطاردتها.

It was easy for Buck to learn how to fight with tooth and speed.

لقد كان من السهل على باك أن يتعلم كيفية القتال بقوة وسرعة.

He used cuts, slashes, and quick snaps just like his ancestors.

لقد استخدم القطع والتشريح والالتقاطات السريعة تمامًا مثل أسلافه.

Those ancestors stirred within him and awoke his wild nature.

لقد تحرك هؤلاء الأجداد في داخله وأيقظوا طبيعته البرية.

Their old skills had passed into him through the bloodline.

لقد انتقلت مهاراتهم القديمة إليه من خلال سلالة الدم.

Their tricks were his now, with no need for practice or effort.

أصبحت حيلهم الآن بين يديه، دون الحاجة إلى التدريب أو بذل الجهد.

On still, cold nights, Buck lifted his nose and howled.

في الليالي الباردة الهادئة، كان باك يرفع أنفه ويصرخ.

He howled long and deep, the way wolves had done long ago.

عوى طويلاً وعميقاً، كما فعل الذئاب منذ زمن بعيد.

Through him, his dead ancestors pointed their noses and howled.

ومن خلاله أشار أسلافه الموتى بأنوفهم وعووا.

They howled down through the centuries in his voice and shape.

لقد صرخوا عبر القرون بصوته وشكلته.

His cadences were theirs, old cries that told of grief and cold.

كانت إيقاعاته هي إيقاعاتهم، صرخات قديمة تحكي عن الحزن والبرد.

They sang of darkness, of hunger, and the meaning of winter.

لقد غنوا عن الظلام، والجوع، ومعنى الشتاء.

Buck proved of how life is shaped by forces beyond oneself,

أثبت باك كيف تتشكل الحياة من خلال قوى خارج الذات،

the ancient song rose through Buck and took hold of his soul.

ارتفعت الأغنية القديمة عبر باك واستولت على روحه.

He found himself because men had found gold in the North.

لقد وجد نفسه لأن الرجال وجدوا الذهب في الشمال.

And he found himself because Manuel, the gardener's helper, needed money.

ووجد نفسه لأن مانويل، مساعد البستاني، كان يحتاج إلى المال.

The Dominant Primordial Beast
الوحش البدائي المسيطر

The dominant primordial beast was as strong as ever in Buck.

كان الوحش البدائي المهيمن قويًا كما كان دائمًا في باك.

But the dominant primordial beast had lain dormant in him.

لكن الوحش البدائي المسيطر كان كامنًا بداخله.

Trail life was harsh, but it strengthened beast inside Buck.

كانت حياة الطريق قاسية، لكنها عززت الوحش داخل باك.

Secretly the beast grew stronger and stronger every day.

في الخفاء، أصبح الوحش أقوى وأقوى كل يوم.

But that inner growth stayed hidden to the outside world.

لكن هذا النمو الداخلي بقي مخفيا عن العالم الخارجي.

A quiet and calm primordial force was building inside Buck.

كانت هناك قوة بدائية هادئة وساكنة تتراكم داخل باك.

New cunning gave Buck balance, calm control, and poise.

لقد أعطى المكر الجديد باك التوازن والتحكم الهادئ والاتزان.

Buck focused hard on adapting, never feeling fully relaxed.

ركز باك بشدة على التكيف، ولم يشعر بالاسترخاء التام أبدًا.

He avoided conflict, never starting fights, nor seeking trouble.

كان يتجنب الصراع، ولا يبدأ القتال أبدًا، ولا يسعى إلى المتاعب.

A slow, steady thoughtfulness shaped Buck's every move.

كان التفكير البطيء والثابت هو الذي شكل كل تحركات باك.

He avoided rash choices and sudden, reckless decisions.

كان يتجنب الاختيارات المتهورة والقرارات المفاجئة المتهورة.

Though Buck hated Spitz deeply, he showed him no aggression.

على الرغم من أن باك كان يكره سبيتز بشدة، إلا أنه لم يظهر له أي عدوان.

Buck never provoked Spitz, and kept his actions restrained.

لم يستفز باك سبيتز أبدًا، وحافظ على أفعاله مقيدة.

Spitz, on the other hand, sensed the growing danger in Buck.

ومن ناحية أخرى، شعر سبيتز بالخطر المتزايد في باك.

He saw Buck as a threat and a serious challenge to his power.

لقد رأى باك كتهديد وتحدي خطير لسلطته.

He used every chance to snarl and show his sharp teeth.

لقد استغل كل فرصة للهجوم وإظهار أسنانه الحادة.

He was trying to start the deadly fight that had to come.

لقد كان يحاول بدء القتال المميت الذي كان لا بد أن يأتي.

Early in the trip, a fight nearly broke out between them.

وفي وقت مبكر من الرحلة، كاد قتال أن يندلع بينهما.

But an unexpected accident stopped the fight from happening.

ولكن حادث غير متوقع منع حدوث القتال.

That evening they set up camp on the bitterly cold Lake Le Barge.

وفي ذلك المساء أقاموا مخيمهم على بحيرة لو بارج شديدة البرودة.

The snow was falling hard, and the wind cut like a knife.

كان الثلج يتساقط بغزارة، والريح تقطع مثل السكين.

The night had come too fast, and darkness surrounded them.

لقد جاء الليل سريعًا جدًا، والظلام يحيط بهم.

They could hardly have chosen a worse place for rest.

لم يكن بإمكانهم اختيار مكان أسوأ للراحة.

The dogs searched desperately for a place to lie down.

بحثت الكلاب بشكل يائس عن مكان للاستلقاء.

A tall rock wall rose steeply behind the small group.

ارتفع جدار صخري طويل بشكل حاد خلف المجموعة الصغيرة.

The tent had been left behind in Dyea to lighten the load.

لقد تم ترك الخيمة في دايا لتخفيف الحمل.

They had no choice but to make the fire on the ice itself.

لم يكن أمامهم خيار سوى إشعال النار على الجليد نفسه.

They spread their sleeping robes directly on the frozen lake.

قاموا بنشر أردية نومهم مباشرة على البحيرة المتجمدة.

A few sticks of driftwood gave them a little bit of fire.

أعطتهم بضعة أعواد من الخشب الطافي القليل من النار.

But the fire was built on the ice, and thawed through it.

لكن النار اشتعلت على الجليد، وذابت من خلاله.

Eventually they were eating their supper in darkness.

وفي النهاية كانوا يتناولون عشاءهم في الظلام.

Buck curled up beside the rock, sheltered from the cold wind.

انحنى باك بجانب الصخرة، محميًا من الرياح الباردة.

The spot was so warm and safe that Buck hated to move away.

كان المكان دافئًا وآمنًا لدرجة أن باك كان يكره الانتقال بعيدًا.

But François had warmed the fish and was handing out rations.

لكن فرانسوا قام بتسخين الأسماك وقام بتوزيع الحصص.

Buck finished eating quickly, and returned to his bed.

انتهى باك من تناول الطعام بسرعة، وعاد إلى سريره.

But Spitz was now laying where Buck had made his bed.

لكن سبيتز كان مستلقيًا الآن حيث صنع باك سريره.

A low snarl warned Buck that Spitz refused to move.

حذرت صرخة منخفضة باك من أن سبيتز رفض التحرك.

Until now, Buck had avoided this fight with Spitz.

حتى الآن، كان باك يتجنب هذه المعركة مع سبيتز.

But deep inside Buck the beast finally broke loose.

ولكن في أعماق باك، انطلق الوحش أخيرًا.

The theft of his sleeping place was too much to tolerate.

لقد كانت سرقة مكان نومه أمراً لا يطاق.

Buck launched himself at Spitz, full of anger and rage.

انقض باك على سبيتز، وكان مليئًا بالغضب والغضب.

Up until not Spitz had thought Buck was just a big dog.

حتى ذلك الوقت كان سبيتز يعتقد أن باك كان مجرد كلب كبير.

He didn't think Buck had survived through his spirit.

لم يعتقد أن باك قد نجا من خلال روحه.

He was expecting fear and cowardice, not fury and revenge.

كان يتوقع الخوف والجبن، وليس الغضب والانتقام.

François stared as both dogs burst from the ruined nest.

حدق فرانسوا بينما خرج الكلبان من العش المدمر.

He understood at once what had started the wild struggle.

لقد فهم على الفور سبب بدء الصراع الوحشي.

"A-a-ah!" François cried out in support of the brown dog.

"آه-آه!" صرخ فرانسوا دعماً للكلب البني.

"Give him a beating! By God, punish that sneaky thief!"

"اضربوه! والله، عاقبوا هذا اللص الماكر!"

Spitz showed equal readiness and wild eagerness to fight.

وأظهر سبيتز استعدادًا مماثلاً وحماسًا شديدًا للقتال.

He cried out in rage while circling fast, seeking an opening.

صرخ بغضب وهو يدور بسرعة، باحثًا عن فرصة.

Buck showed the same hunger to fight, and the same caution.

وأظهر باك نفس الرغبة في القتال، ونفس الحذر.

He circled his opponent as well, trying to gain the upper hand in battle.

كما حاصر خصمه أيضًا، محاولًا كسب اليد العليا في المعركة.

Then something unexpected happened and changed everything.

ثم حدث شيء غير متوقع وغير كل شيء.

That moment delayed the eventual fight for the leadership.

لقد أدت تلك اللحظة إلى تأخير المعركة النهائية على القيادة.

Many miles of trail and struggle still waited before the end.

لا تزال أميال عديدة من الطريق والنضال تنتظر قبل النهاية.

Perrault shouted an oath as a club smacked against bone.

صرخ بيرولت بقسم بينما كانت الهراوة تصطدم بالعظم.

A sharp yelp of pain followed, then chaos exploded all around.

تبع ذلك صرخة حادة من الألم، ثم انفجرت الفوضى في كل مكان.

Dark shapes moved in camp; wild huskies, starved and fierce.

تحركت الأشكال المظلمة في المخيم؛ كلاب الهاسكي البرية، الجائعة والشرسة.

Four or five dozen huskies had sniffed the camp from far away.

كان هناك أربعة أو خمسة عشرات من الكلاب الهاسكي تشم المخيم من بعيد.

They had crept in quietly while the two dogs fought nearby.

لقد تسللوا بهدوء بينما كان الكلبان يتقاتلان في مكان قريب.

François and Perrault charged, swinging clubs at the invaders.

هاجم فرانسوا وبيرو الغزاة، ولوحوا بالهراوات في وجههم.

The starving huskies showed teeth and fought back in frenzy.

أظهرت الكلاب الهاسكي الجائعة أسنانها وقاتلت بشراسة.

The smell of meat and bread had driven them past all fear.

لقد دفعتهم رائحة اللحوم والخبز إلى تجاوز كل الخوف.

Perrault beat a dog that had buried its head in the grub-box.

ضرب بيرولت كلبًا دفن رأسه في صندوق الطعام.

The blow hit hard, and the box flipped, food spilling out.

كانت الضربة قوية، وانقلب الصندوق، وتناثر الطعام خارجه.

In seconds, a score of wild beasts tore into the bread and meat.

في ثوانٍ، هاجمت مجموعة من الوحوش البرية الخبز واللحم.

The men's clubs landed blow after blow, but no dog turned away.

وسددت أندية الرجال ضربة تلو الأخرى، لكن لم يتراجع أحد.

They howled in pain, but fought until no food remained.

لقد صرخوا من الألم، لكنهم قاتلوا حتى لم يبق طعام.

Meanwhile, the sled-dogs had jumped from their snowy beds.

وفي هذه الأثناء، قفزت كلاب الزلاجات من أسرتها الثلجية.

They were instantly attacked by the vicious hungry huskies.

لقد تعرضوا على الفور لهجوم من قبل الكلاب الهاسكي الجائعة الشرسة.

Buck had never seen such wild and starved creatures before.

لم يسبق لباك أن رأى مثل هذه المخلوقات البرية والجائعة من قبل.

Their skin hung loose, barely hiding their skeletons.

كانت جلودهم متدلية، بالكاد تخفي هياكلهم العظمية.

There was a fire in their eyes, from hunger and madness

وكان في عيونهم نار من الجوع والجنون

There was no stopping them; no resisting their savage rush.

لم يكن هناك ما يوقفهم، ولا ما يقاوم اندفاعهم الوحشي.

The sled-dogs were shoved back, pressed against the cliff wall.

تم دفع كلاب الزلاجات إلى الخلف، وضغطها على جدار الجرف.

Three huskies attacked Buck at once, tearing into his flesh.

هاجم ثلاثة كلاب هاسكي باك في وقت واحد، وقاموا بتمزيق لحمه.

Blood poured from his head and shoulders, where he'd been cut.

تدفق الدم من رأسه وكتفيه حيث تم قطعه.

The noise filled the camp; growling, yelps, and cries of pain.

امتلأ المخيم بالضجيج؛ هدير، صراخ، وصراخ الألم.

Billee cried loudly, as usual, caught in the fray and panic.

بكت بيلي بصوت عالٍ، كعادتها، وهي عالقة في المعركة والذعر.

Dave and Solleks stood side by side, bleeding but defiant.

كان ديف وسوليكس واقفين جنبًا إلى جنب، ينزفان ولكنهما متحدان.

Joe fought like a demon, biting anything that came close.

كان جو يقاتل مثل الشيطان، يعض أي شيء يقترب منه.

He crushed a husky's leg with one brutal snap of his jaws.

لقد سحق ساق الهاسكي بضربة وحشية من فكيه.

Pike jumped on the wounded husky and broke its neck instantly.

قفز بايك على الهاسكي الجريح وكسر رقبته على الفور.

Buck caught a husky by the throat and ripped through the vein.

أمسك باك كلب الهاسكي من حلقه ومزقه من خلال الوريد.

Blood sprayed, and the warm taste drove Buck into a frenzy.

تناثر الدم، والطعم الدافئ دفع باك إلى الجنون.

He hurled himself at another attacker without hesitation.

ألقى بنفسه على مهاجم آخر دون تردد.

At the same moment, sharp teeth dug into Buck's own throat.

وفي نفس اللحظة، حفرت أسنان حادة في حلق باك.

Spitz had struck from the side, attacking without warning.

لقد ضرب سبيتز من الجانب، مهاجمًا دون سابق إنذار.

Perrault and François had defeated the dogs stealing the food.

تمكن بيرولت وفرانسوا من هزيمة الكلاب التي كانت تسرق الطعام.

Now they rushed to help their dogs fight back the attackers.

والآن سارعوا لمساعدة كلابهم في محاربة المهاجمين.

The starving dogs retreated as the men swung their clubs.

تراجعت الكلاب الجائعة بينما كان الرجال يهزون هراواتهم.

Buck broke free from the attack, but the escape was brief.

تمكن باك من الهروب من الهجوم، لكن الهروب كان قصيرًا.

The men ran to save their dogs, and the huskies swarmed again.

ركض الرجال لإنقاذ كلابهم، وهاجمتهم الكلاب الهاسكي مرة أخرى.

Billee, frightened into bravery, leapt into the pack of dogs.

بيلي، خائفًا من الشجاعة، قفز إلى مجموعة الكلاب.

But then he fled across the ice, in raw terror and panic.

لكن بعد ذلك هرب عبر الجليد، في حالة من الرعب والذعر.

Pike and Dub followed close behind, running for their lives.

وتبعهما بايك ودب عن كثب، يركضان لإنقاذ حياتهما.

The rest of the team broke and scattered, following after them.

بقية الفريق انكسر وتشتت، وتبعهم.

Buck gathered his strength to run, but then saw a flash.

جمع باك قوته للركض، ولكن بعد ذلك رأى وميضًا.

Spitz lunged at Buck's side, trying to knock him to the ground.

انقض سبيتز على جانب باك، محاولاً إسقاطه على الأرض.

Under that mob of huskies, Buck would have had no escape.

تحت هذا الحشد من الكلاب الهاسكي، لم يكن لدى باك أي فرصة للهروب.

But Buck stood firm and braced for the blow from Spitz.

لكن باك صمد وقاوم الضربة التي وجهها له سبيتز.

Then he turned and ran out onto the ice with the fleeing team.

ثم استدار وركض إلى الجليد مع الفريق الهارب.

Later, the nine sled-dogs gathered in the shelter of the woods.

وفي وقت لاحق، تجمعت الكلاب التسعة في ملجأ الغابة.

No one chased them anymore, but they were battered and wounded.

لم يعد أحد يطاردهم، لكنهم تعرضوا للضرب والجرح.

Each dog had wounds; four or five deep cuts on every body.

كان لدى كل كلب جروح؛ أربعة أو خمسة جروح عميقة في كل جسم.

Dub had an injured hind leg and struggled to walk now.

كان لدى داب إصابة في ساقه الخلفية وكان يكافح من أجل المشي الآن.

Dolly, the newest dog from Dyea, had a slashed throat.

دوللي، أحدث كلب من دايا، أصيب بجرح في الحلق.

Joe had lost an eye, and Billee's ear was cut to pieces

لقد فقد جو إحدى عينيه، وقُطعت أذن بيلي إلى قطع.

All the dogs cried in pain and defeat through the night.

بكت كل الكلاب من الألم والهزيمة طوال الليل.

At dawn they crept back to camp, sore and broken.

وعند الفجرِ، تسللوا عائدين إلى المخيم، متألمين ومكسورين.

The huskies had vanished, but the damage had been done.

لقد اختفت الكلاب الهاسكي، لكن الضرر كان قد وقع.

Perrault and François stood in foul moods over the ruin.

كان بيرولت وفرانسوا واقفين في مزاج سيئ فوق الأنقاض.

Half of the food was gone, snatched by the hungry thieves.

لقد اختفى نصف الطعام، وسرقه اللصوص الجائعون.

The huskies had torn through sled bindings and canvas.

لقد مزقت الكلاب الهاسكي أربطة الزلاجات والقماش.

Anything with a smell of food had been devoured completely.

لقد تم التهام أي شيء له رائحة الطعام بالكامل.

They ate a pair of Perrault's moose-hide traveling boots.

لقد أكلوا زوجًا من أحذية السفر المصنوعة من جلد الموظ الخاصة بـ بيرولت.

They chewed leather reis and ruined straps beyond use.

لقد قاموا بمضغ الريس الجلدي وإتلاف الأشرطة حتى أصبحت غير صالحة للاستخدام.

François stopped staring at the torn lash to check the dogs.

توقف فرانسوا عن النظر إلى الرموش الممزقة للتحقق من الكلاب.

"Ah, my friends," he said, his voice low and filled with worry.

"آه، أصدقائي،" قال بصوت منخفض ومليء بالقلق.

"Maybe all these bites will turn you into mad beasts."

"ربما كل هذه اللدغات سوف تحولك إلى وحوش مجنونة."

"Maybe all mad dogs, sacredam! What do you think, Perrault?"

ربما كل الكلاب المسعورة، يا إلهي! ما رأيك يا بيرولت؟

Perrault shook his head, eyes dark with concern and fear.

هز بيرولت رأسه، وكانت عيناه مظلمتين بالقلق والخوف.

Four hundred miles still lay between them and Dawson.

لا يزال هناك أربعمائة ميل بينهم وبين داوسون.

Dog madness now could destroy any chance of survival.

جنون الكلب الآن قد يدمر أي فرصة للبقاء على قيد الحياة.

They spent two hours swearing and trying to fix the gear.

لقد أمضوا ساعتين في الشتائم ومحاولة إصلاح المعدات.

The wounded team finally left the camp, broken and defeated.

وأخيراً غادر الفريق الجريح المعسكر مكسوراً ومهزوماً.

This was the hardest trail yet, and each step was painful.

لقد كان هذا هو الطريق الأصعب حتى الآن، وكل خطوة كانت مؤلمة.

The Thirty Mile River had not frozen, and was rushing wildly.

لم يتجمد نهر الثلاثين ميلاً، وكان يتدفق بعنف.

Only in calm spots and swirling eddies did ice manage to hold.

لم يتمكن الجليد من الصمود إلا في الأماكن الهادئة والتيارات الدوامية.

Six days of hard labor passed until the thirty miles were done.

لقد مرت ستة أيام من العمل الشاق حتى تم قطع الثلاثين ميلاً.

Each mile of the trail brought danger and the threat of death.

كان كل ميل من الطريق يحمل خطرًا وتهديدًا بالموت.

The men and dogs risked their lives with every painful step.

لقد خاطر الرجال والكلاب بحياتهم مع كل خطوة مؤلمة.

Perrault broke through thin ice bridges a dozen different times.

نجح بيرولت في اختراق الجسور الجليدية الرقيقة عشرات المرات المختلفة.

He carried a pole and let it fall across the hole his body made.

حمل عمودًا وتركه يسقط على الحفرة التي صنعها جسده.

More than once did that pole save Perrault from drowning.

لقد أنقذ هذا العمود بيرولت من الغرق أكثر من مرة.

The cold snap held firm, the air was fifty degrees below zero.

ظلت موجة البرد قوية، وكانت درجة حرارة الهواء خمسين درجة تحت الصفر.

Every time he fell in, Perrault had to light a fire to survive.

في كل مرة كان يسقط فيها، كان على بيرولت أن يشعل النار ليتمكن من البقاء على قيد الحياة.

Wet clothing froze fast, so he dried them near blazing heat.

تجمدت الملابس المبللة بسرعة، لذا قام بتجفيفها بالقرب من الحرارة الشديدة.

No fear ever touched Perrault, and that made him a courier.

لم يكن الخوف يمس بيرولت على الإطلاق، وهذا ما جعله رسولاً.

He was chosen for danger, and he met it with quiet resolve.

لقد تم اختياره لمواجهة الخطر، وقابله بهدوء وتصميم.

He pressed forward into wind, his shriveled face frostbitten.

تقدم للأمام في مواجهة الريح، وكان وجهه المتجعد مغطى بالصقيع.

From faint dawn to nightfall, Perrault led them onward.

من الفجر الخافت حتى حلول الليل، قادهم بيرولت إلى الأمام.

He walked on narrow rim ice that cracked with every step.

كان يمشي على حافة الجليد الضيقة التي كانت تتشقق مع كل خطوة.

They dared not stop—each pause risked a deadly collapse.

لم يجرؤوا على التوقف ـ كل توقف كان يهدد بانهيار مميت.

One time the sled broke through, pulling Dave and Buck in.

في إحدى المرات، اخترقت الزلاجة الطريق، وسحبت ديف وبوك إلى الداخل.

By the time they were dragged free, both were near frozen.

بحلول الوقت الذي تم فيه سحبهما بحرية، كان كلاهما متجمدين تقريبًا.

The men built a fire quickly to keep Buck and Dave alive.

قام الرجال بإشعال النار بسرعة لإبقاء باك وديف على قيد الحياة.

The dogs were coated in ice from nose to tail, stiff as carved wood.

كانت الكلاب مغطاة بالجليد من الأنف إلى الذيل، صلبة مثل الخشب المنحوت.

The men ran them in circles near the fire to thaw their bodies.

قام الرجال بتدويرهم في دوائر بالقرب من النار لتذويب أجسادهم.

They came so close to the flames that their fur was singed.

لقد اقتربوا من النيران لدرجة أن فرائهم احترق.

Spitz broke through the ice next, dragging in the team behind him.

ثم اخترق سبيتز الجليد، وسحب الفريق خلفه.

The break reached all the way up to where Buck was pulling.

وصل الكسر إلى كل الطريق حتى حيث كان باك يسحب.

Buck leaned back hard, paws slipping and trembling on the edge.

انحنى باك إلى الخلف بقوة، وكانت كفوفه تنزلق وترتجف على الحافة.

Dave also strained backward, just behind Buck on the line.

كما بذل ديف جهدًا كبيرًا في التراجع إلى الخلف، خلف باك مباشرة على الخط.

François hauled on the sled, his muscles cracking with effort.

سحب فرانسوا الزلاجة، وكانت عضلاته تتكسر من شدة الجهد.

Another time, rim ice cracked before and behind the sled.

في مرة أخرى، تصدع الجليد على الحافة أمام الزلاجة وخلفها.

They had no way out except to climb a frozen cliff wall.

لم يكن لديهم أي وسيلة للخروج سوى تسلق جدار الجرف المتجمد.

Perrault somehow climbed the wall; a miracle kept him alive.

تمكن بيرولت بطريقة ما من تسلق الجدار؛ وأبقته معجزة على قيد الحياة.

François stayed below, praying for the same kind of luck.

وبقي فرانسوا في الأسفل، وهو يصلي من أجل نفس النوع من الحظ.

They tied every strap, lashing, and trace into one long rope.

قاموا بربط كل حزام، وربط، وأثر في حبل واحد طويل.

The men hauled each dog up, one at a time to the top.

سحب الرجال كل كلب على حدة إلى الأعلى.

François climbed last, after the sled and the entire load.

تسلق فرانسوا أخيرًا، بعد الزلاجة والحمولة بأكملها.

Then began a long search for a path down from the cliffs.

ثم بدأ بحث طويل عن طريق للنزول من المنحدرات.

They finally descended using the same rope they had made.

نزلوا أخيرا باستخدام نفس الحبل الذي صنعوه.

Night fell as they returned to the riverbed, exhausted and sore.

حل الليل عندما عادوا إلى مجرى النهر، مرهقين ومتألمين.

They had taken a full day to cover only a quarter of a mile.

لقد حصلوا على ربع ميل فقط من المكسب خلال اليوم الكامل.

By the time they reached the Hootalinqua, Buck was worn out.

بحلول الوقت الذي وصلوا فيه إلى هوتالينكوا، كان باك مرهقًا.

The other dogs suffered just as badly from the trail conditions.

عانت الكلاب الأخرى بنفس القدر من سوء حالة الطريق.

But Perrault needed to recover time, and pushed them on each day.

لكن بيرولت كان بحاجة إلى استعادة الوقت، وضغط عليهم كل يوم.

The first day they traveled thirty miles to Big Salmon.

في اليوم الأول سافروا مسافة ثلاثين ميلاً إلى بيج سالمون.

The next day they travelled thirty-five miles to Little Salmon.

وفي اليوم التالي سافروا خمسة وثلاثين ميلاً إلى ليتل سالمون.

On the third day they pushed through forty long frozen miles.

وفي اليوم الثالث، تمكنوا من قطع مسافة أربعين ميلاً متجمداً.

By then, they were nearing the settlement of Five Fingers.

وبحلول ذلك الوقت، كانوا يقتربون من مستوطنة فايف فينجرز.

Buck's feet were softer than the hard feet of native huskies.

كانت أقدام باك أكثر نعومة من أقدام الكلاب الهاسكي الأصلية الصلبة.

His paws had grown tender over many civilized generations.

لقد أصبحت أقدامه رقيقة على مر الأجيال المتحضرة.

Long ago, his ancestors had been tamed by river men or hunters.

منذ زمن بعيد، تم ترويض أسلافه من قبل رجال النهر أو الصيادين.

Every day Buck limped in pain, walking on raw, aching paws.

كان باك يعرج كل يوم من الألم، ويمشي على أقدامه الخام المؤلمة.

At camp, Buck dropped like a lifeless form upon the snow.

في المخيم، سقط باك مثل جسد بلا حياة على الثلج.

Though starving, Buck did not rise to eat his evening meal.

على الرغم من الجوع، لم ينهض باك لتناول وجبة العشاء.

François brought Buck his ration, laying fish by his muzzle.

أحضر فرانسوا لبوك حصته من السمك، ووضعه على فمه.

Each night the driver rubbed Buck's feet for half an hour.

كل ليلة كان السائق يدلك قدمي باك لمدة نصف ساعة.

François even cut up his own moccasins to make dog footwear.

حتى أن فرانسوا قام بتقطيع أحذية الموكاسين الخاصة به لصنع أحذية للكلاب.

Four warm shoes gave Buck a great and welcome relief.

أربعة أحذية دافئة منحت باك راحة كبيرة ومرحب بها.

One morning, François forgot the shoes, and Buck refused to rise.

في صباح أحد الأيام، نسي فرانسوا الأحذية، ورفض باك النهوض.

Buck lay on his back, feet in the air, waving them pitifully.

استلقى باك على ظهره، وقدميه في الهواء، ولوح بهما بشكل مثير للشفقة.

Even Perrault grinned at the sight of Buck's dramatic plea.

حتى بيرولت ابتسم عندما رأى نداء باك الدرامي.

Soon Buck's feet grew hard, and the shoes could be discarded.

وسرعان ما أصبحت أقدام باك قاسية، وأصبح من الممكن التخلص من الأحذية.

At Pelly, during harness time, Dolly let out a dreadful howl.

في بيلي، أثناء وقت التسخير، أطلقت دوللي عواءً مروعًا.

The cry was long and filled with madness, shaking every dog.

كانت الصرخة طويلة ومليئة بالجنون، تهز كل كلب.

Each dog bristled in fear without knowing the reason.

كان كل كلب يشعر بالخوف دون أن يعرف السبب.

Dolly had gone mad and hurled herself straight at Buck.

لقد جن جنون دوللي وألقت بنفسها على باك مباشرة.

Buck had never seen madness, but horror filled his heart.

لم يرى باك الجنون أبدًا، لكن الرعب ملأ قلبه.

With no thought, he turned and fled in absolute panic.

وبدون تفكير، استدار وهرب في حالة من الذعر المطلق.

Dolly chased him, her eyes wild, saliva flying from her jaws.

طاردته دوللي، وكانت عيناها متوحشتين، وكان اللعاب يطير من فكيها.

She kept right behind Buck, never gaining and never falling back.

لقد بقيت خلف باك مباشرة، ولم تكسب أبدًا ولم تتراجع أبدًا.

Buck ran through woods, down the island, across jagged ice.

ركض باك عبر الغابات، أسفل الجزيرة، عبر الجليد المتعرج.

He crossed to an island, then another, circling back to the river.

عبر إلى جزيرة، ثم إلى أخرى، ثم عاد في اتجاه النهر.

Still Dolly chased him, her growl close behind at every step.

لا تزال دوللي تطارده، وهديرها قريب من خلفه في كل خطوة.

Buck could hear her breath and rage, though he dared not look back.

كان باك يستطيع سماع أنفاسها وغضبها، على الرغم من أنه لم يجرؤ على النظر إلى الوراء.

François shouted from afar, and Buck turned toward the voice.

صرخ فرانسوا من بعيد، والتفت باك نحو الصوت.

Still gasping for air, Buck ran past, placing all hope in François.

مازال يلهث لالتقاط أنفاسه، ركض باك، واضعًا كل أمله في فرانسوا.

The dog-driver raised an axe and waited as Buck flew past.

رفع سائق الكلب فأسًا وانتظر بينما طار باك.

The axe came down fast and struck Dolly's head with deadly force.

نزل الفأس بسرعة وضرب رأس دوللي بقوة مميتة.

Buck collapsed near the sled, wheezing and unable to move.

انهار باك بالقرب من الزلاجة، وكان يلهث وغير قادر على الحركة.

That moment gave Spitz his chance to strike an exhausted foe.

أعطت تلك اللحظة لسبيتز فرصته لضرب عدو منهك.

Twice he bit Buck, ripping flesh down to the white bone.

لقد عض باك مرتين، مما أدى إلى تمزيق لحمه حتى العظم الأبيض.

François's whip cracked, striking Spitz with full, furious force.

انطلق سوط فرانسوا، وضرب سبيتز بقوة شديدة وعنيفة.

Buck watched with joy as Spitz received his harshest beating yet.

كان باك يراقب بفرح بينما تلقى سبيتز أقسى الضربات التي تلقاها حتى الآن.

"He's a devil, that Spitz," Perrault muttered darkly to himself.

"إنه شيطان، ذلك سبيتز،" تمتم بيرولت في نفسه بصوت قاتم.

"Someday soon, that cursed dog will kill Buck—I swear it."

"في يوم قريب، سوف يقتل هذا الكلب الملعون باك ـ أقسم بذلك."

"That Buck has two devils in him," François replied with a nod.

"هذا باك لديه شيطانان بداخله"، أجاب فرانسوا مع إيماءة.

"When I watch Buck, I know something fierce waits in him."

"عندما أشاهد باك، أعلم أن هناك شيئًا شرسًا ينتظره."

"One day, he'll get mad as fire and tear Spitz to pieces."

"في يوم من الأيام، سوف يجن جنونه كالنار ويمزق سبيتز إلى أشلاء."

"He'll chew that dog up and spit him on the frozen snow."

"سيقوم بمضغ هذا الكلب وبصقه على الثلج المتجمد."

"Sure as anything, I know this deep in my bones."

"من المؤكد أنني أعرف هذا في أعماق عظامي."

From that moment forward, the two dogs were locked in war.

منذ تلك اللحظة، أصبح الكلبان في حالة حرب.

Spitz led the team and held power, but Buck challenged that.

كان سبيتز قائدًا للفريق ويحتفظ بالسلطة، لكن باك تحدى ذلك.

Spitz saw his rank threatened by this odd Southland stranger.

رأى سبيتز أن رتبته مهددة من قبل هذا الغريب من ساوثلاند.

Buck was unlike any southern dog Spitz had known before.

كان باك مختلفًا عن أي كلب جنوبي عرفه سبيتز من قبل.

Most of them failed—too weak to live through cold and hunger.

لقد فشل معظمهم ـ كانوا ضعفاء للغاية لدرجة أنهم لم يتمكنوا من العيش في البرد والجوع.

They died fast under labor, frost, and the slow burn of famine.

لقد ماتوا بسرعة بسبب العمل، والصقيع، والحرق البطيء للمجاعة.

Buck stood apart—stronger, smarter, and more savage each day.

لقد كان باك يقف منفردًا ـ أقوى وأذكى وأكثر وحشية كل يوم.

He thrived on hardship, growing to match the northern huskies.

لقد ازدهر في ظل المشقة، ونما ليصبح منافسًا لكلاب الهاسكي الشمالية.

Buck had strength, wild skill, and a patient, deadly instinct.

كان باك يتمتع بالقوة والمهارة البرية وغريزة قاتلة وصبر.

The man with the club had beaten rashness out of Buck.

لقد ضرب الرجل الذي يحمل النادي باك حتى خرج من حالة التهور.

Blind fury was gone, replaced by quiet cunning and control.

لقد ذهب الغضب الأعمى، وتم استبداله بالمكر الهادئ والسيطرة.

He waited, calm and primal, watching for the right moment.

كان ينتظر بهدوء وتلقائية، يبحث عن اللحظة المناسبة.

Their fight for command became unavoidable and clear.

لقد أصبح صراعهم على القيادة أمراً لا مفر منه وواضحاً.

Buck desired leadership because his spirit demanded it.

لقد رغب باك في القيادة لأن روحه طالبت بذلك.

He was driven by the strange pride born of trail and harness.

لقد كان مدفوعًا بالفخر الغريب الذي ولد من الدرب والحزام.

That pride made dogs pull till they collapsed on the snow.

هذا الفخر جعل الكلاب تسحب نفسها حتى انهارت على الثلج.

Pride lured them into giving all the strength they had.

لقد أغرتهم الكبرياء بإعطاء كل القوة التي لديهم.

Pride can lure a sled-dog even to the point of death.

يمكن للكبرياء أن يغري كلب الزلاجة حتى الموت.

Losing the harness left dogs broken and without purpose.

فقدان الحزام يترك الكلاب مكسورة وبدون هدف.

The heart of a sled-dog can be crushed by shame when they retire.

يمكن أن يُسحق قلب كلب الزلاجة بالخجل عندما يتقاعد.

Dave lived by that pride as he dragged the sled from behind.

لقد عاش ديف بهذا الفخر بينما كان يسحب الزلاجة من الخلف.

Solleks, too, gave his all with grim strength and loyalty.

كما أعطى سوليكس كل ما لديه من قوة وإخلاص.

Each morning, pride turned them from bitter to determined.

في كل صباح، كان الكبرياء يحولهم من مريرين إلى مصممين.

They pushed all day, then dropped silent at the camp's end.

لقد دفعوا طوال اليوم، ثم ساد الصمت في نهاية المخيم.

That pride gave Spitz the strength to beat shirkers into line.

لقد أعطى هذا الكبرياء سبيتز القوة للتغلب على المتقاعسين.

Spitz feared Buck because Buck carried that same deep pride.

كان سبيتز يخشى باك لأن باك كان يحمل نفس الفخر العميق.

Buck's pride now stirred against Spitz, and he did not stop.

لقد تحرك كبرياء باك الآن ضد سبيتز، ولم يتوقف.

Buck defied Spitz's power and blocked him from punishing dogs.

تحدى باك قوة سبيتز ومنعه من معاقبة الكلاب.

When others failed, Buck stepped between them and their leader.

عندما فشل الآخرون، تدخل باك بينهم وبين زعيمهم.

He did this with intent, making his challenge open and clear.

لقد فعل ذلك عن قصد، مما جعل تحديه مفتوحًا وواضحًا.

On one night heavy snow blanketed the world in deep silence.

في إحدى الليالي، غطت الثلوج الكثيفة العالم بصمت عميق.

The next morning, Pike, lazy as ever, did not rise for work.

في صباح اليوم التالي، لم يستيقظ بايك للذهاب إلى العمل، كعادته، لأنه كان كسولاً.

He stayed hidden in his nest beneath a thick layer of snow.

لقد بقي مختبئًا في عشه تحت طبقة سميكة من الثلج.

François called out and searched, but could not find the dog.

نادى فرانسوا وبحث، لكنه لم يتمكن من العثور على الكلب.

Spitz grew furious and stormed through the snow-covered camp.

لقد أصبح سبيتز غاضبًا واقتحم المخيم المغطى بالثلوج.

He growled and sniffed, digging madly with blazing eyes.

لقد هدّر وشمّ، وحفر بجنون مع عيون مشتعلة.

His rage was so fierce that Pike shook under the snow in fear.

كان غضبه شديدًا لدرجة أن بايك كان يرتجف تحت الثلج من الخوف.

When Pike was finally found, Spitz lunged to punish the hiding dog.

عندما تم العثور على بايك أخيرًا، انقض سبيتز لمعاقبة الكلب المختبئ.

But Buck sprang between them with a fury equal to Spitz's own.

لكن باك اندفع بينهما بغضب مماثل لغضب سبيتز.

The attack was so sudden and clever that Spitz fell off his feet.

كان الهجوم مفاجئًا وذكيًا لدرجة أن سبيتز سقط على قدميه.

Pike, who had been shaking, took courage from this defiance.

لقد استمد بايك، الذي كان يرتجف، الشجاعة من هذا التحدي.

He leapt on the fallen Spitz, following Buck's bold example.

لقد قفز على سبيتز الساقط، متبعًا مثال باك الجريء.

Buck, no longer bound by fairness, joined the strike on Spitz.

انضم باك، الذي لم يعد ملزماً بالعدالة، إلى الإضراب ضد سبيتز.

François, amused yet firm in discipline, swung his heavy lash.

كان فرانسوا مسليًا ولكنه حازم في الانضباط، وهو يلوح بسوطه الثقيل.

He struck Buck with all his strength to break up the fight.

ضرب باك بكل قوته لفض القتال.

Buck refused to move and stayed atop the fallen leader.

رفض باك التحرك وبقي فوق الزعيم الساقط.

François then used the whip's handle, hitting Buck hard.

ثم استخدم فرانسوا مقبض السوط، وضرب باك بقوة.

Staggering from the blow, Buck fell back under the assault.

ترنح باك من الضربة، وسقط إلى الخلف تحت الهجوم.

François struck again and again while Spitz punished Pike.

ضرب فرانسوا مرارا وتكرارا بينما عاقب سبيتز بايك.

Days passed, and Dawson City grew nearer and nearer.

ومرت الأيام، وأصبحت مدينة داوسون أقرب فأقرب.

Buck kept interfering, slipping between Spitz and other dogs.

استمر باك في التدخل، والانزلاق بين سبيتز والكلاب الأخرى.

He chose his moments well, always waiting for François to leave.

لقد اختار لحظاته جيدًا، وكان دائمًا ينتظر رحيل فرانسوا.

Buck's quiet rebellion spread, and disorder took root in the team.

انتشرت ثورة باك الهادئة، وترسخت الفوضى في الفريق.

Dave and Solleks stayed loyal, but others grew unruly.

ظل ديف وسوليكس مخلصين، لكن الآخرين أصبحوا غير منضبطين.

The team grew worse—restless, quarrelsome, and out of line.

أصبح الفريق أسوأ ـ مضطربًا، ومتشاجرًا، وخارجًا عن المسار.

Nothing worked smoothly anymore, and fights became common.

لم يعد أي شيء يعمل بسلاسة، وأصبحت المعارك أمرًا شائعًا.

Buck stayed at the heart of the trouble, always provoking unrest.

وبقي باك في قلب المشكلة، مثيرًا للاضطرابات دائمًا.

François stayed alert, afraid of the fight between Buck and Spitz.

ظل فرانسوا متيقظًا، خائفًا من القتال بين باك وسبيتز.

Each night, scuffles woke him, fearing the beginning finally arrived.

في كل ليلة، كانت المشاجرات توقظه، خوفًا من أن تكون البداية قد وصلت أخيرًا.

He leapt from his robe, ready to break up the fight.

قفز من ردائه، مستعدًا لفض القتال.

But the moment never came, and they reached Dawson at last.

ولكن اللحظة لم تأت أبدًا، ووصلوا إلى داوسون أخيرًا.

The team entered the town one bleak afternoon, tense and quiet.

دخل الفريق إلى المدينة في فترة ما بعد الظهيرة الكئيبة، وكان الجو متوتراً وهادئاً.

The great battle for leadership still hung in the frozen air.

لا تزال المعركة الكبرى على القيادة معلقة في الهواء المتجمد.

Dawson was full of men and sled-dogs, all busy with work.

كانت داوسون مليئة بالرجال والكلاب المزلجة، وكان الجميع مشغولين بالعمل.

Buck watched the dogs pull loads from morning until night.

كان باك يراقب الكلاب وهي تسحب الأحمال من الصباح حتى الليل.

They hauled logs and firewood, freighted supplies to the mines.

قاموا بنقل الأخشاب والحطب، ونقلوا الإمدادات إلى المناجم.

Where horses once worked in the Southland, dogs now labored.

حيث كانت الخيول تعمل في السابق في منطقة الجنوب، أصبحت الكلاب تعمل الآن.

Buck saw some dogs from the South, but most were wolf-like huskies.

رأى باك بعض الكلاب من الجنوب، لكن معظمها كانت من نوع الهاسكي التي تشبه الذئاب.

At night, like clockwork, the dogs raised their voices in song.

في الليل، كالعادة، كانت الكلاب ترفع أصواتها بالغناء.

At nine, at midnight, and again at three, the singing began.

وفي الساعة التاسعة، وفي منتصف الليل، ومرة أخرى في الساعة الثالثة، بدأ الغناء.

Buck loved joining their eerie chant, wild and ancient in sound.

كان باك يحب الانضمام إلى ترانيمهم الغريبة، البرية والقديمة في الصوت.

The aurora flamed, stars danced, and snow blanketed the land.

اشتعلت الأضواء الشمالية، ورقصت النجوم، وغطى الثلج الأرض.

The dogs' song rose as a cry against silence and bitter cold.

وارتفعت أغنية الكلاب كصرخة ضد الصمت والبرد القارس.

But their howl held sorrow, not defiance, in every long note.

لكن عواءهم كان يحمل الحزن، وليس التحدي، في كل نغمة طويلة.

Each wailing cry was full of pleading; the burden of life itself.

كانت كل صرخة عويل مليئة بالتوسل، وكان ذلك عبء الحياة نفسها.

That song was old—older than towns, and older than fires

كانت تلك الأغنية قديمة ـ أقدم من المدن، وأقدم من الحرائق

That song was more ancient even than the voices of men.

كانت تلك الأغنية أقدم حتى من أصوات الرجال.

It was a song from the young world, when all songs were sad.

كانت أغنية من عالم الشباب، عندما كانت كل الأغاني حزينة.

The song carried sorrow from countless generations of dogs.

حملت الأغنية الحزن من أجيال لا تعد ولا تحصى من الكلاب.

Buck felt the melody deeply, moaning from pain rooted in the ages.

أحس باك باللحن بعمق، وكان يتأوه من الألم المتجذر في العصور.

He sobbed from a grief as old as the wild blood in his veins.

لقد بكى من حزن قديم مثل الدم البري في عروقه.

The cold, the dark, and the mystery touched Buck's soul.

لقد لمس البرد والظلام والغموض روح باك.

That song proved how far Buck had returned to his origins.

لقد أثبتت هذه الأغنية مدى عودة باك إلى أصوله.

Through snow and howling he had found the start of his own life.

ومن خلال الثلوج والعويل، وجد بداية حياته الخاصة.

Seven days after arriving in Dawson, they set off once again.

وبعد سبعة أيام من وصولهم إلى داوسون، انطلقوا مرة أخرى.

The team dropped from the Barracks down to the Yukon Trail.

نزل الفريق من الثكنات إلى طريق يوكون.

They began the journey back toward Dyea and Salt Water.

بدأوا الرحلة عائدين نحو دايا والمياه المالحة.

Perrault carried dispatches even more urgent than before.

كان بيرولت يحمل رسائل أكثر إلحاحًا من ذي قبل.

He was also seized by trail pride and aimed to set a record.

وقد استولى عليه أيضًا كبرياء المسار وهدف إلى تسجيل رقم قياسي.

This time, several advantages were on Perrault's side.

هذه المرة، كانت هناك عدة مزايا لصالح بيرولت.

The dogs had rested for a full week and regained their strength.

لقد استراحت الكلاب لمدة أسبوع كامل واستعادت قوتها.

The trail they had broken was now hard-packed by others.

لقد كان الطريق الذي فتحوه الآن ممهداً من قبل الآخرين.

In places, police had stored food for dogs and men alike.

وفي بعض الأماكن، قامت الشرطة بتخزين الطعام للكلاب والرجال على حد سواء.

Perrault traveled light, moving fast with little to weigh him down.

كان بيرولت يسافر بخفة، ويتحرك بسرعة مع القليل من الأشياء التي تثقله.

They reached Sixty-Mile, a fifty-mile run, by the first night.

وصلوا إلى مسافة الستين ميلاً، وهي مسافة خمسين ميلاً، في الليلة الأولى.

On the second day, they rushed up the Yukon toward Pelly.

وفي اليوم الثاني، سارعوا إلى يوكون باتجاه بيلي.

But such fine progress came with much strain for François.

لكن هذا التقدم الرائع جاء مصحوبًا بقدر كبير من الضغط على فرانسوا.

Buck's quiet rebellion had shattered the team's discipline.

لقد أدى تمرد باك الهادئ إلى تحطيم انضباط الفريق.

They no longer pulled together like one beast in the reins.

لم يعودوا متحدين مثل وحش واحد في اللجام.

Buck had led others into defiance through his bold example.

لقد قاد باك الآخرين إلى التحدي من خلال مثاله الجريء.

Spitz's command was no longer met with fear or respect.

لم يعد أمر سبيتز يُقابل بالخوف أو الاحترام.

The others lost their awe of him and dared to resist his rule.

لقد فقد الآخرون رهبتهم منه وتجرأوا على مقاومة حكمه.

One night, Pike stole half a fish and ate it under Buck's eye.

في إحدى الليالي، سرق بايك نصف سمكة وأكلها تحت عين باك.

Another night, Dub and Joe fought Spitz and went unpunished.

في ليلة أخرى، خاض داب وجو معركة ضد سبيتز ولم يتعرضا للعقاب.

Even Billee whined less sweetly and showed new sharpness.

حتى بيلي أصبح يتذمر بشكل أقل حلاوة، وأظهر حدة جديدة.

Buck snarled at Spitz every time they crossed paths.

كان باك يزأر في وجه سبيتز في كل مرة عبروا فيها مساراتهم.

Buck's attitude grew bold and threatening, nearly like a bully.

أصبح موقف باك جريئًا ومهددًا، تقريبًا مثل المتنمر.

He paced before Spitz with a swagger, full of mocking menace.

كان يسير جيئة وذهابا أمام سبيتز بتبختر، مليئا بالتهديد الساخر.

That collapse of order also spread among the sled-dogs.

وانتشر انهيار النظام أيضًا بين كلاب الزلاجات.

They fought and argued more than ever, filling camp with noise.

لقد قاتلوا وتجادلوا أكثر من أي وقت مضى، مما ملأ المخيم بالضوضاء.

Camp life turned into a wild, howling chaos each night.

تحولت حياة المخيم إلى فوضى عارمة وصاخبة كل ليلة.

Only Dave and Solleks remained steady and focused.

فقط ديف وسوليكس بقيا ثابتين ومركزين.

But even they became short-tempered from the constant brawls.

ولكن حتى هم أصبحوا سريعي الانفعال بسبب المشاجرات المستمرة.

François cursed in strange tongues and stomped in frustration.

شتم فرانسوا بألسنة غريبة وداس على الأرض بإحباط.

He tore at his hair and shouted while snow flew underfoot.

مزق شعره وصرخ بينما كان الثلج يطير تحت قدميه.

His whip snapped across the pack but barely kept them in line.

انطلق سوطه عبر المجموعة لكنه بالكاد نجح في إبقاءهم في خط واحد.

Whenever his back was turned, the fighting broke out again.

كلما أدار ظهره اندلعت المعارك مرة أخرى.

François used the lash for Spitz, while Buck led the rebels.

استخدم فرانسوا السوط ضد سبيتز، بينما قاد باك المتمردين.

Each knew the other's role, but Buck avoided any blame.

كان كل واحد منهما يعرف دور الآخر، لكن باك تجنب أي لوم.

François never caught Buck starting a fight or shirking his job.

لم يتمكن فرانسوا أبدًا من رؤية باك وهو يبدأ قتالًا أو يتهرب من وظيفته.

Buck worked hard in harness—the toil now thrilled his spirit.

كان باك يعمل بجد في السرج - وكان العمل الشاق الآن يثير روحه.

But he found even more joy in stirring fights and chaos in camp.

ولكنه وجد متعة أكبر في إثارة المعارك والفوضى في المخيم.

At the Tahkeena's mouth one evening, Dub startled a rabbit.

في أحد الأمسيات، عند فم تاكينا، فاجأ داب أرنبًا.

He missed the catch, and the snowshoe rabbit sprang away.

لقد أخطأ في الصيد، وقفز أرنب الثلج بعيدًا.

In seconds, the entire sled team gave chase with wild cries.

في ثوانٍ، قام فريق الزلاجات بأكمله بمطاردته مع صرخات برية.

Nearby, a Northwest Police camp housed fifty husky dogs.

وفي مكان قريب، كان معسكر شرطة الشمال الغربي يضم خمسين كلبًا من فصيلة الهاسكي.

They joined the hunt, surging down the frozen river together.

انضموا إلى الصيد، واندفعوا معًا عبر النهر المتجمد.

The rabbit turned off the river, fleeing up a frozen creek bed.

انحرف الأرنب عن النهر، وهرب إلى مجرى مائي متجمد.

The rabbit skipped lightly over snow while the dogs struggled through.

قفز الأرنب بخفة فوق الثلج بينما كانت الكلاب تكافح من أجل العبور.

Buck led the massive pack of sixty dogs around each twisting bend.

قاد باك المجموعة الضخمة المكونة من ستين كلبًا حول كل منعطف ملتوٍ.

He pushed forward, low and eager, but could not gain ground.

لقد دفع إلى الأمام، منخفضًا ومتحمسًا، لكنه لم يتمكن من كسب الأرض.

His body flashed under the pale moon with each powerful leap.

كان جسده يلمع تحت ضوء القمر الشاحب مع كل قفزة قوية.

Ahead, the rabbit moved like a ghost, silent and too fast to catch.

أمامًا، كان الأرنب يتحرك مثل الشبح، صامتًا وسريعًا جدًا بحيث لا يمكن الإمساك به.

All those old instincts—the hunger, the thrill—rushed through Buck.

كل تلك الغرائز القديمة - الجوع، الإثارة - تسارعت في باك.

Humans feel this instinct at times, driven to hunt with gun and bullet.

يشعر البشر بهذه الغريزة في بعض الأحيان، مما يدفعهم إلى الصيد بالبنادق والرصاص.

But Buck felt this feeling on a deeper and more personal level.

لكن باك شعر بهذا الشعور على مستوى أعمق وأكثر شخصية.

They could not feel the wild in their blood the way Buck could feel it.

لم يتمكنوا من الشعور بالبرية في دمائهم بالطريقة التي شعر بها باك.

He chased living meat, ready to kill with his teeth and taste blood.

كان يطارد اللحوم الحية، مستعدًا للقتل بأسنانه وتذوق الدم.

His body strained with joy, wanting to bathe in warm red life.

كان جسده متوتراً من الفرح، راغباً في الاستحمام في حياة حمراء دافئة.

A strange joy marks the highest point life can ever reach.

فرحة غريبة تمثل أعلى نقطة يمكن أن تصل إليها الحياة على الإطلاق.

The feeling of a peak where the living forget they are even alive.

شعور بالذروة حيث ينسى الأحياء أنهم على قيد الحياة.

This deep joy touches the artist lost in blazing inspiration.

هذا الفرح العميق يلمس الفنان الضائع في الإلهام المشتعل.

This joy seizes the soldier who fights wildly and spares no foe.

هذه الفرحة تسيطر على الجندي الذي يقاتل بضراوة ولا يرحم أحداً من الأعداء.

This joy now claimed Buck as he led the pack in primal hunger.

لقد استحوذ هذا الفرح الآن على باك عندما قاد المجموعة في الجوع البدائي.

He howled with the ancient wolf-cry, thrilled by the living chase.

عوى بصرخة الذئب القديمة، منبهرًا بالمطاردة الحية.

Buck tapped into the oldest part of himself, lost in the wild.

استغل باك الجزء الأقدم من نفسه، المفقود في البرية.

He reached deep within, past memory, into raw, ancient time.

لقد وصل إلى أعماق الذاكرة الماضية، إلى الزمن الخام القديم.

A wave of pure life surged through every muscle and tendon.

تدفقت موجة من الحياة النقية عبر كل عضلة ووتر.

Each leap shouted that he lived, that he moved through death.

كل قفزة كانت تصرخ بأنه عاش، وأنه تحرك عبر الموت.

His body soared joyfully over still, cold land that never stirred.

ارتفع جسده بفرح فوق أرض باردة ثابتة لا تتحرك أبدًا.

Spitz stayed cold and cunning, even in his wildest moments.

ظل سبيتز باردًا وماكرًا، حتى في أكثر لحظاته جنونًا.

He left the trail and crossed land where the creek curved wide.

ترك المسار وعبر الأرض حيث انحنى الخور على نطاق واسع.

Buck, unaware of this, stayed on the rabbit's winding path.

لم يكن باك على علم بهذا، وبقي على المسار المتعرج للأرنب.

Then, as Buck rounded a bend, the ghost-like rabbit was before him.

ثم، عندما انعطف باك حول المنعطف، كان الأرنب الشبح أمامه.

He saw a second figure leap from the bank ahead of the prey.

لقد رأى شخصية ثانية تقفز من البنك أمام الفريسة.

The figure was Spitz, landing right in the path of the fleeing rabbit.

كان هذا الشكل هو سبيتز، الذي هبط مباشرة في طريق الأرنب الهارب.

The rabbit could not turn and met Spitz's jaws in mid-air.

لم يتمكن الأرنب من الدوران والتقى بفكي سبيتز في الهواء.

The rabbit's spine broke with a shriek as sharp as a dying human's cry.

انكسر عمود الأرنب الفقري مع صرخة حادة مثل صرخة إنسان يحتضر.

At that sound—the fall from life to death—the pack howled loud.

عند هذا الصوت ـ السقوط من الحياة إلى الموت ـ عوت المجموعة بصوت عالٍ.

A savage chorus rose from behind Buck, full of dark delight.

ارتفعت جوقة وحشية من خلف باك، مليئة بالبهجة المظلمة.

Buck gave no cry, no sound, and charged straight into Spitz.

لم يصدر باك أي صرخة أو صوت، واندفع مباشرة نحو سبيتز.

He aimed for the throat, but struck the shoulder instead.

كان يهدف إلى الحلق، لكنه ضرب الكتف بدلا من ذلك.

They tumbled through soft snow; their bodies locked in combat.

لقد تدحرجوا عبر الثلج الناعم، وكانت أجسادهم متشابكة في قتال.

Spitz sprang up quickly, as if never knocked down at all.

قفز سبيتز بسرعة، كما لو أنه لم يُسقط على الإطلاق.

He slashed Buck's shoulder, then leaped clear of the fight.

لقد قطع كتف باك، ثم قفز بعيدًا عن القتال.

Twice his teeth snapped like steel traps, lips curled and fierce.

انكسرت أسنانه مرتين مثل مصائد الفولاذ، شفتيه ملتفة وشرسة.

He backed away slowly, seeking firm ground under his feet.

تراجع ببطء، باحثًا عن أرض ثابتة تحت قدميه.

Buck understood the moment instantly and fully.

لقد فهم باك اللحظة على الفور وبشكل كامل.

The time had come; the fight was going to be a fight to the death.

لقد حان الوقت، وكان القتال سيكون قتالًا حتى الموت.

The two dogs circled, growling, ears flat, eyes narrowed.

كان الكلبان يدوران، وهما يزأران، وآذانهما مسطحة، وعيونهما ضيقة.

Each dog waited for the other to show weakness or misstep.

كان كل كلب ينتظر من الآخر أن يظهر الضعف أو الخطأ.

To Buck, the scene felt eerily known and deeply remembered.

بالنسبة لباك، كان المشهد يبدو مألوفًا بشكل مخيف ولا يزال في الذاكرة بعمق.

The white woods, the cold earth, the battle under moonlight.

الغابات البيضاء، والأرض الباردة، والمعركة تحت ضوء القمر.

A heavy silence filled the land, deep and unnatural.

ملأ صمت ثقيل الأرض، عميق وغير طبيعي.

No wind stirred, no leaf moved, no sound broke the stillness.

لم تحرك الرياح، ولم تتحرك الأوراق، ولم يكسر الصمت أي صوت.

The dogs' breaths rose like smoke in the frozen, quiet air.

ارتفعت أنفاس الكلاب مثل الدخان في الهواء المتجمد والهادئ.

The rabbit was long forgotten by the pack of wild beasts.

لقد نسي قطيع الوحوش البرية الأرنب منذ زمن طويل.

These half-tamed wolves now stood still in a wide circle.

الآن، وقفت هذه الذئاب نصف المروضة في دائرة واسعة.

They were quiet, only their glowing eyes revealed their hunger.

لقد كانوا هادئين، فقط عيونهم المتوهجة كشفت عن جوعهم.

Their breath drifted upward, watching the final fight begin.

ارتفع أنفاسهم إلى الأعلى، وهم يشاهدون بداية القتال النهائي.

To Buck, this battle was old and expected, not strange at all.

بالنسبة لباك، كانت هذه المعركة قديمة ومتوقعة، وليست غريبة على الإطلاق.

It felt like a memory of something always meant to happen.

لقد شعرت وكأنها ذكرى لشيء كان من المفترض أن يحدث دائمًا.

Spitz was a trained fighting dog, honed by countless wild brawls.

كان سبيتز كلبًا مدربًا على القتال، وتم صقل مهاراته من خلال المشاركة في عدد لا يحصى من المعارك البرية.

From Spitzbergen to Canada, he had mastered many foes.

من سبيتسبيرجن إلى كندا، كان قد تغلب على العديد من الأعداء.

He was filled with fury, but never gave control to rage.

لقد كان مليئًا بالغضب، لكنه لم يسمح أبدا بالسيطرة على الغضب.

His passion was sharp, but always tempered by hard instinct.

لقد كان شغفه حادًا، لكنه كان دائمًا مخففًا بالغريزة القاسية.

He never attacked until his own defense was in place.

لم يهاجم أبدًا حتى أصبح دفاعه جاهزًا.

Buck tried again and again to reach Spitz's vulnerable neck.

حاول باك مرارا وتكرارا الوصول إلى رقبة سبيتز الضعيفة.

But every strike was met by a slash from Spitz's sharp teeth.

لكن كل ضربة قوبلت بضربة من أسنان سبيتز الحادة.

Their fangs clashed, and both dogs bled from torn lips.

تصادمت أنيابهما، وسقطت الدماء من شفتيهما الممزقتين.

No matter how Buck lunged, he couldn't break the defense.

بغض النظر عن الطريقة التي انقض بها باك، فإنه لم يتمكن من اختراق الدفاع.

He grew more furious, rushing in with wild bursts of power.

لقد أصبح أكثر غضبًا، واندفع نحوها بدفعات جامحة من القوة.

Again and again, Buck struck for the white throat of Spitz.

مرة تلو الأخرى، ضرب باك الحلق الأبيض لسبيتز.

Each time Spitz evaded and struck back with a slicing bite.

في كل مرة كان سبيتز يتجنب ويضرب بقوة.

Then Buck shifted tactics, rushing as if for the throat again.

ثم غيّر باك تكتيكاته، واندفع كما لو كان يتجه نحو الحلق مرة أخرى.

But he pulled back mid-attack, turning to strike from the side.

ولكنه تراجع في منتصف الهجوم، وتحول لضرب من الجانب.

He threw his shoulder into Spitz, aiming to knock him down.

ألقى بكتفه على سبيتز، بهدف إسقاطه.

Each time he tried, Spitz dodged and countered with a slash.

في كل مرة حاول فيها، كان سبيتز يتفادى الهجوم ويرد بضربة.

Buck's shoulder grew raw as Spitz leapt clear after every hit.

أصبح كتف باك خامًا عندما قفز سبيتز بوضوح بعد كل ضربة.

Spitz had not been touched, while Buck bled from many
wounds.

لم يتأثر سبيتز، في حين كان باك ينزف من العديد من الجروح.

Buck's breath came fast and heavy, his body slick with
blood.

كان أنفاس باك سريعة وثقيلة، وكان جسده زلقًا بالدماء.

The fight turned more brutal with each bite and charge.

أصبح القتال أكثر وحشية مع كل عضة وهجمة.

Around them, sixty silent dogs waited for the first to fall.

حولهم، كان هناك ستون كلبًا صامتًا ينتظرون السقوط الأول.

If one dog dropped, the pack were going to finish the fight.

إذا سقط كلب واحد، فإن المجموعة سوف تنهي القتال.

Spitz saw Buck weakening, and began to press the attack.

رأى سبيتز أن باك أصبح ضعيفًا، وبدأ في الضغط على الهجوم.

He kept Buck off balance, forcing him to fight for footing.

لقد أبقى باك خارج التوازن، مما أجبره على القتال من أجل موطئ قدم.

Once Buck stumbled and fell, and all the dogs rose up.

في إحدى المرات، تعثر باك وسقط، فنهضت كل الكلاب.

But Buck righted himself mid-fall, and everyone sank back
down.

لكن باك استعاد توازنه في منتصف السقوط، وسقط الجميع إلى الأسفل.

Buck had something rare—imagination born from deep
instinct.

كان لدى باك شيئًا نادرًا ـ الخيال المولود من غريزة عميقة.

He fought by natural drive, but he also fought with cunning.

لقد قاتل بدافع طبيعي، لكنه قاتل أيضًا بالمكر.

He charged again as if repeating his shoulder attack trick.

لقد هاجم مرة أخرى كما لو كان يكرر خدعة هجوم كتفه.

But at the last second, he dropped low and swept beneath
Spitz.

ولكن في اللحظة الأخيرة، هبط إلى مستوى منخفض وحلق تحت سبيتز.

His teeth locked on Spitz's front left leg with a snap.

انغلقت أسنانه على الساق اليسرى الأمامية لسبيتز بقوة.

Spitz now stood unsteady, his weight on only three legs.

أصبح سبيتز الآن غير مستقر، وكان وزنه يعتمد على ثلاث أرجل فقط.

Buck struck again, tried three times to bring him down.

ضرب باك مرة أخرى، وحاول ثلاث مرات إسقاطه.

On the fourth attempt he used the same move with success

وفي المحاولة الرابعة استخدم نفس الحركة بنجاح

This time Buck managed to bite the right leg of Spitz.

هذه المرة نجح باك في عض الساق اليمنى لسبيتز.

Spitz, though crippled and in agony, kept struggling to survive.

على الرغم من إصابته بالشلل ومعاناته، ظل سبيتز يكافح من أجل البقاء.

He saw the circle of huskies tighten, tongues out, eyes glowing.

لقد رأى دائرة الهاسكي تتقلص، وألسنتها تخرج، وعيون متوهجة.

They waited to devour him, just as they had done to others.

وانتظروا أن يلتهموه، كما فعلوا مع الآخرين.

This time, he stood in the center; defeated and doomed.

هذه المرة، وقف في الوسط؛ مهزومًا ومحكومًا عليه بالهلاك.

There was no option to escape for the white dog now.

لم يعد هناك خيار للهروب بالنسبة للكلب الأبيض الآن.

Buck showed no mercy, for mercy did not belong in the wild.

لم يُظهر باك أي رحمة، لأن الرحمة لا تنتمي إلى البرية.

Buck moved carefully, setting up for the final charge.

تحرك باك بحذر، استعدادًا للهجوم النهائي.

The circle of huskies closed in; he felt their warm breaths.

اقتربت دائرة الهاسكي منه، وشعر بأنفاسهم الدافئة.

They crouched low, prepared to spring when the moment came.

انحنوا منخفضين، مستعدين للقفز عندما تأتي اللحظة.

Spitz quivered in the snow, snarling and shifting his stance.

ارتجف سبيتز في الثلج، وهو يزأر ويغير من موقفه.

His eyes glared, lips curled, teeth flashing in desperate threat.

كانت عيناه متوهجتين، وشفتاه ملتفة، وأسنانه تتألق في تهديد يائس.

He staggered, still trying to hold off the cold bite of death.

لقد ترنح، وهو لا يزال يحاول صد لدغة الموت الباردة.

He had seen this before, but always from the winning side.

لقد رأى هذا من قبل، ولكن دائمًا من الجانب المنتصر.

Now he was on the losing side; the defeated; the prey; death.

الآن أصبح على الجانب الخاسر؛ المهزوم؛ الفريسة؛ الموت.

Buck circled for the final blow, the ring of dogs pressed closer.

دار باك حول نفسه استعدادًا للضربة النهائية، وكانت مجموعة الكلاب تضغط عليه بشكل أقرب.

He could feel their hot breaths; ready for the kill.

كان بإمكانه أن يشعر بأنفاسهم الساخنة؛ مستعدين للقتل.

A stillness fell; all was in its place; time had stopped.

ساد الصمت؛ كل شيء كان في مكانه؛ توقف الزمن.

Even the cold air between them froze for one last moment.

حتى الهواء البارد بينهما تجمد للحظة أخيرة.

Only Spitz moved, trying to hold off his bitter end.

كان سبيتز هو الوحيد الذي تحرك، محاولاً صد نهايته المريرة.

The circle of dogs was closing in around him, as was his destiny.

كانت دائرة الكلاب تقترب منه، كما كان مصيره.

He was desperate now, knowing what was about to happen.

لقد كان يائسًا الآن، لأنه كان يعلم ما كان على وشك الحدوث.

Buck sprang in, shoulder met shoulder one last time.

اندفع باك إلى الداخل، والتقى كتفه بكتفه للمرة الأخيرة.

The dogs surged forward, covering Spitz in the snowy dark.

انطلقت الكلاب إلى الأمام، وغطت سبيتز بالظلام الثلجي.

Buck watched, standing tall; the victor in a savage world.

كان باك يراقب، وهو يقف طويل القامة؛ المنتصر في عالم وحشي.

The dominant primordial beast had made its kill, and it was good.

لقد حقق الوحش البدائي المهيمن هدفه، وكان جيدًا.

He, Who Has Won to Mastership
هو الذي فاز بالسيادة

"Eh? What did I say? I speak true when I say Buck is a devil."

"إيه؟ ماذا قلت؟ صدقت عندما قلت إن باك شيطان."

François said this the next morning after finding Spitz missing.

قال فرانسوا هذا في صباح اليوم التالي بعد العثور على سبيتز في عداد المفقودين.

Buck stood there, covered with wounds from the vicious fight.

كان باك واقفا هناك، مغطى بالجروح من القتال الشرس.

François pulled Buck near the fire and pointed at the injuries.

سحب فرانسوا باك بالقرب من النار وأشار إلى الإصابات.

"That Spitz fought like the Devik," said Perrault, eyeing the deep gashes.

قال بيرولت وهو ينظر إلى الجروح العميقة: "لقد قاتل هذا الشبيتز مثل الديفيك".

"And that Buck fought like two devils," François replied at once.

"وذلك باك قاتل مثل شيطانين"، أجاب فرانسوا على الفور.

"Now we will make good time; no more Spitz, no more trouble."

"الآن سوف نحقق الوقت المناسب؛ لا مزيد من سبيتز، لا مزيد من المتاعب."

Perrault was packing the gear and loaded the sled with care.

كان بيرولت يحزم المعدات ويحمل الزلاجة بعناية.

François harnessed the dogs in preparation for the day's run.

قام فرانسوا بتسخير الكلاب استعدادًا للركض في ذلك اليوم.

Buck trotted straight to the lead position once held by Spitz.

انطلق باك مباشرة إلى موقع الصدارة الذي كان يحتله سبيتز.

But François, not noticing, led Solleks forward to the front.

ولكن فرانسوا، دون أن يلاحظ، قاد سوليكس إلى الأمام.

In François's judgment, Solleks was now the best lead-dog.

في رأي فرانسوا، أصبح سوليكس الآن أفضل كلب قائد.

Buck sprang at Solleks in fury and drove him back in protest.

اندفع باك نحو سولييكس بغضب ودفعه إلى الوراء احتجاجًا.

He stood where Spitz once had stood, claiming the lead position.

لقد وقف حيث كان سبيتز يقف ذات يوم، مدعيًا موقع القيادة.

"Eh? Eh?" cried François, slapping his thighs in amusement.

"إيه؟ إيه؟" صرخ فرانسوا وهو يصفع فخذيه بمرح.

"Look at Buck—he killed Spitz, now he wants to take the job!"

"انظر إلى باك ـ لقد قتل سبيتز، والآن يريد أن يأخذ الوظيفة!"

"Go away, Chook!" he shouted, trying to drive Buck away.

"اذهب بعيدًا يا تشوك!" صرخ محاولًا إبعاد باك.

But Buck refused to move and stood firm in the snow.

لكن باك رفض التحرك وظل ثابتًا في الثلج.

François grabbed Buck by the scruff, dragging him aside.

أمسك فرانسوا باك من قفاه، وسحبه جانبًا.

Buck growled low and threateningly but did not attack.

أطلق باك صوتًا منخفضًا وتهديديًا لكنه لم يهاجم.

François put Solleks back in the lead, trying to settle the dispute

أعاد فرانسوا سوليكس إلى الصدارة، محاولًا تسوية النزاع

The old dog showed fear of Buck and didn't want to stay.

أظهر الكلب العجوز خوفًا من باك ولم يرغب في البقاء.

When François turned his back, Buck drove Solleks out again.

عندما أدار فرانسوا ظهره، أخرج باك سوليكس مرة أخرى.

Solleks did not resist and quietly stepped aside once more.

لم يقاوم سوليكس وتنحى جانبا بهدوء مرة أخرى.

François grew angry and shouted, "By God, I fix you!"

فغضب فرانسوا وصاح: والله إني أشفيك!

He came toward Buck holding a heavy club in his hand.

لقد جاء نحو باك وهو يحمل هراوة ثقيلة في يده.

Buck remembered the man in the red sweater well.

تذكر باك الرجل ذو السترة الحمراء جيدًا.

He retreated slowly, watching François, but growling deeply.

تراجع ببطء، وهو يراقب فرانسوا، لكنه كان يزأر بعمق.

He did not rush back, even when Solleks stood in his place.

ولم يسارع إلى العودة، حتى عندما وقف سوليكس في مكانه.

Buck circled just beyond reach, snarling in fury and protest.

كان باك يدور بعيدًا عن متناول يده، وهو يزأر بغضب واحتجاج.

He kept his eyes on the club, ready to dodge if François threw.

لقد أبقى عينيه على النادي، مستعدًا للتهرب إذا رمى فرانسوا.

He had grown wise and wary in the ways of men with weapons.

لقد أصبح حكيماً وحذراً في التعامل مع الرجال الذين يحملون الأسلحة.

François gave up and called Buck to his former place again.

استسلم فرانسوا واستدعى باك إلى مكانه السابق مرة أخرى.

But Buck stepped back cautiously, refusing to obey the order.

لكن باك تراجع بحذر، رافضًا تنفيذ الأمر.

François followed, but Buck only retreated a few steps more.

وتبعه فرانسوا، لكن باك لم يتراجع إلا بضع خطوات أخرى.

After some time, François threw the weapon down in frustration.

وبعد مرور بعض الوقت، ألقى فرانسوا السلاح أرضًا في إحباط.

He thought Buck feared a beating and was going to come quietly.

اعتقد أن باك كان خائفًا من الضرب وكان سيأتي بهدوء.

But Buck wasn't avoiding punishment—he was fighting for rank.

لكن باك لم يكن يتجنب العقاب، بل كان يقاتل من أجل رتبته.

He had earned the lead-dog spot through a fight to the death

لقد حصل على مكان الكلب الرائد من خلال قتال حتى الموت

he was not going to settle for anything less than being the leader.

لم يكن ليرضى بأقل من أن يكون الزعيم.

Perrault took a hand in the chase to help catch the rebellious Buck.

أخذ بيرولت يده في المطاردة للمساعدة في القبض على باك المتمرد.

Together, they ran him around the camp for nearly an hour.

قاموا معًا بحمله حول المخيم لمدة ساعة تقريبًا.

They hurled clubs at him, but Buck dodged each one skillfully.

لقد ألقوا عليه الهراوات، لكن باك تهرب من كل واحدة منها بمهارة.

They cursed him, his ancestors, his descendants, and every hair on him.

لعنوه، وآبائه، وذريته، وكل شعرة عليه.

But Buck only snarled back and stayed just out of their reach.

لكن باك اكتفى بالهدير وظل بعيدًا عن متناولهم.

He never tried to run away but circled the camp deliberately.

لم يحاول الهروب أبدًا، بل كان يدور حول المخيم عمدًا.

He made it clear he was going to obey once they gave him what he wanted.

وأوضح أنه سوف يطيع بمجرد أن يعطوه ما يريد.

François finally sat down and scratched his head in frustration.

جلس فرانسوا أخيرًا وحك رأسه من الإحباط.

Perrault checked his watch, swore, and muttered about lost time.

تحقق بيرولت من ساعته، وأقسم، وتذمر بشأن الوقت الضائع.

An hour had already passed when they should have been on the trail.

لقد مرت ساعة بالفعل عندما كان من المفترض أن يكونوا على الطريق.

François shrugged sheepishly at the courier, who sighed in defeat.

هز فرانسوا كتفيه بخجل في وجه الرسول الذي تنهد هزيمة.

Then François walked to Solleks and called out to Buck once more.

ثم ذهب فرانسوا إلى سوليكس ونادى على باك مرة أخرى.

Buck laughed like a dog laughs, but kept his cautious distance.

ضحك باك كما يضحك الكلب، لكنه أبقى على مسافة حذرة.

François removed Solleks's harness and returned him to his spot.

قام فرانسوا بإزالة حزام سوليكس وأعاده إلى مكانه.

The sled team stood fully harnessed, with only one spot unfilled.

كان فريق الزلاجات جاهزًا بالكامل، مع وجود مكان واحد فقط شاغرًا.

The lead position remained empty, clearly meant for Buck alone.

ظل موقع الصدارة فارغًا، ومن الواضح أنه مخصص لباك وحده.

François called again, and again Buck laughed and held his ground.

نادى فرانسوا مرة أخرى، وضحك باك مرة أخرى وثبت على موقفه.

"Throw down the club," Perrault ordered without hesitation.

"ألقِ بالنادي أرضًا"، أمر بيرولت دون تردد.

François obeyed, and Buck immediately trotted forward proudly.

أطاع فرانسوا، وركض باك على الفور إلى الأمام بفخر.

He laughed triumphantly and stepped into the lead position.

ضحك منتصرا وصعد إلى موقع القيادة.

François secured his traces, and the sled was broken loose.

قام فرانسوا بتأمين آثاره، وتم تحرير الزلاجة.

Both men ran alongside as the team raced onto the river trail.

ركض الرجلان جنبًا إلى جنب بينما كان الفريق يتسابق نحو مسار النهر.

François had thought highly of Buck's "two devils,"

كان فرانسوا قد فكر كثيرًا في "شيطاني باك"

but he soon realized he had actually underestimated the dog.

ولكنه سرعان ما أدرك أنه في الواقع قد قلل من شأن الكلب.

Buck quickly assumed leadership and performed with excellence.

تولى باك القيادة بسرعة وأدى بشكل ممتاز.

In judgment, quick thinking, and fast action, Buck surpassed Spitz.

في الحكم، والتفكير السريع، والتصرف السريع، تفوق باك على سبيتز.

François had never seen a dog equal to what Buck now displayed.

لم يسبق لفرانسوا أن رأى كلبًا مساوٍ لما يعرضه باك الآن.

But Buck truly excelled in enforcing order and commanding respect.

لكن باك كان متميزًا حقًا في فرض النظام وفرض الاحترام.

Dave and Solleks accepted the change without concern or protest.

لقد تقبل ديف وسوليكس التغيير دون قلق أو احتجاج.

They focused only on work and pulling hard in the reins.

لقد ركزوا فقط على العمل والضغط بقوة على زمام الأمور.

They cared little who led, so long as the sled kept moving.

لم يهتموا كثيرًا بمن يقود، طالما استمرت الزلاجة في الحركة.

Billee, the cheerful one, could have led for all they cared.

كان بإمكان بيلي، البشوش، أن يقود الجميع مهما كان الأمر.

What mattered to them was peace and order in the ranks.

ما كان يهمهم هو السلام والنظام في صفوفهم.

The rest of the team had grown unruly during Spitz's decline.

أصبح بقية الفريق غير منضبط أثناء انحدار سبيتز.

They were shocked when Buck immediately brought them to order.

لقد صدموا عندما أحضرهم باك على الفور إلى النظام.

Pike had always been lazy and dragging his feet behind Buck.

لقد كان بايك دائمًا كسولًا ويجر قدميه خلف باك.

But now was sharply disciplined by the new leadership.

لكن الآن تم تأديبه بشدة من قبل القيادة الجديدة.

And he quickly learned to pull his weight in the team.

وسرعان ما تعلم كيفية تحمل مسؤولياته في الفريق.

By the end of the day, Pike worked harder than ever before.

وبحلول نهاية اليوم، كان بايك يعمل بجهد أكبر من أي وقت مضى.

That night in camp, Joe, the sour dog, was finally subdued.

في تلك الليلة في المخيم، تم إخضاع جو، الكلب الحامض، أخيرًا.

Spitz had failed to discipline him, but Buck did not fail.

لقد فشل سبيتز في تأديبه، لكن باك لم يفشل.

Using his greater weight, Buck overwhelmed Joe in seconds.

وباستخدام وزنه الأكبر، تمكن باك من التغلب على جو في ثوانٍ.

He bit and battered Joe until he whimpered and ceased resisting.

لقد عض جو وضربه حتى أنين وتوقف عن المقاومة.

The whole team improved from that moment on.

لقد تحسن الفريق بأكمله منذ تلك اللحظة.

The dogs regained their old unity and discipline.

استعادت الكلاب وحدتها وانضباطها القديم.

At Rink Rapids, two new native huskies, Teek and Koona, joined.

في رينك رابيدز، انضم اثنان من كلاب الهاسكي الأصلية الجديدة، تيك وكونا.

Buck's swift training of them astonished even François.

لقد أذهل تدريب باك السريع لهم حتى فرانسوا.

"Never was there such a dog as that Buck!" he cried in amazement.

"لم يكن هناك قط كلب مثل هذا باك!" صرخ في دهشة.

"No, never! He's worth one thousand dollars, by God!"

لا، أبدًا! إنه يستحق ألف دولار، والله!

"Eh? What do you say, Perrault?" he asked with pride.

"إيه؟ ماذا تقول يا بيرولت؟" سأل بفخر.

Perrault nodded in agreement and checked his notes.

أومأ بيرولت برأسه موافقًا وراجع ملاحظاته.

We're already ahead of schedule and gaining more each day.

نحن بالفعل متقدمون على الجدول الزمني ونكتسب المزيد كل يوم.

The trail was hard-packed and smooth, with no fresh snow.

كان الطريق ممهدًا وواسعًا، ولم يكن به أي ثلوج جديدة.

The cold was steady, hovering at fifty below zero throughout.

كان البرد مستمرًا، حيث وصلت درجة الحرارة إلى خمسين درجة تحت الصفر في كل مكان.

The men rode and ran in turns to keep warm and make time.

ركب الرجال وركضوا بالتناوب للتدفئة وإيجاد الوقت.

The dogs ran fast with few stops, always pushing forward.

ركضت الكلاب بسرعة مع توقفات قليلة، وكانت دائمًا تدفع إلى الأمام.

The Thirty Mile River was mostly frozen and easy to travel across.

كان نهر الثلاثين ميلاً متجمدًا في معظمه وكان من السهل السفر عبره.

They went out in one day what had taken ten days coming in.

لقد خرجوا في يوم واحد ما استغرق دخوله عشرة أيام.

They made a sixty-mile dash from Lake Le Barge to White Horse.

لقد قاموا برحلة مسافتها ستين ميلاً من بحيرة لو بارج إلى وايت هورس.

Across Marsh, Tagish, and Bennett Lakes they moved incredibly fast.

وعبروا بحيرات مارش وتاجيش وبينيت، تحركوا بسرعة لا تصدق.

The running man towed behind the sled on a rope.

الرجل الذي يركض مسحوبًا خلف الزلاجة بحبل.

On the last night of week two they got to their destination.

وفي الليلة الأخيرة من الأسبوع الثاني وصلوا إلى وجهتهم.

They had reached the top of White Pass together.

لقد وصلوا إلى قمة وايت باس معًا.

They dropped down to sea level with Skaguay's lights below them.

لقد هبطوا إلى مستوى سطح البحر مع أضواء سكاغواي تحتهم.

It had been a record-setting run across miles of cold wilderness.

لقد كان هذا سباقًا قياسيًا عبر أميال من البرية الباردة.

For fourteen days straight, they averaged a strong forty miles.

على مدى أربعة عشر يومًا متواصلة، قطعوا مسافة أربعين ميلًا في المتوسط.

In Skaguay, Perrault and François moved cargo through town.

وفي سكاغواي، قام بيرولت وفرانسوا بنقل البضائع عبر المدينة.

They were cheered and offered many drinks by admiring crowds.

وقد تم الترحيب بهم وتزويدهم بالعديد من المشروبات من قبل الحشود المعجبة.

Dog-busters and workers gathered around the famous dog team.

تجمع صائدو الكلاب والعمال حول فريق الكلاب الشهير.

Then western outlaws came to town and met violent defeat.

ثم جاء الخارجون عن القانون الغربيون إلى المدينة وواجهوا هزيمة عنيفة.

The people soon forgot the team and focused on new drama.

سرعان ما نسي الناس الفريق وركزوا على الدراما الجديدة.

Then came the new orders that changed everything at once.

ثم جاءت الأوامر الجديدة التي غيرت كل شيء دفعة واحدة.

François called Buck to him and hugged him with tearful
pride.

نادى فرانسوا باك عليه وعانقه بفخر دامع.

That moment was the last time Buck ever saw François
again.

كانت تلك اللحظة هي المرة الأخيرة التي رأى فيها باك فرانسوا مرة أخرى.

Like many men before, both François and Perrault were
gone.

وكما حدث مع العديد من الرجال من قبل، فقد رحل كل من فرانسوا وبيرو.

A Scotch half-breed took charge of Buck and his sled dog
teammates.

تولى رجل من أصل اسكتلندي مختلط مسؤولية باك وزملائه في فريق
كلاب الزلاجات.

With a dozen other dog teams, they returned along the trail
to Dawson.

ومع اثني عشر فريقًا آخر منْ الكلاب، عادوا على طول الطريق إلى
داووسن.

It was no fast run now—just heavy toil with a heavy load
each day.

لم يعد الأمر سريعًا الآن - فقط عمل شاق مع حمل ثقيل كل يوم.

This was the mail train, bringing word to gold hunters near
the Pole.

كان هذا قطار البريد، الذي ينقل الأخبار إلى صائدي الذهب بالقرب من
القطب.

Buck disliked the work but bore it well, taking pride in his
effort.

لم يكن باك يحب العمل، لكنه تحمله جيدًا، وكان فخوراً بجهوده.

Like Dave and Solleks, Buck showed devotion to every daily
task.

مثل ديف وسوليكس، أظهر باك تفانيًا في كل مهمة يومية.

He made sure his teammates each pulled their fair weight.

لقد تأكد من أن زملائه في الفريق قاموا بكل ما في وسعهم.

Trail life became dull, repeated with the precision of a
machine.

أصبحت حياة الدرب مملة، تتكرر بدقة الآلة.

Each day felt the same, one morning blending into the next.

كان كل يوم يبدو متشابهاً، كل صباح يمتزج بالصباح التالي.

At the same hour, the cooks rose to build fires and prepare food.

وفي نفس الساعة، نهض الطهاة لإشعال النيران وإعداد الطعام.

After breakfast, some left camp while others harnessed the dogs.

بعد الإفطار، غادر البعض المخيم بينما قام آخرون بتسخير الكلاب.

They hit the trail before the dim warning of dawn touched the sky.

لقد بدأوا رحلتهم قبل أن يلامس ضوء الفجر الخافت السماء.

At night, they stopped to make camp, each man with a set duty.

وفي الليل، توقفوا لإقامة المخيم، وكان لكل رجل منهم مهمة محددة.

Some pitched the tents, others cut firewood and gathered pine boughs.

قام البعض بنصب الخيام، وقام آخرون بقطع الحطب وجمع أغصان الصنوبر.

Water or ice was carried back to the cooks for the evening meal.

تم نقل الماء أو الثلج إلى الطهاة لتناول وجبة العشاء.

The dogs were fed, and this was the best part of the day for them.

تم إطعام الكلاب، وكان هذا أفضل جزء من اليوم بالنسبة لهم.

After eating fish, the dogs relaxed and lounged near the fire.

بعد تناول السمك، استرخى الكلاب وجلسوا بالقرب من النار.

There were a hundred other dogs in the convoy to mingle with.

وكان هناك مائة كلب آخر في القافلة ليختلطوا معهم.

Many of those dogs were fierce and quick to fight without warning.

وكان العديد من تلك الكلاب شرسة وسريعة القتال دون سابق إنذار.

But after three wins, Buck mastered even the fiercest fighters.

لكن بعد ثلاثة انتصارات، تمكن باك من التغلب حتى على أقوى المقاتلين.

Now when Buck growled and showed his teeth, they stepped aside.

والآن عندما زأر باك وأظهر أسنانه، تنحوا جانباً.

Perhaps best of all, Buck loved lying near the flickering campfire.

وربما كان الأفضل من كل هذا هو أن باك كان يحب الاستلقاء بالقرب من نار المخيم المتوهجة.

He crouched with hind legs tucked and front legs stretched ahead.

كان يجلس القرفصاء مع رجليه الخلفيتين مطوية ورجليه الأماميتين ممتدة إلى الأمام.

His head was raised as he blinked softly at the glowing flames.

رفع رأسه وهو يرمش بهدوء عند رؤية النيران المتوهجة.

Sometimes he recalled Judge Miller's big house in Santa Clara.

وفي بعض الأحيان كان يتذكر منزل القاضي ميلر الكبير في سانتا كلارا.

He thought of the cement pool, of Ysabel, and the pug called Toots.

كان يفكر في حوض الأسمنت، وفي إيزابيل، وفي الكلب الصغير الذي يدعى توتس.

But more often he remembered the man with the red sweater's club.

لكن في أغلب الأحيان كان يتذكر الرجل ذو السترة الحمراء.

He remembered Curly's death and his fierce battle with Spitz.

تذكر موت كيرلي ومعركته الشرسة مع سبيتز.

He also recalled the good food he had eaten or still dreamed of.

وتذكر أيضًا الطعام اللذيذ الذي أكله أو ما زال يحلم به.

Buck was not homesick—the warm valley was distant and unreal.

لم يكن باك يشعر بالحنين إلى الوطن ـ كان الوادي الدافئ بعيدًا وغير حقيقي.

Memories of California no longer held any real pull over him.

لم تعد ذكريات كاليفورنيا تشكل له أي تأثير حقيقي.

Stronger than memory were instincts deep in his bloodline.

كانت الغرائز العميقة في سلالته أقوى من الذاكرة.

Habits once lost had returned, revived by the trail and the wild.

لقد عادت العادات التي فقدناها ذات يوم، وأحيتها الطريق والبرية.

As Buck watched the firelight, it sometimes became something else.

بينما كان باك يراقب ضوء النار، كان أحيانًا يتحول إلى شيء آخر.

He saw in the firelight another fire, older and deeper than the present one.

رأى في ضوء النار نارًا أخرى، أقدم وأعمق من النار الحالية.

Beside that other fire crouched a man unlike the half-breed cook.

بجانب تلك النار الأخرى كان يجلس رجل لا يشبه الطاهي الهجين.

This figure had short legs, long arms, and hard, knotted muscles.

كان لهذا الشكل أرجل قصيرة، وأذرع طويلة، وعضلات صلبة ومعقدة.

His hair was long and matted, sloping backward from the eyes.

كان شعره طويلاً ومتشابكًا، وينحدر إلى الخلف بعيدًا عن العينين.

He made strange sounds and stared out in fear at the darkness.

أصدر أصواتًا غريبة وحدق في الظلام بخوف.

He held a stone club low, gripped tightly in his long rough hand.

كان يحمل عصا حجرية منخفضة، ممسكًا بها بإحكام في يده الخشنة الطويلة.

The man wore little; just a charred skin that hung down his back.

كان الرجل يرتدي القليل؛ مجرد جلد متفحم يتدلى على ظهره.

His body was covered with thick hair across arms, chest, and thighs.

كان جسده مغطى بشعر كثيف على ذراعيه وصدره وفخذيه.

Some parts of the hair were tangled into patches of rough fur.

كانت بعض أجزاء الشعر متشابكة في بقع من الفراء الخشن.

He did not stand straight but bent forward from the hips to knees.

لم يكن يقف بشكل مستقيم بل كان ينحني للأمام من الوركين إلى الركبتين.

His steps were springy and catlike, as if always ready to leap.

وكانت خطواته مرنة وخطوات القطط، كما لو كان مستعدًا دائمًا للقفز.

There was a sharp alertness, like he lived in constant fear.

كان هناك يقظة حادة، كما لو كان يعيش في خوف دائم.

This ancient man seemed to expect danger, whether the danger was seen or not.

يبدو أن هذا الرجل القديم كان يتوقع الخطر، سواء كان الخطر مرئيًا أم لا.

At times the hairy man slept by the fire, head tucked between legs.

في بعض الأحيان كان الرجل المشعر ينام بجانب النار، ورأسه بين ساقيه.

His elbows rested on his knees, hands clasped above his head.

كانت مرفقيه مستندة على ركبتيه، ويديه مضمومتين فوق رأسه.

Like a dog he used his hairy arms to shed off the falling rain.

مثل الكلب استخدم ذراعيه المشعرتين للتخلص من المطر المتساقط.

Beyond the firelight, Buck saw twin coals glowing in the dark.

خلف ضوء النار، رأى باك جمرين متوهجين في الظلام.

Always two by two, they were the eyes of stalking beasts of prey.

كانوا دائمًا اثنان اثنان، وكانوا بمثابة عيون الوحوش المفترسة المتسللة.

He heard bodies crash through brush and sounds made in the night.

سمع أصوات أجساد تتحطم وسط الشجيرات وأصواتًا تحدث في الليل.

Lying on the Yukon bank, blinking, Buck dreamed by the fire.

مستلقيا على ضفة نهر يوكون، يرمش، باك يحلم بالنار.

The sights and sounds of that wild world made his hair stand up.

إن مشاهد وأصوات هذا العالم البري جعلت شعره يقف.

The fur rose along his back, his shoulders, and up his neck.

ارتفع الفراء على طول ظهره، وكتفيه، ورقبته.

He whimpered softly or gave a low growl deep in his chest.

كان يئن بهدوء أو يصدر صوت هدير منخفض عميق في صدره.

Then the half-breed cook shouted, "Hey, you Buck, wake up!"

ثم صاح الطاهي ذو السلالة المختلطة، "يا باك، استيقظ!"

The dream world vanished, and real life returned to Buck's eyes.

لقد اختفى عالم الأحلام، وعادت الحياة الحقيقية إلى عيون باك.

He was going to get up, stretch, and yawn, as if woken from a nap.

كان على وشك النهوض، والتمدد، والتثاؤب، وكأنه استيقظ من قيلولة.

The trip was hard, with the mail sled dragging behind them.

كانت الرحلة صعبة، وكان زلاجة البريد تجر خلفهم.

Heavy loads and tough work wore down the dogs each long day.

كانت الأحمال الثقيلة والعمل الشاق يرهق الكلاب كل يوم طويل.

They reached Dawson thin, tired, and needing over a week's rest.

وصلوا إلى داوسون نحيفين، متعبين، ويحتاجون إلى أكثر من أسبوع من الراحة.

But only two days later, they set out down the Yukon again.

ولكن بعد يومين فقط، انطلقوا في رحلة أخرى عبر نهر يوكون.

They were loaded with more letters bound for the outside world.

لقد تم تحميلهم بالمزيد من الرسائل الموجهة إلى العالم الخارجي.

The dogs were exhausted and the men were complaining constantly.

لقد كانت الكلاب منهكة وكان الرجال يشكون باستمرار.

Snow fell every day, softening the trail and slowing the sleds.

كان الثلج يتساقط كل يوم، مما أدى إلى تليين المسار وإبطاء الزلاجات.

This made for harder pulling and more drag on the runners.

أدى هذا إلى زيادة صعوبة السحب وزيادة السحب على العدائين.

Despite that, the drivers were fair and cared for their teams.

وعلى الرغم من ذلك، كان السائقون منصفين وأهتموا بفرقهم.

Each night, the dogs were fed before the men got to eat.

في كل ليلة، يتم إطعام الكلاب قبل أن يحصل الرجال على الطعام.

No man slept before checking the feet of his own dog's.

لم ينم رجل قبل أن يتفقد أقدام كلبه.

Still, the dogs grew weaker as the miles wore on their bodies.

ومع ذلك، أصبحت الكلاب أضعف مع مرور الأميال على أجسادها.

They had traveled eighteen hundred miles through the winter.

لقد سافروا مسافة ألف وثمانمائة ميل خلال فصل الشتاء.

They pulled sleds across every mile of that brutal distance.

لقد سحبوا الزلاجات عبر كل ميل من تلك المسافة الوحشية.

Even the toughest sled dogs feel strain after so many miles.

حتى أقوى كلاب الزلاجات تشعر بالإجهاد بعد كل هذه الأميال.

Buck held on, kept his team working, and maintained discipline.

لقد صمد باك، وأبقى فريقه يعمل، وحافظ على الانضباط.

But Buck was tired, just like the others on the long journey.

لكن باك كان متعبًا، تمامًا مثل الآخرين في الرحلة الطويلة.

Billee whimpered and cried in his sleep each night without fail.

كان بيلي يئن ويبكي أثناء نومه كل ليلة دون انقطاع.

Joe grew even more bitter, and Solleks stayed cold and distant.

أصبح جو أكثر مرارة، وبقي سوليكس باردًا وبعيدًا.

But it was Dave who suffered the worst out of the entire team.

لكن ديف هو الذي عانى أكثر من الفريق بأكمله.

Something had gone wrong inside him, though no one knew what.

لقد حدث خطأ ما في داخله، على الرغم من أن لا أحد يعرف ما هو.

He became moodier and snapped at others with growing anger.

لقد أصبح متقلب المزاج وبدأ يهاجم الآخرين بغضب متزايد.

Each night he went straight to his nest, waiting to be fed.

كل ليلة كان يذهب مباشرة إلى عشه، في انتظار أن يتم إطعامه.

Once he was down, Dave did not get up again till morning.

وبمجرد سقوطه، لم يتمكن ديف من النهوض مرة أخرى حتى الصباح.

On the reins, sudden jerks or starts made him cry out in pain.

على اللجام، الهزات المفاجئة أو الحركات المفاجئة جعلته يصرخ من الألم.

His driver searched for the cause, but found no injury on him.

قام سائقه بالبحث عن السبب، لكنه لم يعثر على أي إصابات.

All the drivers began watching Dave and discussed his case.

بدأ جميع السائقين بمراقبة ديف ومناقشة قضيته.

They talked at meals and during their final smoke of the day.

وتحدثوا أثناء تناول وجبات الطعام وأثناء تدخينهم الأخير في ذلك اليوم.

One night they held a meeting and brought Dave to the fire.

في أحد الليالي عقدوا اجتماعًا وأحضروا ديف إلى النار.

They pressed and probed his body, and he cried out often.

فضغطوا على جسده وفحصوه، وكان يصرخ كثيرًا.

Clearly, something was wrong, though no bones seemed broken.

من الواضح أن هناك خطأ ما، على الرغم من عدم ظهور أي عظام مكسورة.

By the time they reached Cassiar Bar, Dave was falling down.

بحلول الوقت الذي وصلوا فيه إلى بار كاسيار، كان ديف يسقط.

The Scotch half-breed called a halt and removed Dave from the team.

أوقف الفريق ذو السلالة المختلطة الاسكتلندية وأزال ديف من الفريق.

He fastened Solleks in Dave's place, closest to the sled's front.

قام بتثبيت سوليكس في مكان ديف، الأقرب إلى مقدمة الزلاجة.

He meant to let Dave rest and run free behind the moving sled.

كان يقصد أن يترك ديف يستريح ويركض بحرية خلف الزلاجة المتحركة.

But even sick, Dave hated being taken from the job he had owned.

ولكن حتى عندما كان مريضًا، كان ديف يكره أن يتم إبعاده من الوظيفة التي كان يمتلكها.

He growled and whimpered as the reins were pulled from his body.

لقد هدّر وأنين عندما تم سحب اللجام من جسده.

When he saw Solleks in his place, he cried with broken-hearted pain.

عندما رأى سوليكس في مكانه، بكى من الألم الشديد.

The pride of trail work was deep in Dave, even as death approached.

كان فخر العمل على الطريق عميقًا في قلب ديف، حتى مع اقتراب الموت.

As the sled moved, Dave floundered through soft snow near the trail.

وبينما كانت الزلاجة تتحرك، كان ديف يتخبط في الثلج الناعم بالقرب من الطريق.

He attacked Solleks, biting and pushing him from the sled's side.

هاجم سوليكس، فعضه ودفعه من جانب الزلاجة.

Dave tried to leap into the harness and reclaim his working spot.

حاول ديف القفز إلى الحزام واستعادة مكان عمله.

He yelped, whined, and cried, torn between pain and pride in labor.

لقد صرخ، وتذمر، وبكى، ممزقًا بين الألم والفخر بالعمل.

The half-breed used his whip to try driving Dave away from the team.

استخدم الهجين سوطه لمحاولة إبعاد ديف عن الفريق.

But Dave ignored the lash, and the man couldn't strike him harder.

لكن ديف تجاهل السوط، ولم يتمكن الرجل من ضربه بقوة أكبر.

Dave refused the easier path behind the sled, where snow was packed.

رفض ديف المسار الأسهل خلف الزلاجة، حيث كان الثلج كثيفًا.

Instead, he struggled in the deep snow beside the trail, in misery.

وبدلاً من ذلك، كان يكافح في الثلوج العميقة بجانب الطريق، في بؤس.

Eventually, Dave collapsed, lying in the snow and howling in pain.

في النهاية، انهار ديف، مستلقيا على الثلج ويصرخ من الألم.

He cried out as the long train of sleds passed him one by one.

صرخ عندما مر به قطار الزلاجات الطويل واحدًا تلو الآخر.

Still, with what strength remained, he rose and stumbled after them.

ومع ذلك، بما تبقى له من قوة، نهض وتعثر خلفهم.

He caught up when the train stopped again and found his old sled.

لقد لحق به عندما توقف القطار مرة أخرى ووجد زلاجته القديمة.

He floundered past the other teams and stood beside Solleks again.

لقد تخطى الفرق الأخرى ووقف بجانب سوليكس مرة أخرى.

As the driver paused to light his pipe, Dave took his last chance.

وبينما توقف السائق لإشعال غليونه، انتهز ديف فرصته الأخيرة.

When the driver returned and shouted, the team didn't move forward.

وعندما عاد السائق وصاح، لم يتحرك الفريق إلى الأمام.

The dogs had turned their heads, confused by the sudden stoppage.

لقد حركت الكلاب رؤوسها، في حيرة من التوقف المفاجئ.

The driver was shocked too—the sled hadn't moved an inch forward.

لقد صدم السائق أيضًا ـ فالزلاجة لم تتحرك قيد أنملة إلى الأمام.

He called out to the others to come and see what had happened.

ودعا الآخرين إلى الحضور ورؤية ما حدث.

Dave had chewed through Solleks's reins, breaking both apart.

كان ديف قد قضم زمام سوليكس، مما أدى إلى كسر كليهما.

Now he stood in front of the sled, back in his rightful position.

والآن وقف أمام الزلاجة، في مكانه الصحيح.

Dave looked up at the driver, silently pleading to stay in the traces.

نظر ديف إلى السائق، متوسلاً في صمت أن يبقى على المسار.

The driver was puzzled, unsure of what to do for the struggling dog.

كان السائق في حيرة من أمره، وغير متأكد مما يجب فعله للكلب الذي يعاني من صعوبات.

The other men spoke of dogs who had died from being taken out.

وتحدث الرجال الآخرون عن الكلاب التي ماتت بسبب إخراجها.

They told of old or injured dogs whose hearts broke when left behind.

وتحدثوا عن الكلاب العجوز أو المصابة التي تحطمت قلوبها عندما تركت وراءها.

They agreed it was mercy to let Dave die while still in his harness.

واتفقوا على أنه من الرحمة أن يتركوا ديف يموت وهو لا يزال في حزامه.

He was fastened back onto the sled, and Dave pulled with pride.

تم ربطه مرة أخرى على الزلاجة، وسحبه ديف بفخر.

Though he cried out at times, he worked as if pain could be ignored.

رغم أنه كان يبكي في بعض الأحيان، إلا أنه كان يعمل كما لو كان الألم يمكن تجاهله.

More than once he fell and was dragged before rising again.

سقط أكثر من مرة وسُحِب قبل أن ينهض مرة أخرى.

Once, the sled rolled over him, and he limped from that moment on.

في إحدى المرات، انقلبت عليه الزلاجة، وأصبح يعرج منذ تلك اللحظة.

Still, he worked until camp was reached, and then lay by the fire.

ومع ذلك، فقد عمل حتى وصل إلى المخيم، ثم استلقى بجانب النار.

By morning, Dave was too weak to travel or even stand upright.

بحلول الصباح، كان ديف ضعيفًا جدًا بحيث لم يتمكن من السفر أو حتى الوقوف بشكل مستقيم.

At harness-up time, he tried to reach his driver with trembling effort.

عندما حان وقت ربط الحزام، حاول الوصول إلى سائقه بجهد مرتجف.

He forced himself up, staggered, and collapsed onto the snowy ground.

أجبر نفسه على النهوض، وتعثر، وانهار على الأرض الثلجية.

Using his front legs, he dragged his body toward the harnessing area.

استخدم رجليه الأماميتين لسحب جسده نحو منطقة التسخير.

He hitched himself forward, inch by inch, toward the working dogs.

لقد سحب نفسه إلى الأمام، بوصة بوصة، نحو الكلاب العاملة.

His strength gave out, but he kept moving in his last desperate push.

لقد انهارت قوته، لكنه استمر في التحرك في دفعته اليائسة الأخيرة.

His teammates saw him gasping in the snow, still longing to join them.

لقد رأى زملاؤه في الفريق أنه يلهث في الثلج، ولا يزال يتوقون للانضمام إليهم.

They heard him howling with sorrow as they left the camp behind.

سمعوه يصرخ من الحزن عندما غادروا المخيم خلفهم.

As the team vanished into trees, Dave's cry echoed behind them.

وبينما اختفى الفريق بين الأشجار، تردد صدى صرخة ديف خلفهم.

The sled train halted briefly after crossing a stretch of river timber.

توقف قطار الزلاجات لفترة وجيزة بعد عبور جزء من نهر الأخشاب.

The Scotch half-breed walked slowly back toward the camp behind.

سار الهجين الاسكتلندي ببطء نحو المخيم خلفه.

The men stopped speaking when they saw him leave the sled train.

توقف الرجال عن الكلام عندما رأوه يغادر قطار الزلاجات.

Then a single gunshot rang out clear and sharp across the trail.

ثم سمعت طلقة نارية واحدة واضحة وحادة عبر الطريق.

The man returned quickly and took up his place without a word.

عاد الرجل بسرعة وجلس في مكانه دون أن يقول كلمة.

Whips cracked, bells jingled, and the sleds rolled on through snow.

انطلقت أصوات السياط، ورنّ الأجراس، وتدحرجت الزلاجات عبر الثلوج.

But Buck knew what had happened—and so did every other dog.

لكن باك كان يعلم ما حدث، وكان كل كلب آخر يعلم ذلك أيضًا.

The Toil of Reins and Trail
عناء اللجام والطريق

Thirty days after leaving Dawson, the Salt Water Mail reached Skaguay.

بعد ثلاثين يومًا من مغادرة داوسون، وصلت سفينة بريد المياه المالحة إلى سكاجواي.

Buck and his teammates pulled the lead, arriving in pitiful condition.

باك وزملاؤه حققوا التقدم، ووصلوا في حالة يرثى لها.

Buck had dropped from one hundred forty to one hundred fifteen pounds.

انخفض وزن باك من مائة وأربعين إلى مائة وخمسة عشر رطلاً.

The other dogs, though smaller, had lost even more body weight.

أما الكلاب الأخرى، على الرغم من صغر حجمها، فقد فقدت المزيد من وزن الجسم.

Pike, once a fake limper, now dragged a truly injured leg behind him.

بايك، الذي كان يعرج في السابق بشكل مزيف، يسحب الآن ساقًا مصابة حقًا خلفه.

Solleks was limping badly, and Dub had a wrenched shoulder blade.

كان سوليكس يعرج بشدة، وكان دوب يعاني من تمزق في لوح كتفه.

Every dog in the team was footsore from weeks on the frozen trail.

كان كل كلب في الفريق يعاني من آلام في قدميه بسبب الأسابيع التي قضاها على الطريق المتجمد.

They had no spring left in their steps, only slow, dragging motion.

لم يعد لديهم أي نشاط في خطواتهم، فقط حركة بطيئة ومتثاقلة.

Their feet hit the trail hard, each step adding more strain to their bodies.

ضربت أقدامهم الطريق بقوة، وكانت كل خطوة تضيف المزيد من الضغط على أجسادهم.

They were not sick, only drained beyond all natural recovery.

لم يكونوا مرضى، بل كانوا مستنزفين إلى حد لا يمكن الشفاء منه بشكل طبيعي.

This was not tiredness from one hard day, cured with a night's rest.

لم يكن هذا تعبًا من يوم شاق، تم علاجه بالراحة الليلية.

It was exhaustion built slowly through months of grueling effort.

لقد كان إرهاقًا تراكم ببطء عبر أشهر من الجهد الشاق.

No reserve strength remained—they had used up every bit they had.

لم يتبق لديهم أي احتياطي من القوة ـ فقد استنفدوا كل ما لديهم.

Every muscle, fiber, and cell in their bodies was spent and worn.

لقد استُنفدت كل عضلة وليفة وخلية في أجسادهم.

And there was a reason—they had covered twenty-five hundred miles.

وكان هناك سبب ـ لقد قطعوا مسافة ألفين وخمسمائة ميل.

They had rested only five days during the last eighteen hundred miles.

لقد استراحوا لمدة خمسة أيام فقط خلال الثمانية عشر ميلاً الأخيرة.

When they reached Skaguay, they looked barely able to stand upright.

عندما وصلوا إلى سكاجواي، بدا أنهم بالكاد قادرين على الوقوف بشكل مستقيم.

They struggled to keep the reins tight and stay ahead of the sled.

لقد كافحوا من أجل إبقاء زمام الأمور مشدودة والبقاء في المقدمة أمام الزلاجة.

On downhill slopes, they only managed to avoid being run over.

على المنحدرات، تمكنوا فقط من تجنب التعرض للدهس.

"March on, poor sore feet," the driver said as they limped along.

"استمروا في السير، أيها المسكين ذو الأقدام المؤلمة"، قال السائق بينما كانوا يعرجون على الطريق.

"This is the last stretch, then we all get one long rest, for sure."

"هذه هي المرحلة الأخيرة، وبعدها سنحصل جميعًا على قسط من الراحة الطويلة، بالتأكيد."

"One truly long rest," he promised, watching them stagger forward.

"راحة طويلة حقًا"، وعدهم وهو يراقبهم وهم يتقدمون للأمام.

The drivers expected they were going to now get a long, needed break.

وكان السائقون يتوقعون الآن أنهم سيحصلون على استراحة طويلة وضرورية.

They had traveled twelve hundred miles with only two days' rest.

لقد سافروا مسافة ألف ومائتي ميل مع يومين راحة فقط.

By fairness and reason, they felt they had earned time to relax.

ومن باب الإنصاف والمنطق، فقد شعروا أنهم استحقوا الوقت للاسترخاء.

But too many had come to the Klondike, and too few had stayed home.

لكن الكثيرين جاؤوا إلى كلوندايك، وقليل منهم بقي في المنزل.

Letters from families flooded in, creating piles of delayed mail.

تدفقت الرسائل من العائلات، مما أدى إلى أكوام من البريد المتأخر.

Official orders arrived—new Hudson Bay dogs were going to take over.

وصلت الأوامر الرسمية ـ كان من المقرر أن يتولى كلاب هدسون باي الجدد المسؤولية.

The exhausted dogs, now called worthless, were to be disposed of.

كان من المقرر التخلص من الكلاب المنهكة، والتي أصبحت الآن عديمة القيمة.

Since money mattered more than dogs, they were going to be sold cheaply.

وبما أن المال كان أكثر أهمية من الكلاب، فقد كان من المقرر بيعها بثمن بخس.

Three more days passed before the dogs felt just how weak they were.

مرت ثلاثة أيام أخرى قبل أن يشعر الكلاب بمدى ضعفهم.

On the fourth morning, two men from the States bought the whole team.

وفي صباح اليوم الرابع، اشترى رجلان من الولايات المتحدة الفريق بأكمله.

The sale included all the dogs, plus their worn harness gear.

شمل البيع جميع الكلاب، بالإضافة إلى أحزمة الأمان التي كانت تستخدمها.

The men called each other "Hal" and "Charles" as they completed the deal.

أطلق الرجال على بعضهم البعض اسم "هال" و"تشارلز" عندما أكملوا الصفقة.

Charles was middle-aged, pale, with limp lips and fierce mustache tips.

كان تشارلز في منتصف العمر، شاحبًا، بشفاه مترهلة وشاربه كثيف.

Hal was a young man, maybe nineteen, wearing a cartridge-stuffed belt.

كان هال شابًا، ربما يبلغ من العمر تسعة عشر عامًا، يرتدي حزامًا محشوًا بالخرطوش.

The belt held a big revolver and a hunting knife, both unused.

كان الحزام يحمل مسدسًا كبيرًا وسكين صيد، وكلاهما لم يستخدما.

It showed how inexperienced and unfit he was for northern life.

وأظهر ذلك مدى قلة خبرته وعدم ملاءمته للحياة الشمالية.

Neither man belonged in the wild; their presence defied all reason.

لم يكن أي من الرجلين ينتمي إلى البرية؛ فوجودهما يتحدى كل المنطق.

Buck watched as money exchanged hands between buyer and agent.

كان باك يراقب الأموال وهي تنتقل بين المشتري والوكيل.

He knew the mail-train drivers were leaving his life like the rest.

لقد علم أن سائقي قطار البريد يغادرون حياته مثل بقية الناس.

They followed Perrault and François, now gone beyond recall.

وتبعوا بيرولت وفرانسوا، اللذين أصبحا الآن في وضع لا يمكن تذكره.

Buck and the team were led to their new owners' sloppy camp.

تم أخذ باك وفريقه إلى المعسكر غير المنظم لأصحابهم الجدد.

The tent sagged, dishes were dirty, and everything lay in disarray.

كانت الخيمة مترهلة، والأطباق متسخة، وكل شيء في حالة من الفوضى.

Buck noticed a woman there too—Mercedes, Charles's wife and Hal's sister.

لاحظ باك وجود امرأة هناك أيضًا ـ مرسيدس، زوجة تشارلز وشقيقة هال.

They made a complete family, though far from suited to the trail.

لقد شكلوا عائلة متكاملة، رغم أنهم لم يكونوا مناسبين للمسار.

Buck watched nervously as the trio started packing the supplies.

كان باك يراقب بتوتر بينما بدأ الثلاثي في تعبئة الإمدادات.

They worked hard but without order—just fuss and wasted effort.

لقد عملوا بجد ولكن دون نظام ـ مجرد ضجة وجهد ضائع.

The tent was rolled into a bulky shape, far too large for the sled.

تم لف الخيمة إلى شكل ضخم، أكبر بكثير من الزلاجة.

Dirty dishes were packed without being cleaned or dried at all.

تم تعبئة الأطباق المتسخة دون تنظيفها أو تجفيفها على الإطلاق.

Mercedes fluttered about, constantly talking, correcting, and meddling.

كانت مرسيدس ترفرف هنا وهناك، وتتحدث باستمرار، وتصحح، وتتدخل.

When a sack was placed on front, she insisted it go on the back.

عندما تم وضع الكيس في المقدمة، أصرت على وضعه في الخلف.

She packed the sack in the bottom, and the next moment she needed it.

وضعت الكيس في الأسفل، وفي اللحظة التالية احتاجته.

So the sled was unpacked again to reach the one specific bag.

لذلك تم تفريغ الزلاجة مرة أخرى للوصول إلى الحقيبة المحددة.

Nearby, three men stood outside a tent, watching the scene unfold.

وفي مكان قريب، كان هناك ثلاثة رجال يقفون خارج خيمة، يراقبون المشهد.

They smiled, winked, and grinned at the newcomers' obvious confusion.

ابتسموا، وغمزوا، وضحكوا على الارتباك الواضح الذي أصاب الوافدين الجدد.

"You've got a right heavy load already," said one of the men.

"لقد حصلت على حمل ثقيل بالفعل"، قال أحد الرجال.

"I don't think you should carry that tent, but it's your choice."

"لا أعتقد أنه يجب عليك حمل تلك الخيمة، لكن هذا اختيارك."

"Undreamed of!" cried Mercedes, throwing up her hands in despair.

"لم أحلم به!" صرخت مرسيدس وهي ترفع يديها في يأس.

"How could I possibly travel without a tent to stay under?"

"كيف يمكنني أن أسافر دون خيمة للبقاء تحتها؟"

"It's springtime—you won't see cold weather again," the man replied.

"إنه فصل الربيع، ولن ترى الطقس البارد مرة أخرى"، أجاب الرجل.

But she shook her head, and they kept piling items onto the sled.

لكنها هزت رأسها، واستمروا في تكديس الأشياء على الزلاجة.

The load towered dangerously high as they added the final things.

ارتفعت الأحمال بشكل خطير عندما أضافوا الأشياء النهائية.

"Think the sled will ride?" asked one of the men with a skeptical look.

"هل تعتقد أن الزلاجة سوف تتحرك؟" سأل أحد الرجال بنظرة متشككة.

"Why shouldn't it?" Charles snapped back with sharp annoyance.

"لماذا لا نفعل ذلك؟" رد تشارلز بانزعاج حاد.

"Oh, that's all right," the man said quickly, backing away from offense.

"أوه، لا بأس بذلك،" قال الرجل بسرعة، متراجعًا عن الإساءة.

"I was only wondering—it just looked a bit too top-heavy to me."

"كنت أتساءل فقط ـ لقد بدا الأمر ثقيلًا بعض الشيء بالنسبة لي."

Charles turned away and tied down the load as best as he could.

استدار تشارلز وربط الحمولة بأفضل ما استطاع.

But the lashings were loose and the packing poorly done overall.

لكن الربط كان فضفاضًا والتعبئة كانت سيئة بشكل عام.

"Sure, the dogs will pull that all day," another man said sarcastically.

"بالتأكيد، الكلاب ستفعل ذلك طوال اليوم"، قال رجل آخر ساخرًا.

"Of course," Hal replied coldly, grabbing the sled's long gee-pole.

"بالطبع،" أجاب هال ببرود، وهو يمسك بعمود الزلاجة الطويل.

With one hand on the pole, he swung the whip in the other.

وبإحدى يديه على العمود، كان يلوح بالسوط في اليد الأخرى.

"Let's go!" he shouted. "Move it!" urging the dogs to start.

"هيا بنا!" صرخ. "تحركوا!" حاثًا الكلاب على الانطلاق.

The dogs leaned into the harness and strained for a few moments.

انحنت الكلاب إلى الحزام وتوترت لعدة لحظات.

Then they stopped, unable to budge the overloaded sled an inch.

ثم توقفوا، غير قادرين على تحريك الزلاجة المحملة قيد أنملة.

"The lazy brutes!" Hal yelled, lifting the whip to strike them.

"الوحوش الكسالى!" صرخ هال، ورفع السوط ليضربهم.

But Mercedes rushed in and seized the whip from Hal's hands.

لكن مرسيدس هرعت وانتزعت السوط من يد هال.

"Oh, Hal, don't you dare hurt them," she cried in alarm.

"أوه، هال، لا تجرؤ على إيذائهم،" صرخت في حالة من الفزع.

"Promise me you'll be kind to them, or I won't go another step."

"وعدني بأنك ستكون لطيفًا معهم، وإلا فلن أتخذ خطوة أخرى."

"You don't know a thing about dogs," Hal snapped at his sister.

"أنت لا تعرفين شيئًا عن الكلاب"، قال هال لأخته.

"They're lazy, and the only way to move them is to whip them."

"إنهم كسالى، والطريقة الوحيدة لتحريكهم هي ضربهم بالسوط."

"Ask anyone—ask one of those men over there if you doubt me."

"اسأل أي شخص، اسأل أحد هؤلاء الرجال هناك إذا كنت تشك بي."

Mercedes looked at the onlookers with pleading, tearful eyes.

نظرت مرسيدس إلى المتفرجين بعيون متوسلة مليئة بالدموع.

Her face showed how deeply she hated the sight of any pain.

أظهر وجهها مدى كرهها لرؤية أي ألم.

"They're weak, that's all," one man said. "They're worn out."

"إنهم ضعفاء، هذا كل ما في الأمر"، قال أحد الرجال. "لقد أُنهكوا".

"They need rest—they've been worked too long without a break."

"إنهم يحتاجون إلى الراحة ـ لقد عملوا لفترة طويلة دون انقطاع."

"Rest be cursed," Hal muttered with his lip curled.

"الباقي ملعون" تمتم هال مع شفتيه ملتفة.

Mercedes gasped, clearly pained by the coarse word from him.

شهقت مرسيدس، من الواضح أنها شعرت بالألم بسبب الكلمة البذيئة التي قالها لها.

Still, she stayed loyal and instantly defended her brother.

ومع ذلك، ظلت مخلصة ودافعت عن شقيقها على الفور.

"Don't mind that man," she said to Hal. "They're our dogs."

"لا تهتمّ لهذا الرجل"، قالت لهال. "إنهم كلابنا".

"You drive them as you see fit—do what you think is right."

"أنت تقودهم كما تراه مناسبًا ـ افعل ما تعتقد أنه صحيح."

Hal raised the whip and struck the dogs again without mercy.

رفع هال السوط وضرب الكلاب مرة أخرى دون رحمة.

They lunged forward, bodies low, feet pushing into the snow.

اندفعوا إلى الأمام، أجسادهم منخفضة، وأقدامهم تدفع في الثلج.

All their strength went into the pull, but the sled wasn't moving.

لقد بذلوا كل قوتهم في السحب، لكن الزلاجة لم تكن تتحرك.

The sled stayed stuck, like an anchor frozen into the packed snow.

ظلت الزلاجة عالقة، مثل مرساة متجمدة في الثلج المتراكم.

After a second effort, the dogs stopped again, panting hard.

وبعد محاولة ثانية، توقفت الكلاب مرة أخرى، وهي تلهث بشدة.

Hal raised the whip once more, just as Mercedes interfered again.

رفع هال السوط مرة أخرى، في الوقت الذي تدخلت فيه مرسيدس مرة أخرى.

She dropped to her knees in front of Buck and hugged his neck.

نزلت على ركبتيها أمام باك وعانقت رقبته.

Tears filled her eyes as she pleaded with the exhausted dog.

امتلأت عيناها بالدموع وهي تتوسل إلى الكلب المنهك.

"You poor dears," she said, "why don't you just pull harder?"

"يا مساكين،" قالت، "لماذا لا تسحبون بقوة أكبر؟"

"If you pull, then you won't get to be whipped like this."

"إذا قمت بالسحب، فلن يتم جلدك بهذه الطريقة."

Buck disliked Mercedes, but he was too tired to resist her now.

لم يكن باك يحب مرسيدس، لكنه كان متعبًا جدًا بحيث لم يتمكن من مقاومتها الآن.

He accepted her tears as just another part of the miserable day.

لقد تقبل دموعها باعتبارها جزءًا آخر من يومه البائس.

One of the watching men finally spoke after holding back his anger.

تحدث أحد الرجال الذين كانوا يراقبون أخيرًا بعد أن تمكن من كبت غضبه.

"I don't care what happens to you folks, but those dogs matter."

"لا يهمني ما يحدث لكم أيها الناس، ولكن تلك الكلاب مهمة."

"If you want to help, break that sled loose—it's frozen to the snow."

"إذا كنت تريد المساعدة، قم بكسر تلك الزلاجة - فهي متجمدة في الثلج."

"Push hard on the gee-pole, right and left, and break the ice seal."

"اضغط بقوة على عمود الجي، يمينًا ويسارًا، واكسر ختم الجليد."

A third attempt was made, this time following the man's suggestion.

وتم إجراء محاولة ثالثة، هذه المرة بناء على اقتراح الرجل.

Hal rocked the sled from side to side, breaking the runners loose.

هز هال الزلاجة من جانب إلى آخر، مما أدى إلى تحرير العدائين.

The sled, though overloaded and awkward, finally lurched forward.

رغم أن الزلاجة كانت مثقلة وخرقاء، إلا أنها اندفعت إلى الأمام في النهاية.

Buck and the others pulled wildly, driven by a storm of whiplashes.

سحب باك والآخرون أنفسهم بعنف، تحت وطأة عاصفة من الضربات العنيفة.

A hundred yards ahead, the trail curved and sloped into the street.

على بعد مائة ياردة إلى الأمام، انحنى المسار وانحدر إلى الشارع.

It was going to have taken a skilled driver to keep the sled upright.

كان من المفترض أن يحتاج الأمر إلى سائق ماهر للحفاظ على الزلاجة في وضع مستقيم.

Hal was not skilled, and the sled tipped as it swung around the bend.

لم يكن هال ماهرًا، وانقلبت الزلاجة عندما تأرجحت حول المنحنى.

Loose lashings gave way, and half the load spilled onto the snow.

انهارت الأربطة، وسقط نصف الحمولة على الثلج.

The dogs did not stop; the lighter sled flew along on its side.

لم تتوقف الكلاب، وكانت الزلاجة الخفيفة تطير على جانبها.

Angry from abuse and the heavy burden, the dogs ran faster.

غاضبين من الإساءة والعبء الثقيل، ركضت الكلاب بشكل أسرع.

Buck, in fury, broke into a run, with the team following behind.

اندفع باك في غضب شديد، وتبعه الفريق.

Hal shouted "Whoa! Whoa!" but the team paid no attention to him.

صرخ هال "واو! واو!" لكن الفريق لم ينتبه له.

He tripped, fell, and was dragged along the ground by the harness.

لقد تعثر وسقط وسحبه الحزام على الأرض.

The overturned sled bumped over him as the dogs raced on ahead.

ارتطمت الزلاجة المقلوبة به بينما كانت الكلاب تتسابق أمامه.

The rest of the supplies scattered across Skaguay's busy street.

بقية الإمدادات متناثرة في شوارع سكاغواي المزدحمة.

Kind-hearted people rushed to stop the dogs and gather the gear.

هرع الناس طيبو القلوب لإيقاف الكلاب وجمع المعدات.

They also gave advice, blunt and practical, to the new travelers.

كما قدموا نصائح مباشرة وعملية للمسافرين الجدد.

"If you want to reach Dawson, take half the load and double the dogs."

"إذا كنت تريد الوصول إلى داوسون، خذ نصف الحمولة وضاعف عدد الكلاب."

Hal, Charles, and Mercedes listened, though not with enthusiasm.

استمع هال، وتشارلز، ومرسيدس، ولكن ليس بحماس.

They pitched their tent and started sorting through their supplies.

قاموا بنصب خيمتهم وبدأوا بفرز إمداداتهم.

Out came canned goods, which made onlookers laugh aloud.

وخرجت الأطعمة المعلبة، مما جعل المتفرجين يضحكون بصوت عالٍ.

"Canned stuff on the trail? You'll starve before that melts," one said.

"معلبات على الطريق؟ ستموت جوعًا قبل أن تذوب"، قال أحدهم.

"Hotel blankets? You're better off throwing them all out."

بطانيات الفنادق؟ من الأفضل التخلص منها جميعًا.

"Ditch the tent, too, and no one washes dishes here."

"تخلص من الخيمة أيضًا، ولن يغسل أحد الأطباق هنا."

"You think you're riding a Pullman train with servants on board?"

"هل تعتقد أنك تركب قطار بولمان مع الخدم على متنه؟"

The process began—every useless item was tossed to the side.

بدأت العملية ـ تم إلقاء كل عنصر عديم الفائدة جانبًا.

Mercedes cried when her bags were emptied onto the snowy ground.

بكت مرسيدس عندما أفرغت حقائبها على الأرض الثلجية.

She sobbed over every item thrown out, one by one without pause.

كانت تبكي بشدة على كل قطعة تم إلقاؤها، واحدة تلو الأخرى، دون توقف.

She vowed not to go one more step—not even for ten Charleses.

لقد أقسمت على عدم الذهاب خطوة أخرى ـ حتى ولو لعشرة تشارلز.

She begged each person nearby to let her keep her precious things.

وتوسلت إلى كل شخص قريب منها أن يسمح لها بالاحتفاظ بأشياءها الثمينة.

At last, she wiped her eyes and began tossing even vital clothes.

وأخيراً مسحت عينيها وبدأت تتخلص حتى من الملابس الحيوية.

When done with her own, she began emptying the men's supplies.

عندما انتهت من أعمالها، بدأت في إفراغ إمدادات الرجال.

Like a whirlwind, she tore through Charles and Hal's belongings.

مثل عاصفة، مزقت ممتلكات تشارلز وهال.

Though the load was halved, it was still far heavier than needed.

على الرغم من أن الحمل انخفض إلى النصف، إلا أنه كان لا يزال أثقل بكثير من اللازم.

That night, Charles and Hal went out and bought six new dogs.

في تلك الليلة، خرج تشارلز وهال واشتريا ستة كلاب جديدة.

These new dogs joined the original six, plus Teek and Koona.

انضمت هذه الكلاب الجديدة إلى الكلاب الستة الأصلية، بالإضافة إلى تيك وكونا.

Together they made a team of fourteen dogs hitched to the sled.

لقد شكلوا معًا فريقًا مكونًا من أربعة عشر كلبًا مربوطين بالزلاجة.

But the new dogs were unfit and poorly trained for sled work.

لكن الكلاب الجديدة كانت غير صالحة للعمل على الزلاجات ولم يتم تدريبها بشكل جيد.

Three of the dogs were short-haired pointers, and one was a Newfoundland.

ثلاثة من الكلاب كانت من نوع المؤشرات ذات الشعر القصير، وكان واحد منها من نوع نيوفاوندلاند.

The final two dogs were mutts of no clear breed or purpose at all.

كان الكلبان الأخيران من الكلاب الهجينة التي ليس لها سلالة واضحة أو غرض على الإطلاق.

They didn't understand the trail, and they didn't learn it quickly.

لم يفهموا المسار، ولم يتعلموه بسرعة.

Buck and his mates watched them with scorn and deep irritation.

كان باك وأصدقاؤه يراقبونهم بازدراء وانزعاج عميق.

Though Buck taught them what not to do, he could not teach duty.

على الرغم من أن باك علمهم ما لا ينبغي لهم فعله، إلا أنه لم يكن قادرًا على تعليمهم الواجب.

They didn't take well to trail life or the pull of reins and sleds.

لم يتقبلوا بشكل جيد تتبع الحياة أو سحب اللجام والزلاجات.

Only the mongrels tried to adapt, and even they lacked fighting spirit.

حاول الهجينون فقط التكيف، وحتى هم كانوا يفتقرون إلى روح القتال.

The other dogs were confused, weakened, and broken by their new life.

كانت الكلاب الأخرى مرتبكة، ضعيفة، ومنكسرة بسبب حياتها الجديدة.

With the new dogs clueless and the old ones exhausted, hope was thin.

مع الكلاب الجديدة التي كانت في حيرة من أمرها والكلاب القديمة المنهكة، كان الأمل ضئيلاً.

Buck's team had covered twenty-five hundred miles of harsh trail.

لقد قطع فريق باك مسافة ألفين وخمسمائة ميل من الطريق القاسي.

Still, the two men were cheerful and proud of their large dog team.

ومع ذلك، كان الرجلان مبتهجين وفخورين بفريق الكلاب الكبير الخاص بهم.

They thought they were traveling in style, with fourteen dogs hitched.

ظنوا أنهم يسافرون بأناقة، مع أربعة عشر كلبًا مربوطين.

They had seen sleds leave for Dawson, and others arrive from it.

لقد شاهدوا زلاجات تغادر إلى داوسون، وأخرى تصل منها.

But never had they seen one pulled by as many as fourteen dogs.

لكنهم لم يروا قط واحدًا يسحبه ما يصل إلى أربعة عشر كلبًا.

There was a reason such teams were rare in the Arctic wilderness.

وكان هناك سبب لكون مثل هذه الفرق نادرة في البرية القطبية الشمالية.

No sled could carry enough food to feed fourteen dogs for the trip.

لم يكن بمقدور أي مزلجة أن تحمل ما يكفي من الطعام لإطعام أربعة عشر كلبًا طوال الرحلة.

But Charles and Hal didn't know that—they had done the math.

لكن تشارلز وهال لم يعرفا ذلك ـ لقد أجريا الحسابات.

They penciled out the food: so much per dog, so many days, done.

لقد خططوا للطعام: كمية محددة لكل كلب، وعدد محدد من الأيام، وتم الانتهاء من ذلك.

Mercedes looked at their figures and nodded as if it made sense.

نظرت مرسيدس إلى أرقامهم وأومأت برأسها كما لو كان الأمر منطقيًا.

It all seemed very simple to her, at least on paper.

لقد بدا الأمر كله بسيطًا جدًا بالنسبة لها، على الأقل على الورق.

The next morning, Buck led the team slowly up the snowy street.

وفي صباح اليوم التالي، قاد باك الفريق ببطء إلى الشارع الثلجي.

There was no energy or spirit in him or the dogs behind him.

لم تكن هناك طاقة أو روح فيه أو في الكلاب خلفه.

They were dead tired from the start—there was no reserve left.

لقد كانوا متعبين للغاية منذ البداية ـ لم يتبق لديهم أي احتياطي.

Buck had made four trips between Salt Water and Dawson already.

لقد قام باك بأربع رحلات بين سولت ووتر وداوسون بالفعل.

Now, faced with the same trail again, he felt nothing but bitterness.

والآن، عندما واجه نفس المسار مرة أخرى، لم يشعر إلا بالمرارة.

His heart was not in it, nor were the hearts of the other dogs.

لم يكن قلبه فيه، ولا قلوب الكلاب الأخرى.

The new dogs were timid, and the huskies lacked all trust.

كانت الكلاب الجديدة خجولة، وكانت كلاب الهاسكي تفتقر إلى الثقة.

Buck sensed he could not rely on these two men or their sister.

أحس باك أنه لا يستطيع الاعتماد على هذين الرجلين أو أختهما.

They knew nothing and showed no signs of learning on the trail.

لم يعرفوا شيئًا ولم يظهروا أي علامات على التعلم أثناء الرحلة.

They were disorganized and lacked any sense of discipline.

لقد كانوا غير منظمين ويفتقرون إلى أي حس بالانضباط.

It took them half the night to set up a sloppy camp each time.

استغرق الأمر منهم نصف الليل لإقامة معسكر غير منظم في كل مرة.

And half the next morning they spent fumbling with the sled again.

وفي الصباح التالي قضوا نصف الوقت في محاولة التعامل مع الزلاجة مرة أخرى.

By noon, they often stopped just to fix the uneven load.

بحلول الظهر، كانوا يتوقفون في كثير من الأحيان فقط لإصلاح الحمل غير المتساوي.

On some days, they traveled less than ten miles in total.

وفي بعض الأيام، سافروا مسافة أقل من عشرة أميال إجمالاً.

Other days, they didn't manage to leave camp at all.

وفي أيام أخرى، لم يتمكنوا من مغادرة المخيم على الإطلاق.

They never came close to covering the planned food-distance.

ولم يقتربوا أبدًا من تغطية مسافة الغذاء المخطط لها.

As expected, they ran short on food for the dogs very quickly.

كما كان متوقعًا، نفد الطعام المخصص للكلاب بسرعة كبيرة.

They made matters worse by overfeeding in the early days.

لقد جعلوا الأمور أسوأ بسبب الإفراط في التغذية في الأيام الأولى.

This brought starvation closer with every careless ration.

وقد أدى هذا إلى تقريب المجاعة منا مع كل حصة غير مدروسة.

The new dogs had not learned to survive on very little.

لم تتعلم الكلاب الجديدة كيفية البقاء على قيد الحياة على القليل جدًا.

They ate hungrily, with appetites too large for the trail.

لقد أكلوا بشراهة، وكانت شهيتهم كبيرة جدًا بالنسبة للطريق.

Seeing the dogs weaken, Hal believed the food wasn't enough.

عندما رأى هال الكلاب تضعف، اعتقد أن الطعام لم يكن كافيا.

He doubled the rations, making the mistake even worse.

لقد ضاعف الحصص، مما جعل الخطأ أسوأ.

Mercedes added to the problem with tears and soft pleading.

أضافت مرسيدس إلى المشكلة دموعها وتوسلاتها الناعمة.

When she couldn't convince Hal, she fed the dogs in secret.

عندما لم تتمكن من إقناع هال، قامت بإطعام الكلاب سراً.

She stole from the fish sacks and gave it to them behind his back.

سرقت من أكياس السمك وأعطتها لهم من وراء ظهره.

But what the dogs truly needed wasn't more food—it was rest.

لكن ما يحتاجه الكلاب حقًا لم يكن المزيد من الطعام، بل الراحة.

They were making poor time, but the heavy sled still dragged on.

لقد كانوا يحققون وقتًا سيئًا، لكن الزلاجة الثقيلة كانت لا تزال مستمرة.

That weight alone drained their remaining strength each day.

كان هذا الوزن وحده يستنزف قوتهم المتبقية كل يوم.

Then came the stage of underfeeding as the supplies ran low.

ثم جاءت مرحلة نقص التغذية حيث انخفضت الإمدادات.

Hal realized one morning that half the dog food was already gone.

أدرك هال في أحد الصباحات أن نصف طعام الكلب قد نفد بالفعل.

They had only traveled a quarter of the total trail distance.

لقد سافروا ربع المسافة الإجمالية للمسار فقط.

No more food could be bought, no matter what price was offered.

لم يعد من الممكن شراء المزيد من الطعام، بغض النظر عن السعر المعروض.

He reduced the dogs' portions below the standard daily ration.

لقد خفض حصص الكلاب إلى ما دون الحصة اليومية القياسية.

At the same time, he demanded longer travel to make up for loss.

وفي الوقت نفسه، طالب برحلة أطول لتعويض الخسارة.

Mercedes and Charles supported this plan, but failed in execution.

وقد دعم مرسيدس وتشارلز هذه الخطة، لكنهما فشلا في تنفيذها.

Their heavy sled and lack of skill made progress nearly impossible.

إن زلاجاتهم الثقيلة وافتقارهم إلى المهارة جعل التقدم مستحيلاً تقريباً.

It was easy to give less food, but impossible to force more effort.

كان من السهل تقديم كمية أقل من الطعام، ولكن من المستحيل إجبار الناس على بذل المزيد من الجهد.

They couldn't start early, nor could they travel for extra hours.

لم يتمكنوا من البدء مبكرًا، ولم يتمكنوا من السفر لساعات إضافية.

They didn't know how to work the dogs, nor themselves, for that matter.

لم يعرفوا كيفية التعامل مع الكلاب، ولا حتى مع أنفسهم، في هذا الشأن.

The first dog to die was Dub, the unlucky but hardworking thief.

كان الكلب الأول الذي مات هو دوب، اللص غير المحظوظ ولكنه مجتهد.

Though often punished, Dub had pulled his weight without complaint.

على الرغم من معاقبته في كثير من الأحيان، كان داب يحمل ثقله دون شكوى.

His injured shoulder grew worse without care or needed rest.

ازدادت إصابة كتفه سوءًا دون رعاية أو حاجة للراحة.

Finally, Hal used the revolver to end Dub's suffering.

وأخيرًا، استخدم هال المسدس لإنهاء معاناة داب.

A common saying claimed that normal dogs die on husky rations.

هناك مقولة شائعة تقول أن الكلاب الطبيعية تموت على حصص الهاسكي.

Buck's six new companions had only half the husky's share of food.

كان لدى رفاق باك الستة الجدد نصف حصة الهاسكي من الطعام فقط.

The Newfoundland died first, then the three short-haired pointers.

مات نيوفاوندلاند أولاً، ثم الكلاب الثلاثة ذات الشعر القصير.

The two mongrels held on longer but finally perished like the rest.

صمدت السلالتان الهجينتان لفترة أطول ولكن في النهاية هلكتا مثل البقية.

By this time, all the amenities and gentleness of the Southland were gone.

بحلول هذا الوقت، اختفت كل وسائل الراحة واللطف التي كانت موجودة في منطقة الجنوب.

The three people had shed the last traces of their civilized upbringing.

لقد تخلص الأشخاص الثلاثة من آخر آثار تربيتهم المتحضرة.

Stripped of glamour and romance, Arctic travel became brutally real.

بعد أن جردوها من السحر والرومانسية، أصبحت السفر إلى القطب الشمالي حقيقة واقعة.

It was a reality too harsh for their sense of manhood and womanhood.

لقد كان الواقع قاسياً للغاية بالنسبة لإحساسهم بالرجولة والأنوثة.

Mercedes no longer wept for the dogs, but now wept only for herself.

لم تعد مرسيدس تبكي على الكلاب، بل أصبحت تبكي على نفسها فقط.

She spent her time crying and quarreling with Hal and Charles.

لقد أمضت وقتها في البكاء والشجار مع هال وتشارلز.

Quarreling was the one thing they were never too tired to do.

كان الشجار هو الشيء الوحيد الذي لم يتعبوا من فعله أبدًا.

Their irritability came from misery, grew with it, and surpassed it.

إن انفعالهم كان نابعاً من البؤس، ونما معه، وتجاوزه.

The patience of the trail, known to those who toil and suffer kindly, never came.

إن صبر الطريق، المعروف لدى أولئك الذين يتعبون ويعانون بلطف، لم يأتِ أبدًا.

That patience, which keeps speech sweet through pain, was unknown to them.

إن الصبر الذي يحفظ الكلام حلواً رغم الألم لم يكن معروفاً لهم.

They had no hint of patience, no strength drawn from suffering with grace.

لم يكن لديهم أدنى قدر من الصبر، ولم تكن لديهم القوة التي تستمد من المعاناة بالنعمة.

They were stiff with pain—aching in their muscles, bones, and hearts.

كانوا متيبسين من الألم - وجع في عضلاتهم وعظامهم وقلوبهم.

Because of this, they grew sharp of tongue and quick with harsh words.

وبسبب هذا، أصبحوا حادي اللسان وسريعي الكلام القاسي.

Each day began and ended with angry voices and bitter complaints.

كان كل يوم يبدأ وينتهي بأصوات غاضبة وشكاوى مريرة.

Charles and Hal wrangled whenever Mercedes gave them a chance.

كان تشارلز وهال يتجادلان كلما أعطتهم مرسيدس فرصة.

Each man believed he did more than his fair share of the work.

كان كل رجل يعتقد أنه قام بأكثر من نصيبه العادل من العمل.

Neither ever missed a chance to say so, again and again.

ولم يفوت أي منهما فرصة ليقول ذلك مرارا وتكرارا.

Sometimes Mercedes sided with Charles, sometimes with Hal.

في بعض الأحيان كانت مرسيدس تقف إلى جانب تشارلز، وفي بعض الأحيان تقف إلى جانب هال.

This led to a grand and endless quarrel among the three.

وأدى هذا إلى شجار كبير لا نهاية له بين الثلاثة.

A dispute over who should chop firewood grew out of control.

نشأ نزاع حول من يجب أن يقوم بتقطيع الحطب إلى حد خارج عن السيطرة.

Soon, fathers, mothers, cousins, and dead relatives were named.

وبعد قليل، تم ذكر أسماء الآباء والأمهات وأبناء العمومة والأقارب المتوفين.

Hal's views on art or his uncle's plays became part of the fight.

أصبحت آراء هال حول الفن أو مسرحيات عمه جزءًا من القتال.

Charles's political beliefs also entered the debate.

ودخلت المعتقدات السياسية لتشارلز أيضًا في المناقشة.

To Mercedes, even her husband's sister's gossip seemed relevant.

بالنسبة لمرسيدس، حتى ثرثرة أخت زوجها بدت ذات صلة.

She aired opinions on that and on many of Charles's family's flaws.

وقد أعربت عن آرائها حول هذا الموضوع وحول العديد من عيوب عائلة تشارلز.

While they argued, the fire stayed unlit and camp half set.

بينما كانوا يتجادلون، ظلت النار مطفأة والمخيم نصف مشتعل.

Meanwhile, the dogs remained cold and without any food.

وفي هذه الأثناء، ظلت الكلاب باردة وبدون أي طعام.

Mercedes held a grievance she considered deeply personal.

كان لدى مرسيدس شكوى اعتبرتها شخصية للغاية.

She felt mistreated as a woman, denied her gentle privileges.

لقد شعرت بالمعاملة السيئة كامرأة، وحُرمت من امتيازاتها اللطيفة.

She was pretty and soft, and used to chivalry all her life.

لقد كانت جميلة وناعمة، وكانت معتادة على الفروسية طوال حياتها.

But her husband and brother now treated her with impatience.

لكن زوجها وشقيقها الآن يعاملانها بفارغ الصبر.

Her habit was to act helpless, and they began to complain.

كانت عادتها أن تتصرف بعجز، فبدأوا يشكون.

Offended by this, she made their lives all the more difficult.

لقد أساءت إليهم، مما جعل حياتهم أكثر صعوبة.

She ignored the dogs and insisted on riding the sled herself.

تجاهلت الكلاب وأصرت على ركوب الزلاجة بنفسها.

Though light in looks, she weighed one hundred twenty pounds.

رغم مظهرها الخفيف، كان وزنها مائة وعشرين رطلاً.

That added burden was too much for the starving, weak dogs.

كان هذا العبء الإضافي أكثر مما تستطيع الكلاب الجائعة والضعيفة أن تتحمله.

Still, she rode for days, until the dogs collapsed in the reins.

ومع ذلك، فقد ظلت تركب لعدة أيام، حتى انهارت الكلاب في اللجام.

The sled stood still, and Charles and Hal begged her to walk.

ظلت الزلاجة واقفة في مكانها، وتوسل تشارلز وهال إليها أن تمشي.

They pleaded and entreated, but she wept and called them cruel.

لقد توسلوا إليها وتوسلوا إليها، لكنها بكت ووصفتهم بالقسوة.

On one occasion, they pulled her off the sled with sheer force and anger.

في إحدى المرات، سحبوها من الزلاجة بقوة شديدة وغضب.

They never tried again after what happened that time.

ولم يحاولوا مرة أخرى بعد ما حدث تلك المرة.

She went limp like a spoiled child and sat in the snow.

أصبحت مترهلة مثل طفل مدلل وجلست في الثلج.

They moved on, but she refused to rise or follow behind.

لقد تحركوا، لكنها رفضت أن تنهض أو تتبعهم.

After three miles, they stopped, returned, and carried her back.

وبعد ثلاثة أميال، توقفوا، وعادوا، وحملوها.

They reloaded her onto the sled, again using brute strength.

ثم أعادوا تحميلها على الزلاجة، مستخدمين القوة الغاشمة مرة أخرى.

In their deep misery, they were callous to the dogs' suffering.

في بؤسهم العميق، كانوا قساة القلب تجاه معاناة الكلاب.

Hal believed one must get hardened and forced that belief on others.

كان هال يعتقد أنه يجب على الإنسان أن يصبح أكثر صلابة ويفرض هذا الاعتقاد على الآخرين.

He first tried to preach his philosophy to his sister

حاول أولاً أن يبشر أخته بفلسفته

and then, without success, he preached to his brother-in-law.

وبعد ذلك، دون جدوى، قام بالوعظ إلى صهره.

He had more success with the dogs, but only because he hurt them.

لقد حقق نجاحا أكبر مع الكلاب، ولكن فقط لأنه كان يؤذيهم.

At Five Fingers, the dog food ran out of food completely.

في مطعم فايف فينجرز، نفد طعام الكلاب بالكامل.

A toothless old squaw sold a few pounds of frozen horse-hide

باعت امرأة عجوز بلا أسنان بضعة أرطال من جلود الخيول المجمدة

Hal traded his revolver for the dried horse-hide.

قام هال بتبديل مسدسه بجلد الحصان المجفف.

The meat had come from starved horses of cattlemen months before.

لقد جاء اللحم من خيول مربي الماشية الجائعة قبل أشهر.

Frozen, the hide was like galvanized iron; tough and inedible.

كان الجلد متجمدًا مثل الحديد المجلفن، قاسيًا وغير صالح للأكل.

The dogs had to chew endlessly at the hide to eat it.

كان على الكلاب أن تمضغ الجلد بلا نهاية حتى تأكله.

But the leathery strings and short hair were hardly nourishment.

لكن الأوتار الجلدية والشعر القصير لم يكونا غذاءً على الإطلاق.

Most of the hide was irritating, and not food in any true sense.

كانت معظم الجلود مزعجة، ولم تكن طعامًا بالمعنى الحقيقي للكلمة.

And through it all, Buck staggered at the front, like in a nightmare.

وعلى الرغم من كل ذلك، ظل باك يترنح في المقدمة، كما لو كان في كابوس.

He pulled when able; when not, he lay until whip or club raised him.

كان يسحب عندما يكون قادرًا على ذلك، وعندما لا يكون قادرًا على ذلك، كان يظل مستلقيًا حتى يرفعه السوط أو الهراوة.

His fine, glossy coat had lost all stiffness and sheen it once had.

لقد فقد معطفه الناعم اللامع كل صلابته ولمعانه الذي كان يتمتع به من قبل.

His hair hung limp, draggled, and clotted with dried blood from the blows.

كان شعره متدليًا، متطايرًا، ومتخثرًا بالدم الجاف من الضربات.

His muscles shrank to cords, and his flesh pads were all worn away.

تقلصت عضلاته إلى حبال، وتآكلت جميع وسادات لحمه.

Each rib, each bone showed clearly through folds of wrinkled skin.

كل ضلع وكل عظمة ظهرت بوضوح من خلال طيات الجلد المتجعد.

It was heartbreaking, yet Buck's heart could not break.

لقد كان الأمر مفجعًا، لكن قلب باك لم يستطع أن ينكسر.

The man in the red sweater had tested that and proved it long ago.

لقد اختبر الرجل ذو السترة الحمراء ذلك وأثبته منذ زمن طويل.

As it was with Buck, so it was with all his remaining teammates.

كما كان الحال مع باك، كذلك كان الحال مع جميع زملائه المتبقين في الفريق.

There were seven in total, each one a walking skeleton of misery.

كان هناك سبعة في المجموع، كل واحد منهم عبارة عن هيكل عظمي متحرك من البؤس.

They had grown numb to lash, feeling only distant pain.

لقد أصبحوا مخدرين للجلد، ويشعرون بألم بعيد فقط.

Even sight and sound reached them faintly, as through a thick fog.

حتى أن البصر والصوت وصلا إليهما بشكل خافت، كما لو كانا من خلال ضباب كثيف.

They were not half alive—they were bones with dim sparks inside.

لم يكونوا على قيد الحياة إلى النصف، بل كانوا عظامًا تحمل شرارات خافتة في داخلها.

When stopped, they collapsed like corpses, their sparks almost gone.

عندما توقفوا، انهاروا مثل الجثث، واختفت شراراتهم تقريبًا.

And when the whip or club struck again, the sparks fluttered weakly.

وعندما ضرب السوط أو الهراوة مرة أخرى، تطايرت الشرارات بشكل ضعيف.

Then they rose, staggered forward, and dragged their limbs ahead.

ثم نهضوا، وتقدموا متعثرين، وجرروا أطرافهم إلى الأمام.

One day kind Billee fell and could no longer rise at all.

ذات يوم سقط بيلي اللطيف ولم يعد قادرًا على النهوض على الإطلاق.

Hal had traded his revolver, so he used an axe to kill Billee instead.

لقد قام هال بتبديل مسدسه، لذلك استخدم فأسًا لقتل بيلي بدلاً من ذلك.

He struck him on the head, then cut his body free and dragged it away.

ضربه على رأسه، ثم قطع جسده وسحبه بعيدًا.

Buck saw this, and so did the others; they knew death was near.

لقد رأى باك هذا، ورأى الآخرون أيضًا؛ لقد عرفوا أن الموت كان قريبًا.

Next day Koona went, leaving just five dogs in the starving team.

في اليوم التالي ذهب كونا، ولم يترك سوى خمسة كلاب في الفريق الجائع.

Joe, no longer mean, was too far gone to be aware of much at all.

جو لم يعد سيئًا، لكنه أصبح بعيدًا جدًا عن الوعي بأي شيء على الإطلاق.

Pike, no longer faking his injury, was barely conscious.

لم يعد بايك يتظاهر بالإصابة، وكان فاقدًا للوعي تقريبًا.

Solleks, still faithful, mourned he had no strength to give.

كان سوليكس لا يزال مخلصًا، لكنه حزن لأنه لم يعد لديه القوة ليقدمها.

Teek was beaten most because he was fresher, but fading fast.

لقد تعرض تيك للضرب أكثر من غيره لأنه كان أكثر نضارة، لكنه كان يتلاشى بسرعة.

And Buck, still in the lead, no longer kept order or enforced it.

وباك، الذي لا يزال في المقدمة، لم يعد يحافظ على النظام أو ينفذه.

Half blind with weakness, Buck followed the trail by feel alone.

كان باك نصف أعمى من الضعف، فتبع المسار بمفرده.

It was beautiful spring weather, but none of them noticed it.

لقد كان الطقس ربيعيًا جميلًا، لكن لم يلاحظه أحد منهم.

Each day the sun rose earlier and set later than before.

كل يوم تشرق الشمس مبكرا وتغرب متأخرا عن ذي قبل.

By three in the morning, dawn had come; twilight lasted till nine.

بحلول الساعة الثالثة صباحًا، جاء الفجر، واستمر الشفق حتى الساعة التاسعة.

The long days were filled with the full blaze of spring sunshine.

كانت الأيام الطويلة مليئة بأشعة شمس الربيع الساطعة.

The ghostly silence of winter had changed into a warm murmur.

لقد تحول الصمت الشبحي للشتاء إلى همهمة دافئة.

All the land was waking, alive with the joy of living things.

كانت الأرض كلها تستيقظ، على قيد الحياة بفرحة الكائنات الحية.

The sound came from what had lain dead and still through winter.

لقد جاء الصوت من شيء كان ميتًا وساكنًا طوال الشتاء.

Now, those things moved again, shaking off the long frost sleep.

الآن، تحركت تلك الأشياء مرة أخرى، متخلصة من نوم الصقيع الطويل.

Sap was rising through the dark trunks of the waiting pine trees.

كان النسغ يرتفع من خلال جذوع أشجار الصنوبر المظلمة المنتظرة.

Willows and aspens burst out bright young buds on each twig.

تنبت براعم صغيرة لامعة على كل غصن من أشجار الصفصاف والحور الرجراج.

Shrubs and vines put on fresh green as the woods came alive.

أصبحت الشجيرات والكروم خضراء اللون بينما أصبحت الغابات حية.

Crickets chirped at night, and bugs crawled in daylight sun.

كانت الصراصير تزقزق في الليل، وكانت الحشرات تزحف في ضوء الشمس في النهار.

Partridges boomed, and woodpeckers knocked deep in the trees.

كانت طيور الحجل تدوي، وكان نقار الخشب يطرق الأشجار بعمق.

Squirrels chattered, birds sang, and geese honked over the dogs.

ثرثرت السناجب، وغنت الطيور، وأطلقت الأوز أصواتها فوق الكلاب.

The wild-fowl came in sharp wedges, flying up from the south.

جاءت الطيور البرية في أسافين حادة، تطير من الجنوب.

From every hillside came the music of hidden, rushing streams.

من كل سفح تل جاءت موسيقى الجداول المتدفقة المخفية.

All things thawed and snapped, bent and burst back into motion.

كل الأشياء ذابت وانكسرت وانحنت ثم عادت إلى الحركة.

The Yukon strained to break the cold chains of frozen ice.

بذلت منطقة يوكون قصارى جهدها لكسر السلاسل الباردة من الجليد المتجمد.

The ice melted underneath, while the sun melted it from above.

ذاب الجليد من تحته، بينما أذابته الشمس من الأعلى.

Air-holes opened, cracks spread, and chunks fell into the river.

فتحت ثقوب الهواء، وانتشرت الشقوق، وسقطت قطع منها في النهر.

Amid all this bursting and blazing life, the travelers staggered.

وفي وسط كل هذه الحياة الصاخبة والمشتعلة، تعثر المسافرون.

Two men, a woman, and a pack of huskies walked like the dead.

كان هناك رجلان وامرأة ومجموعة من الكلاب الهاسكي يمشون كالأموات.

The dogs were falling, Mercedes wept, but still rode the sled.

كانت الكلاب تتساقط، وبكت مرسيدس، لكنها لا تزال تركب الزلاجة.

Hal cursed weakly, and Charles blinked through watering eyes.

لعن هال بصوت ضعيف، وأغمض تشارلز عينيه الدامعتين.

They stumbled into John Thornton's camp by White River's mouth.

لقد تعثروا في معسكر جون ثورنتون عند مصب نهر وايت.

When they stopped, the dogs dropped flat, as if all struck dead.

عندما توقفوا، سقطت الكلاب على الأرض، كما لو أنهم جميعًا ماتوا.

Mercedes wiped her tears and looked across at John Thornton.

مسحت مرسيدس دموعها ونظرت إلى جون ثورنتون.

Charles sat on a log, slowly and stiffly, aching from the trail.

جلس تشارلز على جذع شجرة، ببطء وبصعوبة، وهو يتألم من الطريق.

Hal did the talking as Thornton carved the end of an axe-handle.

كان هال يتحدث بينما كان ثورنتون يقطع نهاية مقبض الفأس.

He whittled birch wood and answered with brief, firm replies.

قام بنحت خشب البتولا وأجاب بإجابات موجزة وحازمة.

When asked, he gave advice, certain it wasn't going to be followed.

عندما سئل، أعطى النصيحة، متأكدًا من أنها لن يتم اتباعها.

Hal explained, "They told us the trail ice was dropping out."

وأوضح هال قائلاً: "لقد أخبرونا أن الجليد على الطريق كان يتساقط".

"They said we should stay put—but we made it to White River."

"قالوا لنا أنه يجب علينا البقاء في مكاننا ـ لكننا وصلنا إلى وايت ريفر."

He ended with a sneering tone, as if to claim victory in hardship.

وانتهى كلامه بنبرة ساخرة، وكأنه يريد أن يدعي النصر في محنة.

"And they told you true," John Thornton answered Hal quietly.

"وقالوا لك الحقيقة"، أجاب جون ثورنتون هال بهدوء.

"The ice may give way at any moment—it's ready to drop out."

"قد ينهار الجليد في أي لحظة، فهو جاهز للسقوط."

"Only blind luck and fools could have made it this far alive."

"فقط الحظ الأعمى والحمقى كان بإمكانهم الوصول إلى هذه المرحلة على قيد الحياة."

"I tell you straight, I wouldn't risk my life for all Alaska's gold."

"سأقول لك بصراحة، أنا لن أخاطر بحياتي من أجل كل ذهب ألاسكا."

"That's because you're not a fool, I suppose," Hal answered.

"هذا لأنك لست أحمقًا، على ما أعتقد،" أجاب هال.

"All the same, we'll go on to Dawson." He uncoiled his whip.

"على أية حال، سنذهب إلى داوسون." فك سوطه.

"Get up there, Buck! Hi! Get up! Go on!" he shouted harshly.

"اصعد يا باك! أهلاً! انهض! هيا!" صرخ بعنف.

Thornton kept whittling, knowing fools won't hear reason.

واصل ثورنتون النحت، لأنه كان يعلم أن الحمقى لن يستمعوا إلى المنطق.

To stop a fool was futile—and two or three fooled changed nothing.

إن إيقاف الأحمق كان أمراً غير مجدٍ، وخداع اثنين أو ثلاثة لن يغير شيئاً.

But the team didn't move at the sound of Hal's command.

لكن الفريق لم يتحرك عند سماع أمر هال.

By now, only blows could make them rise and pull forward.

بحلول هذا الوقت، لم يعد هناك ما يمكن أن يجعلهم ينهضون ويتقدمون إلى الأمام سوى الضربات.

The whip snapped again and again across the weakened dogs.

انطلقت السوط مرارا وتكرارا عبر الكلاب الضعيفة.

John Thornton pressed his lips tightly and watched in silence.

ضغط جون ثورنتون على شفتيه بقوة وراقب في صمت.

Solleks was the first to crawl to his feet under the lash.

كان سوليكس هو أول من زحف إلى قدميه تحت السوط.

Then Teek followed, trembling. Joe yelped as he stumbled up.

ثم تبعه تيك وهو يرتجف. صرخ جو وهو يتعثر.

Pike tried to rise, failed twice, then finally stood unsteadily.

حاول بايك النهوض، لكنه فشل مرتين، ثم وقف أخيرا غير ثابت.

But Buck lay where he had fallen, not moving at all this time.

لكن باك ظل مستلقيا حيث سقط، ولم يتحرك على الإطلاق هذه المرة.

The whip slashed him over and over, but he made no sound.

لقد ضربه السوط مرارا وتكرارا، لكنه لم يصدر أي صوت.

He did not flinch or resist, simply remained still and quiet.

لم يتراجع أو يقاوم، بل ظل ساكنًا وهادئًا.

Thornton stirred more than once, as if to speak, but didn't.

تحرك ثورنتون أكثر من مرة، وكأنه يريد أن يتكلم، لكنه لم يفعل.

His eyes grew wet, and still the whip cracked against Buck.

أصبحت عيناه مبللة، وما زالت السوط تتكسر في وجه باك.

At last, Thornton began pacing slowly, unsure of what to do.

وأخيرا، بدأ ثورنتون في المشي ببطء، غير متأكد مما يجب فعله.

It was the first time Buck had failed, and Hal grew furious.

لقد كانت هذه هي المرة الأولى التي يفشل فيها باك، مما أثار غضب هال.

He threw down the whip and picked up the heavy club instead.

ألقى بالسوط والتقط الهراوة الثقيلة بدلاً من ذلك.

The wooden club came down hard, but Buck still did not rise to move.

سقطت العصا الخشبية بقوة، لكن باك لم يتمكن من النهوض للتحرك.

Like his teammates, he was too weak—but more than that.

مثل زملائه في الفريق، كان ضعيفًا جدًا - ولكن أكثر من ذلك.

Buck had decided not to move, no matter what came next.

قرر باك عدم التحرك، بغض النظر عما سيأتي بعد ذلك.

He felt something dark and certain hovering just ahead.

لقد شعر بشيء مظلم ومؤكد يحوم في الأفق.

That dread had seized him as soon as he reached the riverbank.

لقد استولى عليه هذا الرعب بمجرد وصوله إلى ضفة النهر.

The feeling had not left him since he felt the ice thin under his paws.

لم يتركه هذا الشعور منذ أن شعر بالجليد الرقيق تحت كفوفه.

Something terrible was waiting—he felt it just down the trail.

لقد كان هناك شيء فظيع في انتظاره ـ شعر به في نهاية الطريق.

He wasn't going to walk towards that terrible thing ahead

لم يكن ينوي السير نحو ذلك الشيء الرهيب الذي أمامه

He was not going to obey any command that took him to that thing.

لم يكن ليطيع أي أمر يأخذه إلى هذا الشيء.

The pain of the blows hardly touched him now—he was too far gone.

لم يعد ألم الضربات يؤثر عليه الآن ـ لقد كان بعيدًا جدًا.

The spark of life flickered low, dimmed beneath each cruel strike.

كانت شرارة الحياة تتلألأ، وتتلاشى تحت كل ضربة قاسية.

His limbs felt distant; his whole body seemed to belong to another.

كان يشعر وكأن أطرافه بعيدة، لكن جسده كله بدا وكأنه ينتمي إلى شخص آخر.

He felt a strange numbness as the pain faded out completely.

لقد شعر بخدر غريب حيث اختفى الألم تمامًا.

From far away, he sensed he was being beaten, but barely knew.

من بعيد، شعر أنه يتعرض للضرب، لكنه لم يكن يعلم.

He could hear the thuds faintly, but they no longer truly hurt.

كان بإمكانه سماع الضربات الخفيفة، لكنها لم تعد تؤلمه حقًا.

The blows landed, but his body no longer seemed like his own.

لقد هبطت الضربات عليه، لكن جسده لم يعد يبدو وكأنه ملكه.

Then suddenly, without warning, John Thornton gave a wild cry.

ثم فجأة، وبدون سابق إنذار، أطلق جون ثورنتون صرخة جنونية.

It was inarticulate, more the cry of a beast than of a man.

لقد كان صراخًا غير قابل للتعبير، أشبه بصراخ وحش أكثر من صراخ إنسان.

He leapt at the man with the club and knocked Hal backward.

قفز على الرجل الذي يحمل النادي وضرب هال على ظهره.

Hal flew as if struck by a tree, landing hard upon the ground.

طار هال كما لو أنه أصيب بشجرة، فهبط بقوة على الأرض.

Mercedes screamed aloud in panic and clutched at her face.

صرخت مرسيدس بصوت عالي في حالة من الذعر وأمسكت بوجهها.

Charles only looked on, wiped his eyes, and stayed seated.

كان تشارلز ينظر فقط، ويمسح عينيه، ويبقى جالسًا.

His body was too stiff with pain to rise or help in the fight.

كان جسده متيبسًا للغاية بسبب الألم ولم يتمكن من النهوض أو المساعدة في القتال.

Thornton stood over Buck, trembling with fury, unable to speak.

وقف ثورنتون فوق باك، يرتجف من الغضب، غير قادر على الكلام.

He shook with rage and fought to find his voice through it.

لقد ارتجف من الغضب وحارب ليجد صوته من خلاله.

"If you strike that dog again, I'll kill you," he finally said.

"إذا ضربت هذا الكلب مرة أخرى، سأقتلك"، قال أخيرًا.

Hal wiped blood from his mouth and came forward again.

مسح هال الدم من فمه وتقدم إلى الأمام مرة أخرى.

"It's my dog," he muttered. "Get out of the way, or I'll fix you."

"إنه كلبي،" تمتم. "ابتعد عن الطريق، وإلا سأصلحك."

"I'm going to Dawson, and you're not stopping me," he added.

"سأذهب إلى داوسون، ولن تمنعني"، أضاف.

Thornton stood firm between Buck and the angry young man.

وقف ثورنتون بثبات بين باك والشاب الغاضب.

He had no intention of stepping aside or letting Hal pass.

لم يكن لديه أي نية للتنحي جانباً أو السماح لهال بالمرور.

Hal pulled out his hunting knife, long and dangerous in hand.

أخرج هال سكين الصيد الخاص به، الطويل والخطير في يده.

Mercedes screamed, then cried, then laughed in wild hysteria.

صرخت مرسيدس، ثم بكت، ثم ضحكت في هستيريا جامحة.

Thornton struck Hal's hand with his axe-handle, hard and fast.

ضرب ثورنتون يد هال بمقبض الفأس، بقوة وبسرعة.

The knife was knocked loose from Hal's grip and flew to the ground.

لقد تم انتزاع السكين من قبضة هال وطار إلى الأرض.

Hal tried to pick the knife up, and Thornton rapped his knuckles again.

حاول هال التقاط السكين، وضربه ثورنتون على مفاصله مرة أخرى.

Then Thornton stooped down, grabbed the knife, and held it.

ثم انحنى ثورنتون، وأمسك بالسكين، وأبقى عليه.

With two quick chops of the axe-handle, he cut Buck's reins.

وبضربتين سريعتين بمقبض الفأس، قطع زمام باك.

Hal had no fight left in him and stepped back from the dog.

لم يعد لدى هال أي قدرة على القتال وتراجع عن الكلب.

Besides, Mercedes needed both arms now to keep her upright.

وبالإضافة إلى ذلك، أصبحت مرسيدس بحاجة إلى ذراعيها الآن لتتمكن من البقاء منتصبة.

Buck was too near death to be of use for pulling a sled again.

كان باك قريبًا جدًا من الموت لدرجة أنه لم يعد قادرًا على سحب الزلاجة مرة أخرى.

A few minutes later, they pulled out, heading down the river.

وبعد دقائق قليلة، انسحبوا، متجهين إلى أسفل النهر.

Buck raised his head weakly and watched them leave the bank.

رفع باك رأسه ضعيفًا وشاهدهم يغادرون البنك.

Pike led the team, with Solleks at the rear in the wheel spot.

كان بايك على رأس الفريق، بينما كان سوليكس في الخلف في مركز القيادة.

Joe and Teek walked between, both limping with exhaustion.

كان جو وتيك يمشيان بينهما، وكلاهما يعرج من الإرهاق.

Mercedes sat on the sled, and Hal gripped the long gee-pole.

جلست مرسيدس على الزلاجة، وأمسك هال بالعمود الطويل.

Charles stumbled behind, his steps clumsy and uncertain.

تعثر تشارلز في الخلف، وكانت خطواته خرقاء وغير مؤكدة.

Thornton knelt by Buck and gently felt for broken bones.

ركع ثورنتون بجانب باك وشعر بلطف بالعظام المكسورة.

His hands were rough but moved with kindness and care.

كانت يداه خشنة ولكنها كانت تتحرك بلطف وعناية.

Buck's body was bruised but showed no lasting injury.

كان جسد باك مصابًا بكدمات ولكن لم تظهر عليه أي إصابة دائمة.

What remained was terrible hunger and near-total weakness.

كل ما تبقى كان الجوع الشديد والضعف شبه الكامل.

By the time this was clear, the sled had gone far downriver.

بحلول الوقت الذي أصبح فيه الأمر واضحًا، كانت الزلاجة قد ذهبت بعيدًا في مجرى النهر.

Man and dog watched the sled slowly crawl over the cracking ice.

كان الرجل والكلب يراقبان الزلاجة وهي تزحف ببطء فوق الجليد المتصدع.

Then, they saw the sled sink down into a hollow.

ثم رأوا الزلاجة تغرق في حفرة.

The gee-pole flew up, with Hal still clinging to it in vain.

طار العمود الجي إلى الأعلى، وكان هال لا يزال متشبثًا به دون جدوى.

Mercedes's scream reached them across the cold distance.

وصل صراخ مرسيدس إليهم عبر المسافة الباردة.

Charles turned and stepped back—but he was too late.

استدار تشارلز وتراجع إلى الوراء ـ لكنه كان متأخرًا جدًا.

A whole ice sheet gave way, and they all dropped through.

انهارت طبقة جليدية بأكملها، وسقطوا جميعًا من خلالها.

Dogs, sled, and people vanished into the black water below.

اختفت الكلاب والزلاجات والأشخاص في المياه السوداء أدناه.

Only a wide hole in the ice was left where they had passed.

لم يبق سوى حفرة واسعة في الجليد حيث مروا.

The trail's bottom had dropped out—just as Thornton warned.

لقد انخفض قاع الطريق ـ تمامًا كما حذر ثورنتون.

Thornton and Buck looked at one another, silent for a moment.

نظر ثورنتون وبوك إلى بعضهما البعض، وظلا صامتين لبعض الوقت.

"You poor devil," said Thornton softly, and Buck licked his hand.

"أيها الشيطان المسكين"، قال ثورنتون بهدوء، ولعق باك يده.

For the Love of a Man
من أجل حب الرجل

John Thornton froze his feet in the cold of the previous December.

تجمد جون ثورنتون قدميه في البرد في شهر ديسمبر الماضي.

His partners made him comfortable and left him to recover alone.

لقد جعله شركاؤه مرتاحًا وتركوه يتعافى بمفرده.

They went up the river to gather a raft of saw-logs for Dawson.

لقد صعدوا إلى النهر لجمع مجموعة من جذوع الأشجار لداووسن.

He was still limping slightly when he rescued Buck from death.

كان لا يزال يعرج قليلاً عندما أنقذ باك من الموت.

But with warm weather continuing, even that limp disappeared.

ولكن مع استمرار الطقس الدافئ، اختفى هذا العرج أيضًا.

Lying by the riverbank during long spring days, Buck rested.

أثناء أيام الربيع الطويلة، كان باك يستريح على ضفة النهر.

He watched the flowing water and listened to birds and insects.

كان يراقب المياه المتدفقة ويستمع إلى الطيور والحشرات.

Slowly, Buck regained his strength under the sun and sky.

ببطء، استعاد باك قوته تحت الشمس والسماء.

A rest felt wonderful after traveling three thousand miles.

كان الحصول على قسط من الراحة أمرًا رائعًا بعد السفر لمسافة ثلاثة آلاف ميل.

Buck became lazy as his wounds healed and his body filled out.

أصبح باك كسولًا حيث شُفِيت جروحه وامتلئ جسده.

His muscles grew firm, and flesh returned to cover his bones.

أصبحت عضلاته مشدودة، وعاد اللحم ليغطي عظامه.

They were all resting—Buck, Thornton, Skeet, and Nig.

وكانوا جميعًا يستريحون - باك، ثورنتون، سكيت، ونيج.

They waited for the raft that was going to carry them down to Dawson.

لقد انتظروا الطوافة التي ستحملهم إلى داوسون.

Skeet was a small Irish setter who made friends with Buck.

كان سكيت كلبًا أيرلنديًا صغيرًا أصبح صديقًا لبوك.

Buck was too weak and ill to resist her at their first meeting.

كان باك ضعيفًا ومريضًا للغاية بحيث لم يتمكن من مقاومتها في لقائهما الأول.

Skeet had the healer trait that some dogs naturally possess.

كان لدى سكيت سمة الشفاء التي يمتلكها بعض الكلاب بشكل طبيعي.

Like a mother cat, she licked and cleaned Buck's raw wounds.

مثل قطة الأم، قامت بلعق وتنظيف جروح باك الخام.

Every morning after breakfast, she repeated her careful work.

كل صباح بعد الإفطار، كانت تكرر عملها الدقيق.

Buck came to expect her help as much as he did Thornton's.

لقد أصبح باك يتوقع مساعدتها بقدر ما كان يتوقع مساعدة ثورنتون.

Nig was friendly too, but less open and less affectionate.

كان نيج ودودًا أيضًا، لكنه كان أقل انفتاحًا وأقل عاطفية.

Nig was a big black dog, part bloodhound and part deerhound.

كان نيج كلبًا أسودًا كبيرًا، نصفه كلب صيد ونصفه كلب صيد الغزلان.

He had laughing eyes and endless good nature in his spirit.

كان لديه عيون ضاحكة وطبيعة طيبة لا نهاية لها في روحه.

To Buck's surprise, neither dog showed jealousy toward him.

لدهشة باك، لم يظهر أي من الكلبين الغيرة تجاهه.

Both Skeet and Nig shared the kindness of John Thornton.

لقد تقاسم كل من سكيت ونيج لطف جون ثورنتون.

As Buck got stronger, they lured him into foolish dog games.

عندما أصبح باك أقوى، قاموا بإغرائه بألعاب الكلاب الحمقاء.

Thornton often played with them too, unable to resist their joy.

وكان ثورنتون يلعب معهم في كثير من الأحيان أيضًا، غير قادر على مقاومة فرحتهم.

In this playful way, Buck moved from illness to a new life.

بهذه الطريقة المرحة، انتقل باك من المرض إلى حياة جديدة.

Love—true, burning, and passionate love—was his at last.

الحب ـ الحب الحقيقي، المشتعل، والعاطفي ـ أصبح ملكه في النهاية.

He had never known this kind of love at Miller's estate.

لم يكن قد عرف هذا النوع من الحب في منزل ميلر من قبل.

With the Judge's sons, he had shared work and adventure.

وكان يتقاسم العمل والمغامرة مع أبناء القاضي.

With the grandsons, he saw stiff and boastful pride.

مع الأحفاد رأى الكبرياء المتصلب والمتبجح.

With Judge Miller himself, he had a respectful friendship.

وكانت تربطه بالقاضي ميلر صداقة محترمة.

But love that was fire, madness, and worship came with Thornton.

لكن الحب الذي كان نارًا وجنونًا وعبادة جاء مع ثورنتون.

This man had saved Buck's life, and that alone meant a great deal.

لقد أنقذ هذا الرجل حياة باك، وهذا وحده كان يعني الكثير.

But more than that, John Thornton was the ideal kind of master.

ولكن أكثر من ذلك، كان جون ثورنتون هو النوع المثالي من المعلمين.

Other men cared for dogs out of duty or business necessity.

كان الرجال الآخرون يهتمون بالكلاب من باب الواجب أو ضرورة العمل.

John Thornton cared for his dogs as if they were his children.

كان جون ثورنتون يهتم بكلابه كما لو كانوا أبنائه.

He cared for them because he loved them and simply could not help it.

لقد اهتم بهم لأنه أحبهم ولم يكن يستطيع مساعدة أنفسهم.

John Thornton saw even further than most men ever managed to see.

لقد رأى جون ثورنتون أبعد مما تمكن معظم الرجال من رؤيته.

He never forgot to greet them kindly or speak a cheering word.

لم ينسَ أبدًا أن يحييهم بلطف أو يتحدث إليهم بكلمة تشجيع.

He loved sitting down with the dogs for long talks, or "gassy," as he said.

كان يحب الجلوس مع الكلاب لإجراء محادثات طويلة، أو "الغازات"، كما قال.

He liked to seize Buck's head roughly between his strong hands.

كان يحب أن يمسك رأس باك بقوة بين يديه القويتين.

Then he rested his own head against Buck's and shook him gently.

ثم أراح رأسه على رأس باك وهزه بلطف.

All the while, he called Buck rude names that meant love to Buck.

في هذه الأثناء، كان يطلق على باك أسماءً فظة كانت تعني الحب بالنسبة له.

To Buck, that rough embrace and those words brought deep joy.

بالنسبة لباك، تلك العناق الخشن وتلك الكلمات جلبت له فرحة عميقة.

His heart seemed to shake loose with happiness at each movement.

بدا قلبه وكأنه يرتجف من السعادة عند كل حركة.

When he sprang up afterward, his mouth looked like it laughed.

وعندما قفز بعد ذلك، بدا فمه وكأنه يضحك.

His eyes shone brightly and his throat trembled with unspoken joy.

أشرقت عيناه ببراعة وارتجف حلقه بفرح غير منطوق.

His smile stood still in that state of emotion and glowing affection.

ظلت ابتسامته ثابتة في تلك الحالة من العاطفة والمودة المتوهجة.

Then Thornton exclaimed thoughtfully, "God! he can almost speak!"

ثم صاح ثورنتون متأملاً: "يا إلهي! إنه يستطيع التحدث تقريبًا!"

Buck had a strange way of expressing love that nearly caused pain.

كان لدى باك طريقة غريبة للتعبير عن الحب والتي كادت أن تسبب الألم.

He often griped Thornton's hand in his teeth very tightly.

كان يمسك بيد ثورنتون بين أسنانه بقوة في كثير من الأحيان.

The bite was going to leave deep marks that stayed for some time after.

كانت العضة ستترك علامات عميقة ستبقى لبعض الوقت بعد ذلك.

Buck believed those oaths were love, and Thornton knew the same.

كان باك يعتقد أن هذه القسمات هي الحب، وكان ثورنتون يعرف الشيء نفسه.

Most often, Buck's love showed in quiet, almost silent adoration.

في أغلب الأحيان، كان حب باك يظهر في عبادة هادئة وصامتة تقريبًا.

Though thrilled when touched or spoken to, he did not seek attention.

على الرغم من أنه كان يشعر بسعادة غامرة عندما يلمسه أحد أو يتحدث إليه، إلا أنه لم يسعى إلى جذب الانتباه.

Skeet nudged her nose under Thornton's hand until he petted her.

دفعت سكيت أنفها تحت يد ثورنتون حتى قام بمداعبتها.

Nig walked up quietly and rested his large head on Thornton's knee.

صعد نيج بهدوء وأراح رأسه الكبير على ركبة ثورنتون.

Buck, in contrast, was satisfied to love from a respectful distance.

على النقيض من ذلك، كان باك راضيًا بالحب من مسافة محترمة.

He lied for hours at Thornton's feet, alert and watching closely.

لقد ظل مستلقيا لساعات عند قدمي ثورنتون، متيقظا ويراقب عن كثب.

Buck studied every detail of his master's face and slightest motion.

درس باك كل تفاصيل وجه سيده وأدنى حركة.

Or lied farther away, studying the man's shape in silence.

أو كذب في مكان أبعد، يدرس شكل الرجل في صمت.

Buck watched each small move, each shift in posture or gesture.

كان باك يراقب كل حركة صغيرة، وكل تحول في الوضعية أو الإيماءة.

So powerful was this connection that often pulled Thornton's gaze.

لقد كانت هذه الصلة قوية جدًا لدرجة أنها جذبت انتباه ثورنتون في كثير من الأحيان.

He met Buck's eyes with no words, love shining clearly through.

التقت عيون باك دون أي كلمات، وكان الحب يتألق بوضوح من خلال عيونه.

For a long while after being saved, Buck never let Thornton out of sight.

لمدة طويلة بعد أن تم إنقاذه، لم يترك باك ثورنتون خارج نطاق رؤيته أبدًا.

Whenever Thornton left the tent, Buck followed him closely outside.

كلما غادر ثورنتون الخيمة، كان باك يتبعه عن كثب إلى الخارج.

All the harsh masters in the Northland had made Buck afraid to trust.

لقد جعل كل الأسياد القساة في نورثلاند باك خائفًا من الثقة.

He feared no man could remain his master for more than a short time.

كان يخشى ألا يتمكن أي رجل من البقاء سيدًا لنفسه لأكثر من فترة قصيرة.

He feared John Thornton was going to vanish like Perrault and François.

كان يخشى أن يختفي جون ثورنتون مثل بيرولت وفرانسوا.

Even at night, the fear of losing him haunted Buck's restless sleep.

حتى في الليل، كان الخوف من فقدانه يطارد نوم باك المضطرب.

When Buck woke, he crept out into the cold, and went to the tent.

عندما استيقظ باك، تسلل إلى البرد، وذهب إلى الخيمة.

He listened carefully for the soft sound of breathing inside.

كان يستمع بعناية إلى صوت التنفس الناعم في الداخل.

Despite Buck's deep love for John Thornton, the wild stayed alive.

على الرغم من حب باك العميق لجون ثورنتون، إلا أن البرية ظلت على قيد الحياة.

That primitive instinct, awakened in the North, did not disappear.

إن تلك الغريزة البدائية التي استيقظت في الشمال لم تختفِ.

Love brought devotion, loyalty, and the fire-side's warm bond.

جلب الحب الإخلاص والولاء والرابطة الدافئة بجانب النار.

But Buck also kept his wild instincts, sharp and ever alert.

لكن باك احتفظ أيضًا بغرائزه البرية، حادة ومتيقظة دائمًا.

He was not just a tamed pet from the soft lands of civilization.

لم يكن مجرد حيوان أليف مروض من الأراضي الناعمة للحضارة.

Buck was a wild being who had come in to sit by Thornton's fire.

كان باك كائنًا بريًا جاء ليجلس بجوار نار ثورنتون.

He looked like a Southland dog, but wildness lived within him.

لقد كان يبدو مثل كلب من ساوثلاند، لكن البرية كانت تعيش بداخله.

His love for Thornton was too great to allow theft from the man.

كان حبه لثورنتون كبيرًا جدًا لدرجة أنه لم يسمح له بالسرقة من الرجل.

But in any other camp, he would steal boldly and without pause.

لكن في أي معسكر آخر، كان يسرق بجرأة ودون توقف.

He was so clever in stealing that no one could catch or accuse him.

لقد كان ذكيًا جدًا في السرقة لدرجة أنه لم يتمكن أحد من القبض عليه أو اتهامه.

His face and body were covered in scars from many past fights.

كان وجهه وجسده مغطيين بالندوب من العديد من المعارك الماضية.

Buck still fought fiercely, but now he fought with more cunning.

لا يزال باك يقاتل بشراسة، لكنه الآن يقاتل بمكر أكثر.

Skeet and Nig were too gentle to fight, and they were Thornton's.

كان سكيت ونيج لطيفين للغاية بحيث لا يستطيعان القتال، وكانا تابعين لثورنتون.

But any strange dog, no matter how strong or brave, gave way.

لكن أي كلب غريب، مهما كان قوياً أو شجاعاً، استسلم.

Otherwise, the dog found itself battling Buck; fighting for its life.

وإلا، وجد الكلب نفسه يقاتل باك؛ يقاتل من أجل حياته.

Buck had no mercy once he chose to fight against another dog.

لم يكن لدى باك أي رحمة عندما اختار القتال ضد كلب آخر.

He had learned well the law of club and fang in the Northland.

لقد تعلم جيدًا قانون النادي والأنياب في نورثلاند.

He never gave up an advantage and never backed away from battle.

لم يتنازل أبدًا عن أي ميزة ولم يتراجع أبدًا عن المعركة.

He had studied Spitz and the fiercest dogs of mail and police.

لقد درس سبيتز وأشرس كلاب البريد والشرطة.

He knew clearly there was no middle ground in wild combat.

لقد كان يعلم بوضوح أنه لا يوجد منطقة وسطى في القتال البري.

He must rule or be ruled; showing mercy meant showing weakness.

يجب عليه أن يحكم أو يُحكم؛ إظهار الرحمة يعني إظهار الضعف.

Mercy was unknown in the raw and brutal world of survival.

لم تكن الرحمة معروفة في عالم البقاء القاسي والوحشي.

To show mercy was seen as fear, and fear led quickly to death.

كان يُنظر إلى إظهار الرحمة على أنه خوف، والخوف يؤدي سريعًا إلى الموت.

The old law was simple: kill or be killed, eat or be eaten.

كان القانون القديم بسيطًا: اقتل أو تُقتل، كل أو تؤكل.

That law came from the depths of time, and Buck followed it fully.

لقد جاء هذا القانون من أعماق الزمن، وقد اتبعه باك بشكل كامل.

Buck was older than his years and the number of breaths he took.

كان باك أكبر من عمره وعدد الأنفاس التي أخذها.

He connected the ancient past with the present moment clearly.

لقد ربط الماضي القديم باللحظة الحالية بشكل واضح.

The deep rhythms of the ages moved through him like the tides.

تحركت فيه إيقاعات العصور العميقة مثل المد والجزر.

Time pulsed in his blood as surely as seasons moved the earth.

كان الزمن ينبض في دمه مثلما تتحرك الفصول في الأرض.

He sat by Thornton's fire, strong-chested and white-fanged.

كان يجلس بجانب نار ثورنتون، قوي الصدر وأنيابه بيضاء.

His long fur waved, but behind him the spirits of wild dogs watched.

كان فراءه الطويل يلوح، ولكن خلفه كانت أرواح الكلاب البرية تراقب.

Half-wolves and full wolves stirred within his heart and senses.

تحركت الذئاب النصفية والذئاب الكاملة في قلبه وحواسه.

They tasted his meat and drank the same water that he did.

فتذوقوا لحمه وشربوا نفس الماء الذي شربه.

They sniffed the wind alongside him and listened to the forest.

كانوا يشتمون الريح بجانبه ويستمعون إلى الغابة.

They whispered the meanings of the wild sounds in the darkness.

لقد همسوا بمعاني الأصوات البرية في الظلام.

They shaped his moods and guided each of his quiet reactions.

لقد شكلوا مزاجه وأرشدوا كل ردود أفعاله الهادئة.

They lay with him as he slept and became part of his deep dreams.

لقد ظلوا معه أثناء نومه وأصبحوا جزءًا من أحلامه العميقة.

They dreamed with him, beyond him, and made up his very spirit.

لقد حلموا معه، وأبعد منه، وصنعوا روحه.

The spirits of the wild called so strongly that Buck felt pulled.

لقد نادت أرواح البرية بقوة لدرجة أن باك شعر بالانجذاب.

Each day, mankind and its claims grew weaker in Buck's heart.

يوما بعد يوم، أصبحت البشرية ومطالبها أضعف في قلب باك.

Deep in the forest, a strange and thrilling call was going to rise.

في أعماق الغابة، كان من المقرر أن يرتفع نداء غريب ومثير.

Every time he heard the call, Buck felt an urge he could not resist.

في كل مرة سمع فيها النداء، شعر باك برغبة لا يستطيع مقاومتها.

He was going to turn from the fire and from the beaten human paths.

وكان ينوي أن يبتعد عن النار وعن الطرق البشرية المهترئة.

He was going to plunge into the forest, going forward without knowing why.

كان ينوي أن يقفز إلى الغابة، ويمضي قدمًا دون أن يعرف السبب.

He did not question this pull, for the call was deep and powerful.

ولم يشكك في هذا الجذب، لأن الدعوة كانت عميقة وقوية.

Often, he reached the green shade and soft untouched earth

في كثير من الأحيان، وصل إلى الظل الأخضر والأرض الناعمة غير الملموسة

But then the strong love for John Thornton pulled him back to the fire.

ولكن بعد ذلك، أعاده حبه القوي لجون ثورنتون إلى النار.

Only John Thornton truly held Buck's wild heart in his grasp.

كان جون ثورنتون هو الوحيد الذي امتلك قلب باك الجامح حقًّا.

The rest of mankind had no lasting value or meaning to Buck.

لم يكن لبقية البشرية أي قيمة أو معنى دائم بالنسبة لباك.

Strangers might praise him or stroke his fur with friendly hands.

قد يمدحه الغرباء أو يداعبون فروه بأيديهم الودودة.

Buck remained unmoved and walked off from too much affection.

ظل باك ثابتًا ومشى بعيدًا بسبب كثرة المودة.

Hans and Pete arrived with the raft that had long been awaited

وصل هانز وبيت مع الطوافة التي طال انتظارها

Buck ignored them until he learned they were close to Thornton.

تجاهلهم باك حتى علم أنهم قريبون من ثورنتون.

After that, he tolerated them, but never showed them full warmth.

وبعد ذلك، تحملهم، لكنه لم يظهر لهم الدفء الكامل أبدًا.

He took food or kindness from them as if doing them a favor.

كان يأخذ منهم الطعام أو المعروف كأنه يقدم لهم معروفًا.

They were like Thornton—simple, honest, and clear in thought.

لقد كانوا مثل ثورنتون - بسيطين، صادقين، وواضحين في أفكارهم.

All together they traveled to Dawson's saw-mill and the great eddy

سافروا جميعًا معًا إلى منشرة داوسون والدوامة العظيمة

On their journey the learned to understand Buck's nature deeply.

خلال رحلتهم، تعلموا فهم طبيعة باك بشكل عميق.

They did not try to grow close like Skeet and Nig had done.

لم يحاولوا أن يصبحوا قريبين من بعضهم مثلما فعل سكيت ونيج.

But Buck's love for John Thornton only deepened over time.

لكن حب باك لجون ثورنتون تعمق مع مرور الوقت.

Only Thornton could place a pack on Buck's back in the summer.

كان ثورنتون وحده القادر على حمل حقيبة على ظهر باك في الصيف.

Whatever Thornton commanded, Buck was willing to do fully.

مهما كان ما أمر به ثورنتون، كان باك على استعداد للقيام به بالكامل.

One day, after they left Dawson for the headwaters of the Tanana,

ذات يوم، بعد أن غادروا داوسون إلى منابع نهر تانانا،

the group sat on a cliff that dropped three feet to bare bedrock.

جلست المجموعة على جرف ينخفض ثلاثة أقدام إلى الصخر الأساسي العاري.

John Thornton sat near the edge, and Buck rested beside him.

جلس جون ثورنتون بالقرب من الحافة، واستراح باك بجانبه.

Thornton had a sudden thought and called the men's attention.

خطرت في ذهن ثورنتون فكرة مفاجئة، فلفت انتباه الرجال.

He pointed across the chasm and gave Buck a single command.

وأشار عبر الهاوية وأعطى باك أمرًا واحدًا.

"Jump, Buck!" he said, swinging his arm out over the drop.

"اقفز يا باك!" قال وهو يلوح بذراعه فوق السقوط.

In a moment, he had to grab Buck, who was leaping to obey.

في لحظة، كان عليه أن يمسك باك، الذي كان يقفز ليطيعه.

Hans and Pete rushed forward and pulled both back to safety.

اندفع هانز وبيت إلى الأمام وسحباهما إلى مكان آمن.

After all ended, and they had caught their breath, Pete spoke up.

وبعد أن انتهى كل شيء، وبعد أن التقطوا أنفاسهم، تحدث بيت.

"The love's uncanny," he said, shaken by the dog's fierce devotion.

"الحب غريب"، قال وهو يرتجف من إخلاص الكلب الشديد.

Thornton shook his head and replied with calm seriousness.

هز ثورنتون رأسه وأجاب بهدوء وجدية.

"No, the love is splendid," he said, "but also terrible."

"لا، الحب رائع"، قال، "ولكنه فظيع أيضًا".

"Sometimes, I must admit, this kind of love makes me afraid."

"في بعض الأحيان، يجب أن أعترف، هذا النوع من الحب يجعلني خائفًا."

Pete nodded and said, "I'd hate to be the man who touches you."

أومأ بيت برأسه وقال، "لا أرغب في أن أكون الرجل الذي يلمسك".

He looked at Buck as he spoke, serious and full of respect.

نظر إلى باك وهو يتحدث، وكان جادًا ومليئًا بالاحترام.

"Py Jingo!" said Hans quickly. "Me either, no sir."

قال هانز بسرعة: "باي جينجو!". "وأنا أيضًا، لا يا سيدي."

Before the year ended, Pete's fears came true at Circle City.

قبل نهاية العام، تحققت مخاوف بيت في سيركل سيتي.

A cruel man named Black Burton picked a fight in the bar.

رجل قاسي يدعى بلاك بيرتون بدأ قتالاً في الحانة.

He was angry and malicious, lashing out at a new tenderfoot.

لقد كان غاضبًا وخبيثًا، يهاجم المبتدئين الجدد.

John Thornton stepped in, calm and good-natured as always.

تدخل جون ثورنتون بهدوء وحسن الطباع كما هو الحال دائمًا.

Buck lay in a corner, head down, watching Thornton closely.

كان باك مستلقيا في الزاوية، رأسه لأسفل، يراقب ثورنتون عن كثب.

Burton suddenly struck, his punch sending Thornton spinning.

وجه بيرتون ضربة مفاجئة، حيث أدت لكمته إلى دوران ثورنتون.

Only the bar's rail kept him from crashing hard to the ground.

فقط درابزين الشريط هو الذي منعه من الاصطدام بقوة بالأرض.

The watchers heard a sound that was not bark or yelp

سمع المراقبون صوتًا لم يكن نباحًا أو عواءً

a deep roar came from Buck as he launched toward the man.

خرج هدير عميق من باك عندما انطلق نحو الرجل.

Burton threw his arm up and barely saved his own life.

رفع بيرتون ذراعه إلى الأعلى وبالكاد أنقذ حياته.

Buck crashed into him, knocking him flat onto the floor.

اصطدم به باك، مما أدى إلى سقوطه على الأرض.

Buck bit deep into the man's arm, then lunged for the throat.

عض باك ذراع الرجل بعمق، ثم انقض على الحلق.

Burton could only partly block, and his neck was torn open.

لم يتمكن بيرتون إلا من الصد جزئيًا، وكان رقبته ممزقة.

Men rushed in, clubs raised, and drove Buck off the bleeding man.

اندفع الرجال، ورفعوا الهراوات، وطردوا باك من الرجل النازف.

A surgeon worked quickly to stop the blood from flowing out.

عمل الجراح بسرعة على إيقاف تدفق الدم.

Buck paced and growled, trying to attack again and again.

كان باك يذرع المكان ذهابًا وإيابًا ويصدر صوتًا حادًا، محاولًا الهجوم مرارًا وتكرارًا.

Only swinging clubs kept him back from reaching Burton.

لم يمنعه سوى الهراوات المتأرجحة من الوصول إلى بيرتون.

A miners' meeting was called and held right there on the spot.

تم عقد اجتماع لعمال المناجم في نفس المكان.

They agreed Buck had been provoked and voted to set him free.

واتفقوا على أن باك كان مستفزًا وصوتوا على إطلاق سراحه.

But Buck's fierce name now echoed in every camp in Alaska.

لكن اسم باك الشرس أصبح الآن يتردد صداه في كل معسكر في ألاسكا.

Later that fall, Buck saved Thornton again in a new way.

وفي وقت لاحق من ذلك الخريف، أنقذ باك ثورنتون مرة أخرى بطريقة جديدة.

The three men were guiding a long boat down rough rapids.

كان الرجال الثلاثة يقودون قاربًا طويلًا عبر منحدرات خشنة.

Thornton maned the boat, calling directions to the shoreline.

كان ثورنتون يقود القارب، ويعطي الاتجاهات إلى الشاطئ.

Hans and Pete ran on land, holding a rope from tree to tree.

ركض هانز وبيت على الأرض، ممسكين بحبل من شجرة إلى شجرة.

Buck kept pace on the bank, always watching his master.

واصل باك السير على الضفة، وكان يراقب سيده دائمًا.

At one nasty place, rocks jutted out under the fast water.

في أحد الأماكن القبيحة، برزت الصخور تحت المياه السريعة.

Hans let go of the rope, and Thornton steered the boat wide.

أطلق هانز الحبل، وقاد ثورنتون القارب إلى اتجاه واسع.

Hans sprinted to catch the boat again past the dangerous rocks.

انطلق هانز مسرعًا ليلحق بالقارب مرة أخرى متجاوزًا الصخور الخطيرة.

The boat cleared the ledge but hit a stronger part of the current.

تمكن القارب من تجاوز الحافة لكنه اصطدم بجزء أقوى من التيار.

Hans grabbed the rope too quickly and pulled the boat off balance.

أمسك هانز بالحبل بسرعة كبيرة وسحب القارب إلى حالة من عدم التوازن.

The boat flipped over and slammed into the bank, bottom up.

انقلب القارب واصطدم بالضفة من الأسفل إلى الأعلى.

Thornton was thrown out and swept into the wildest part of the water.

تم طرد ثورنتون وجرفته المياه إلى الجزء الأكثر وحشية من المياه.

No swimmer could have survived in those deadly, racing waters.

لم يكن بإمكان أي سباح أن ينجو في تلك المياه المميتة المتسارعة.

Buck jumped in instantly and chased his master down the river.

قفز باك على الفور وطارد سيده أسفل النهر.

After three hundred yards, he reached Thornton at last.

وبعد ثلاثمائة ياردة، وصل أخيرا إلى ثورنتون.

Thornton grabbed Buck's tail, and Buck turned for the shore.

أمسك ثورنتون بذيل باك، ثم اتجه باك نحو الشاطئ.

He swam with full strength, fighting the water's wild drag.

كان يسبح بكل قوته، محاربًا مقاومة الماء الجامحة.

They moved downstream faster than they could reach the shore.

لقد تحركوا باتجاه مجرى النهر بسرعة أكبر من قدرتهم على الوصول إلى الشاطئ.

Ahead, the river roared louder as it fell into deadly rapids.

أمام النهر، كان صوت هديره أعلى وهو ينحدر إلى المنحدرات المميتة.

Rocks sliced through the water like the teeth of a huge comb.

الصخور تشق طريقها عبر الماء مثل أسنان مشط ضخم.

The pull of the water near the drop was savage and inescapable.

كانت قوة جذب المياه بالقرب من القطرة وحشية ولا مفر منها.

Thornton knew they could never make the shore in time.

أدرك ثورنتون أنهم لن يتمكنوا أبدًا من الوصول إلى الشاطئ في الوقت المناسب.

He scraped over one rock, smashed across a second,

لقد خدش صخرة واحدة، وحطم صخرة ثانية،

And then he crashed into a third rock, grabbing it with both hands.

ثم اصطدم بالصخرة الثالثة، وأمسك بها بكلتا يديه.

He let go of Buck and shouted over the roar, "Go, Buck! Go!"

أطلق سراح باك وصاح فوق الزئير، "اذهب، باك! اذهب!"

Buck could not stay afloat and was swept down by the current.

لم يتمكن باك من البقاء طافيًا وجرفته التيارات المائية.

He fought hard, struggling to turn, but made no headway at all.

لقد حارب بشدة، وكافح من أجل التحول، لكنه لم يحقق أي تقدم على الإطلاق.

Then he heard Thornton repeat the command over the river's roar.

ثم سمع ثورنتون يكرر الأمر على الرغم من هدير النهر.

Buck reared out of the water, raised his head as if for a last look.

خرج باك من الماء، ورفع رأسه كما لو كان يلقي نظرة أخيرة.

then turned and obeyed, swimming toward the bank with resolve.

ثم استدار وأطاع، وسبح نحو الضفة بعزم.

Pete and Hans pulled him ashore at the final possible moment.

قام بيت وهانز بسحبه إلى الشاطئ في اللحظة الأخيرة الممكنة.

They knew Thornton could cling to the rock for only minutes more.

لقد عرفوا أن ثورنتون لن يتمكن من التشبث بالصخرة إلا لبضع دقائق أخرى.

They ran up the bank to a spot far above where he was hanging.

ركضوا إلى أعلى البنك حتى وصلوا إلى مكان بعيد عن المكان الذي كان معلقًا فيه.

They tied the boat's line to Buck's neck and shoulders carefully.

قاموا بربط خط القارب حول رقبة باك وكتفيه بعناية.

The rope was snug but loose enough for breathing and movement.

كان الحبل مريحًا ولكنه فضفاض بدرجة كافية للتنفس والحركة.

Then they launched him into the rushing, deadly river again.

ثم ألقوه مرة أخرى في النهر المتدفق القاتل.

Buck swam boldly but missed his angle into the stream's force.

سبح باك بجرأة لكنه أخطأ زاوية دخوله إلى تيار الماء.

He saw too late that he was going to drift past Thornton.

لقد أدرك متأخرًا أنه سوف ينجرف بعيدًا عن ثورنتون.

Hans jerked the rope tight, as if Buck were a capsizing boat.

سحب هانز الحبل بقوة، كما لو كان باك قاربًا ينقلب.

The current pulled him under, and he vanished below the surface.

سحبه التيار إلى الأسفل، واختفى تحت السطح.

His body struck the bank before Hans and Pete pulled him out.

ارتطم جسده بالبنك قبل أن يقوم هانز وبيت بسحبه للخارج.

He was half-drowned, and they pounded the water out of him.

لقد غرق نصفًا، وقاموا بضرب الماء عليه حتى خرج.

Buck stood, staggered, and collapsed again onto the ground.

وقف باك، وتعثر، ثم انهار مرة أخرى على الأرض.

Then they heard Thornton's voice faintly carried by the wind.

ثم سمعوا صوت ثورنتون يحمله الريح بشكل خافت.

Though the words were unclear, they knew he was near death.

ورغم أن الكلمات لم تكن واضحة، إلا أنهم عرفوا أنه كان على وشك الموت.

The sound of Thornton's voice hit Buck like an electric jolt.

لقد ضرب صوت ثورنتون باك مثل صدمة كهربائية.

He jumped up and ran up the bank, returning to the launch point.

قفز وركض نحو الضفة، وعاد إلى نقطة الانطلاق.

Again they tied the rope to Buck, and again he entered the stream.

وربطوا الحبل مرة أخرى إلى باك، ودخل مرة أخرى إلى النهر.

This time, he swam directly and firmly into the rushing water.

هذه المرة، سبح مباشرة وبثبات في المياه المتدفقة.

Hans let out the rope steadily while Pete kept it from tangling.

أطلق هانز الحبل بثبات بينما منعه بيت من التشابك.

Buck swam hard until he was lined up just above Thornton.

سبح باك بقوة حتى اصطف فوق ثورنتون مباشرة.

Then he turned and charged down like a train in full speed.

ثم استدار وانطلق بسرعة هائلة مثل القطار.

Thornton saw him coming, braced, and locked arms around his neck.

لقد رأى ثورنتون أنه قادم، فقام برفع ذراعيه ووضعها حول رقبته.

Hans tied the rope fast around a tree as both were pulled under.

قام هانز بربط الحبل حول شجرة بقوة بينما كان كلاهما يسحبان تحتها.

They tumbled underwater, smashing into rocks and river debris.

لقد سقطوا تحت الماء، واصطدموا بالصخور وحطام النهر.

One moment Buck was on top, the next Thornton rose gasping.

في لحظة كان باك في الأعلى، وفي اللحظة التالية نهض ثورنتون وهو يلهث.

Battered and choking, they veered to the bank and safety.

أصيبوا بالصدمة والاختناق، فانحرفوا إلى الضفة والأمان.

Thornton regained consciousness, lying across a drift log.

استعاد ثورنتون وعيه، وهو مستلقٍ على جذع شجرة.

Hans and Pete worked him hard to bring back breath and life.

لقد عمل هانز وبيت بجد حتى يتمكن من استعادة أنفاسه وحياته.

His first thought was for Buck, who lay motionless and limp.

كان تفكيره الأول هو باك، الذي كان مستلقيا بلا حراك ومرتخيا.

Nig howled over Buck's body, and Skeet licked his face gently.

عوى نيج فوق جسد باك، ولعق سكيت وجهه بلطف.

Thornton, sore and bruised, examined Buck with careful hands.

قام ثورنتون بفحص باك بكل حذر، وكان جسده مليئا بالكدمات.

He found three ribs broken, but no deadly wounds in the dog.

ووجد أن ثلاثة أضلاع مكسورة، لكن لم توجد جروح مميتة في الكلب.

"That settles it," Thornton said. "We camp here." And they did.

قال ثورنتون: "هذا يُحسم الأمر. نُخيّم هنا". وهذا ما فعلوه.

They stayed until Buck's ribs healed and he could walk again.

لقد بقوا حتى شُفيت أضلاع باك وأصبح قادرًا على المشي مرة أخرى.

That winter, Buck performed a feat that raised his fame further.

في ذلك الشتاء، قام باك بإنجاز أدى إلى زيادة شهرته بشكل أكبر.

It was less heroic than saving Thornton, but just as impressive.

لقد كان الأمر أقل بطولية من إنقاذ ثورنتون، لكنه كان مثيرًا للإعجاب بنفس القدر.

At Dawson, the partners needed supplies for a distant journey.

في داوسون، احتاج الشركاء إلى إمدادات لرحلة بعيدة.

They wanted to travel East, into untouched wilderness lands.

أرادوا السفر شرقًا، إلى الأراضي البرية غير المستكشفة.

Buck's deed in the Eldorado Saloon made that trip possible.

لقد جعلت أفعال باك في صالون إلدورادو هذه الرحلة ممكنة.

It began with men bragging about their dogs over drinks.

بدأ الأمر مع الرجال الذين يتفاخرون بكلابهم أثناء شرب المشروبات.

Buck's fame made him the target of challenges and doubt.

لقد جعلت شهرة باك منه هدفًا للتحديات والشكوك.

Thornton, proud and calm, stood firm in defending Buck's name.

وقف ثورنتون بفخر وهدوء، وظل ثابتًا في الدفاع عن اسم باك.

One man said his dog could pull five hundred pounds with ease.

قال أحد الرجال إن كلبه يستطيع سحب خمسمائة رطل بسهولة.

Another said six hundred, and a third bragged seven hundred.

وقال آخر ستمائة، وقال ثالث سبعمائة.

"Pfft!" said John Thornton, "Buck can pull a thousand pound sled."

"بفت!" قال جون ثورنتون، "يستطيع باك سحب زلاجة تزن ألف رطل."

Matthewson, a Bonanza King, leaned forward and challenged him.

انحنى ماثيوسون، ملك بونانزا، إلى الأمام وتحداه.

"You think he can put that much weight into motion?"

"هل تعتقد أنه قادر على وضع هذا القدر من الوزن في الحركة؟"

"And you think he can pull the weight a full hundred yards?"

"وهل تعتقد أنه قادر على رفع الوزن لمسافة مائة ياردة كاملة؟"

Thornton replied coolly, "Yes. Buck is dog enough to do it."

أجاب ثورنتون ببرود: "نعم. باك جبانٌ بما يكفي ليفعل ذلك."

"He'll put a thousand pounds into motion, and pull it a hundred yards."

"سيضع ألف جنيه في الحركة، ويسحبها لمسافة مائة ياردة."

Matthewson smiled slowly and made sure all men heard his words.

ابتسم ماثيوسون ببطء وتأكد من أن جميع الرجال سمعوا كلماته.

"I've got a thousand dollars that says he can't. There it is."

"لديّ ألف دولار تُشير إلى أنه لا يستطيع. ها هو ذا."

He slammed a sack of gold dust the size of sausage on the bar.

ضرب كيسًا من غبار الذهب بحجم السجق على البار.

Nobody said a word. The silence grew heavy and tense around them.

لم ينطق أحد بكلمة. ساد الصمت بينهم توتر وثقل.

Thornton's bluff—if it was one—had been taken seriously.

لقد تم أخذ خدعة ثورنتون ـ إن كانت حقيقية ـ على محمل الجد.

He felt heat rise in his face as blood rushed to his cheeks.

شعر بارتفاع الحرارة في وجهه بينما اندفع الدم إلى خديه.

His tongue had gotten ahead of his reason in that moment.

لقد سبق لسانه عقله في تلك اللحظة.

He truly didn't know if Buck could move a thousand pounds.

إنه حقا لا يعرف إذا كان باك قادرا على نقل ألف جنيه.

Half a ton! The size of it alone made his heart feel heavy.

نصف طن! حجمه وحده أثقل قلبه.

He had faith in Buck's strength and had thought him capable.

لقد كان لديه ثقة في قوة باك وكان يعتقد أنه قادر.

But he had never faced this kind of challenge, not like this.

ولكنه لم يواجه هذا النوع من التحدي من قبل، ليس بهذه الطريقة.

A dozen men watched him quietly, waiting to see what he'd do.

كان هناك عشرة رجال يراقبونه بهدوء، في انتظار رؤية ما سيفعله.

He didn't have the money—neither did Hans or Pete.

لم يكن لديه المال ـ ولا هانز أو بيت.

"I've got a sled outside," said Matthewson coldly and direct.

"لقد حصلت على مزلجة بالخارج"، قال ماثيوسون ببرود وبشكل مباشر.

"It's loaded with twenty sacks, fifty pounds each, all flour.

"إنها محملة بعشرين كيسًا، كل كيس يزن خمسين رطلاً، كلها من الدقيق.

So don't let a missing sled be your excuse now," he added.

وأضاف "لذا لا تدع فقدان الزلاجة يكون عذرك الآن".

Thornton stood silent. He didn't know what words to offer.

وقف ثورنتون صامتًا. لم يعرف الكلمات التي سيقولها.

He looked around at the faces without seeing them clearly.

كان ينظر حوله إلى الوجوه دون أن يراها بوضوح.

He looked like a man frozen in thought, trying to restart.

لقد بدا وكأنه رجل متجمد في أفكاره، يحاول البدء من جديد.

Then he saw Jim O'Brien, a friend from the Mastodon days.

ثم رأى جيم أوبراين، وهو صديق من أيام ماستودون.

That familiar face gave him courage he didn't know he had.

لقد أعطاه هذا الوجه المألوف الشجاعة التي لم يكن يعلم أنه يمتلكها.

He turned and asked in a low voice, "Can you lend me a thousand?"

ثم التفت وسأل بصوت منخفض: هل يمكنك أن تقرضني ألفًا؟

"Sure," said O'Brien, dropping a heavy sack by the gold already.

"بالتأكيد،" قال أوبراين، وهو يسقط كيسًا ثقيلًا بجوار الذهب بالفعل.

"But truthfully, John, I don't believe the beast can do this."

"لكن الحقيقة يا جون، أنا لا أعتقد أن الوحش قادر على فعل هذا."

Everyone in the Eldorado Saloon rushed outside to see the event.

هرع الجميع في صالون إلدورادو إلى الخارج لمشاهدة الحدث.

They left tables and drinks, and even the games were paused.

لقد تركوا الطاولات والمشروبات، وحتى الألعاب توقفت.

Dealers and gamblers came to witness the bold wager's end.

حضر التجار والمقامرون ليشهدوا نهاية الرهان الجريء.

Hundreds gathered around the sled in the icy open street.

تجمع المئات حول الزلاجة في الشارع المفتوح الجليدي.

Matthewson's sled stood with a full load of flour sacks.

كانت زلاجة ماثيوسون تحمل حمولة كاملة من أكياس الدقيق.

The sled had been sitting for hours in minus temperatures.

ظلت الزلاجة جالسة لعدة ساعات في درجات حرارة منخفضة تحت الصفر.

The sled's runners were frozen tight to the packed-down snow.

كانت عجلات الزلاجة متجمدة بإحكام بسبب الثلوج المتراكمة.

Men offered two-to-one odds that Buck could not move the sled.

وقد عرض الرجال احتمالات بنسبة اثنين إلى واحد بأن باك لن يتمكن من تحريك الزلاجة.

A dispute broke out about what "break out" really meant.

لقد نشأ نزاع حول ما يعنيه "الاندلاع" في الواقع.

O'Brien said Thornton should loosen the sled's frozen base.

قال أوبراين أن ثورنتون يجب أن يخفف قاعدة الزلاجة المتجمدة.

Buck could then "break out" from a solid, motionless start.

وقد يتمكن باك بعد ذلك من "الانطلاق" من بداية ثابتة ثابتة.

Matthewson argued the dog must break the runners free too.

وزعم ماثيوسون أن الكلب يجب أن يحرر العدائين أيضًا.

The men who had heard the bet agreed with Matthewson's view.

واتفق الرجال الذين سمعوا الرهان مع وجهة نظر ماثيوسون.

With that ruling, the odds jumped to three-to-one against Buck.

ومع هذا القرار، ارتفعت احتمالات الفوز ضد باك إلى ثلاثة مقابل واحد.

No one stepped forward to take the growing three-to-one odds.

ولم يتقدم أحد ليأخذ فرص الفوز المتزايدة التي وصلت إلى ثلاثة مقابل واحد.

Not a single man believed Buck could perform the great feat.

لم يعتقد أي رجل أن باك قادر على تحقيق هذا الإنجاز العظيم.

Thornton had been rushed into the bet, heavy with doubts.

لقد تم دفع ثورنتون إلى الرهان، وهو مثقل بالشكوك.

Now he looked at the sled and the ten-dog team beside it.

والآن نظر إلى الزلاجة وفريق الكلاب العشرة بجانبها.

Seeing the reality of the task made it seem more impossible.

إن رؤية حقيقة المهمة جعلتها تبدو أكثر استحالة.

Matthewson was full of pride and confidence in that moment.

كان ماثيوسون مليئًا بالفخر والثقة في تلك اللحظة.

"Three to one!" he shouted. "I'll bet another thousand, Thornton!

"ثلاثة إلى واحد!" صرخ. "أراهن بألف أخرى يا ثورنتون!"

What do you say?" he added, loud enough for all to hear.

"ماذا تقول؟" أضاف بصوت عالٍ بما يكفي ليسمعه الجميع.

Thornton's face showed his doubts, but his spirit had risen.

أظهر وجه ثورنتون شكوكه، لكن روحه ارتفعت.

That fighting spirit ignored odds and feared nothing at all.

لقد تجاهلت روح القتال الصعاب ولم تخش شيئًا على الإطلاق.

He called Hans and Pete to bring all their cash to the table.

اتصل بهانز وبيت ليحضرا كل أموالهما إلى الطاولة.

They had little left—only two hundred dollars combined.

لم يتبق لديهم سوى القليل - مائتي دولار فقط.

This small sum was their total fortune during hard times.

وكان هذا المبلغ الصغير هو مجموع ثروتهم خلال الأوقات الصعبة.

Still, they laid all of the fortune down against Matthewson's bet.

ومع ذلك، فقد وضعوا كل ثروتهم ضد رهان ماثيويسون.

The ten-dog team was unhitched and moved away from the sled.

تم فك ربط فريق الكلاب العشرة وتحرك بعيدًا عن الزلاجة.

Buck was placed in the reins, wearing his familiar harness.

تم وضع باك في اللجام، مرتديًا حزامه المألوف.

He had caught the energy of the crowd and felt the tension.

لقد التقط طاقة الحشد وشعر بالتوتر.

Somehow, he knew he had to do something for John Thornton.

بطريقة ما، كان يعلم أنه يجب عليه أن يفعل شيئًا من أجل جون ثورنتون.

People murmured with admiration at the dog's proud figure.

همس الناس بإعجاب عند رؤية شكل الكلب الفخور.

He was lean and strong, without a single extra ounce of flesh.

لقد كان نحيفًا وقويًا، ولم يكن لديه ذرة إضافية من اللحم.

His full weight of hundred fifty pounds was all power and endurance.

كان وزنه الكامل الذي بلغ مائة وخمسين رطلاً هو القوة والقدرة على التحمل.

Buck's coat gleamed like silk, thick with health and strength.

كان معطف باك لامعًا مثل الحرير، سميكًا بالصحة والقوة.

The fur along his neck and shoulders seemed to lift and bristle.

بدا الفراء على طول رقبته وكتفيه وكأنه يرتفع وينتفخ.

His mane moved slightly, each hair alive with his great energy.

تحرك شعره قليلاً، وكل شعرة منه مليئة بطاقته العظيمة.

His broad chest and strong legs matched his heavy, tough frame.

صدره العريض وساقيه القويتين يتناسبان مع جسده الثقيل والقوي.

Muscles rippled under his coat, tight and firm as bound iron.

كانت عضلاته تتقلص تحت معطفه، مشدودة وقوية مثل الحديد المقيد.

Men touched him and swore he was built like a steel machine.

لمسه الرجال وأقسموا أنه كان مبنيًا مثل آلة فولاذية.

The odds dropped slightly to two to one against the great dog.

انخفضت الاحتمالات قليلاً إلى اثنين إلى واحد ضد الكلب العظيم.

A man from the Skookum Benches pushed forward, stuttering.

تقدم رجل من مقاعد سكوكوم إلى الأمام، متلعثمًا.

"Good, sir! I offer eight hundred for him—before the test, sir!"

حسنًا يا سيدي! أعرض عليه ثمانمائة جنيه قبل الاختبار يا سيدي!

"Eight hundred, as he stands right now!" the man insisted.

"ثمانمائة، كما هو واقفًا الآن!" أصر الرجل.

Thornton stepped forward, smiled, and shook his head calmly.

تقدم ثورنتون للأمام، وابتسم، وهز رأسه بهدوء.

Matthewson quickly stepped in with a warning voice and frown.

تدخل ماثيوسون بسرعة بصوت تحذيري وعبوس.

"You must step away from him," he said. "Give him space."

قال: «يجب أن تبتعد عنه، وأعطه مساحة».

The crowd grew silent; only gamblers still offered two to one.

ساد الصمت بين الحشد؛ ولم يبق إلا المقامرون الذين عرضوا رهان اثنين إلى واحد.

Everyone admired Buck's build, but the load looked too great.

أعجب الجميع ببنية باك، لكن الحمل بدا ثقيلاً للغاية.

Twenty sacks of flour—each fifty pounds in weight—seemed far too much.

بدت عشرون كيسًا من الدقيق ـ يزن كل منها خمسين رطلاً ـ أكثر مما يمكن تحمله.

No one was willing to open their pouch and risk their money.

لم يكن أحد على استعداد لفتح حقيبته والمخاطرة بأمواله.

Thornton knelt beside Buck and took his head in both hands.

ركع ثورنتون بجانب باك وأمسك رأسه بكلتا يديه.

He pressed his cheek against Buck's and spoke into his ear.

ضغط خده على خد باك وتحدث في أذنه.

There was no playful shaking or whispered loving insults now.

لم يعد هناك اهتزاز مرح أو إهانات محبة همسًا الآن.

He only murmured softly, "As much as you love me, Buck."

لقد همس بهدوء، "بقدر ما تحبني، باك."

Buck let out a quiet whine, his eagerness barely restrained.

أطلق باك صرخة هادئة، وكان حماسه بالكاد مقيدًا.

The onlookers watched with curiosity as tension filled the air.

كان المتفرجون يراقبون بفضول بينما كان التوتر يملأ الهواء.

The moment felt almost unreal, like something beyond reason.

كانت تلك اللحظة تبدو غير واقعية تقريبًا، وكأنها شيء خارج عن المنطق.

When Thornton stood, Buck gently took his hand in his jaws.

عندما وقف ثورنتون، أمسك باك يده بلطف بين فكيه.

He pressed down with his teeth, then let go slowly and gently.

ضغط عليها بأسنانه، ثم أطلقها ببطء ولطف.

It was a silent answer of love, not spoken, but understood.

لقد كان جوابا صامتا للحب، لم يتم التحدث عنه، بل تم فهمه.

Thornton stepped well back from the dog and gave the signal.

ابتعد ثورنتون خطوة إلى الوراء قليلاً عن الكلب وأعطى الإشارة.

"Now, Buck," he said, and Buck responded with focused calm.

"حسنًا، باك"، قال، ورد باك بهدوء وتركيز.

Buck tightened the traces, then loosened them by a few inches.

شد باك المسارات، ثم خففها ببضعة بوصات.

This was the method he had learned; his way to break the sled.

كانت هذه هي الطريقة التي تعلمها، طريقته في كسر الزلاجة.

"Gee!" Thornton shouted, his voice sharp in the heavy silence.

"جي!" صرخ ثورنتون بصوت حاد في الصمت الثقيل.

Buck turned to the right and lunged with all of his weight.

اتجه باك إلى اليمين وانقض بكل وزنه.

The slack vanished, and Buck's full mass hit the tight traces.

اختفى التراخي، وضربت كتلة باك الكاملة الآثار الآثار الضيقة.

The sled trembled, and the runners made a crisp crackling sound.

ارتجفت الزلاجة، وأصدر المتسابقون صوت طقطقة واضح.

"Haw!" Thornton commanded, shifting Buck's direction again.

"هاو!" أمر ثورنتون، وهو يغير اتجاه باك مرة أخرى.

Buck repeated the move, this time pulling sharply to the left.

كرر باك الحركة، هذه المرة سحب بقوة إلى اليسار.

The sled cracked louder, the runners snapping and shifting.

تصاعد صوت الزلاجة بشكل أعلى، وبدأ العدائون في التحرك والتحرك.

The heavy load slid slightly sideways across the frozen snow.

انزلق الحمل الثقيل قليلاً إلى الجانب عبر الثلج المتجمد.

The sled had broken free from the grip of the icy trail!

لقد انطلقت الزلاجة من قبضة الطريق الجليدي!

Men held their breath, unaware they were not even breathing.

حبس الرجال أنفاسهم، دون أن يدركوا أنهم لا يتنفسون.

"Now, PULL!" Thornton cried out across the frozen silence.

"الآن، اسحب!" صرخ ثورنتون عبر الصمت المتجمد.

Thornton's command rang out sharp, like the crack of a whip.

لقد كان أمر ثورنتون حادًا، مثل صوت السوط.

Buck hurled himself forward with a fierce and jarring lunge.

ألقى باك بنفسه إلى الأمام بهجوم شرس ومزعج.

His whole frame tensed and bunched for the massive strain.

كان جسده بأكمله متوترًا ومتجمعًا بسبب الضغط الهائل.

Muscles rippled under his fur like serpents coming alive.

تموجت العضلات تحت فروه مثل الثعابين التي تنبض بالحياة.

His great chest was low, head stretched forward toward the sled.

كان صدره الكبير منخفضًا، ورأسه ممتدًا للأمام نحو الزلاجة.

His paws moved like lightning, claws slicing the frozen ground.

تحركت مخالبه مثل البرق، ومخالبه تقطع الأرض المتجمدة.

Grooves were cut deep as he fought for every inch of traction.

تم قطع الأخاديد عميقًا أثناء محاولته الحصول على كل بوصة من الجر.

The sled rocked, trembled, and began a slow, uneasy motion.

بدأت الزلاجة تتأرجح، وترتجف، وبدأت حركة بطيئة وغير مريحة.

One foot slipped, and a man in the crowd groaned aloud.

انزلقت إحدى القدمين، وأطلق أحد الرجال من بين الحشد أنينًا بصوت عالٍ.

Then the sled lunged forward in a jerking, rough movement.

ثم اندفعت الزلاجة إلى الأمام في حركة متقطعة وخشنة.

It didn't stop again—half an inch...an inch...two inches more.

ولم تتوقف مرة أخرى - نصف بوصة... بوصة... بوصتين أكثر.

The jerks became smaller as the sled began to gather speed.

أصبحت الهزات أصغر عندما بدأت الزلاجة تكتسب السرعة.

Soon Buck was pulling with smooth, even, rolling power.

وبعد قليل أصبح باك يسحب بقوة متدحرجة سلسة ومتساوية.

Men gasped and finally remembered to breathe again.

شهق الرجال وأخيراً تذكروا أن يتنفسوا مرة أخرى.

They had not noticed their breath had stopped in awe.

ولم يلاحظوا أن أنفاسهم توقفت من الرهبة.

Thornton ran behind, calling out short, cheerful commands.

ركض ثورنتون خلفه، وهو يصدر أوامر قصيرة ومبهجة.

Ahead was a stack of firewood that marked the distance.

كان أمامنا كومة من الحطب تشير إلى المسافة.

As Buck neared the pile, the cheering grew louder and louder.

وعندما اقترب باك من الكومة، أصبح الهتاف أعلى وأعلى.

The cheering swelled into a roar as Buck passed the end point.

ارتفعت الهتافات إلى هدير عندما تجاوز باك نقطة النهاية.

Men jumped and shouted, even Matthewson broke into a grin.

قفز الرجال وصاحوا، حتى أن ماثيوسون ابتسم.

Hats flew into the air, mittens were tossed without thought or aim.

طارت القبعات في الهواء، وألقيت القفازات دون تفكير أو هدف.

Men grabbed each other and shook hands without knowing who.

أمسك الرجال ببعضهم البعض وتصافحوا دون أن يعرفوا من هو.

The whole crowd buzzed in wild, joyful celebration.

كان الحشد بأكمله يحتفل بفرحة غامرة.

Thornton dropped to his knees beside Buck with trembling hands.

سقط ثورنتون على ركبتيه بجانب باك ويداه ترتعشان.

He pressed his head to Buck's and shook him gently back and forth.

ضغط رأسه على رأس باك وهزه بلطف ذهابًا وإيابًا.

Those who approached heard him curse the dog with quiet love.

سمع الذين اقتربوا منه يلعن الكلب بحب هادئ.

He swore at Buck for a long time—softly, warmly, with emotion.

لقد أقسم على باك لفترة طويلة - بهدوء، بحرارة، وبعاطفة.

"Good, sir! Good, sir!" cried the Skookum Bench king in a rush.

"حسنًا، سيدي! حسنًا، سيدي!" صرخ ملك مقعد سكوكوم مسرعًا.

"I'll give you a thousand—no, twelve hundred—for that dog, sir!"

"سأعطيك ألفًا - لا، ألفًا ومائتين - مقابل هذا الكلب يا سيدي!"

Thornton rose slowly to his feet, his eyes shining with emotion.

نهض ثورنتون ببطء على قدميه، وكانت عيناه تتألقان بالعاطفة.

Tears streamed openly down his cheeks without any shame.

تدفقت الدموع على خديه بكل حرية دون أي خجل.

"Sir," he said to the Skookum Bench king, steady and firm

"سيدي،" قال لملك مقعد سكوكوم، بثبات وحزم

"No, sir. You can go to hell, sir. That's my final answer."

لا يا سيدي. اذهب إلى الجحيم يا سيدي. هذا جوابي النهائي.

Buck grabbed Thornton's hand gently in his strong jaws.

أمسك باك يد ثورنتون بلطف بفكيه القويين.

Thornton shook him playfully, their bond deep as ever.

هزه ثورنتون بطريقة مرحة، وكانت علاقتهما عميقة كما كانت دائمًا.

The crowd, moved by the moment, stepped back in silence.

تحرك الحشد في تلك اللحظة وتراجع إلى الوراء في صمت.

From then on, none dared interrupt such sacred affection.

ومنذ ذلك الحين، لم يجرؤ أحد على مقاطعة هذا المودة المقدسة.

The Sound of the Call
صوت النداء

Buck had earned sixteen hundred dollars in five minutes.

لقد ربح باك ستة عشر مائة دولار في خمس دقائق.

The money let John Thornton pay off some of his debts.

مكّنت الأموال جون ثورنتون من سداد بعض ديونه.

With the rest of the money he headed East with his partners.

وببقية الأموال توجه شرقًا مع شركائه.

They sought a fabled lost mine, as old as the country itself.

لقد بحثوا عن منجم مفقود أسطوري، قديم قدم البلد نفسه.

Many men had looked for the mine, but few had ever found it.

لقد بحث العديد من الرجال عن المنجم، لكن قليل منهم من وجدوه.

More than a few men had vanished during the dangerous quest.

لقد اختفى أكثر من رجل خلال المهمة الخطيرة.

This lost mine was wrapped in both mystery and old tragedy.

كان هذا المنجم المفقود محاطًا بالغموض والمأساة القديمة.

No one knew who the first man to find the mine had been.

لم يكن أحد يعلم من هو الرجل الأول الذي عثر على المنجم.

The oldest stories don't mention anyone by name.

القصص القديمة لا تذكر أحداً بالاسم.

There had always been an ancient ramshackle cabin there.

لقد كان هناك دائمًا كوخًا قديمًا متهالكًا هناك.

Dying men had sworn there was a mine next to that old cabin.

أقسم الرجال المحتضرون أن هناك منجمًا بجوار تلك الكابينة القديمة.

They proved their stories with gold like none found elsewhere.

لقد أثبتوا قصصهم بالذهب كما لم نجد مثله في أي مكان آخر.

No living soul had ever looted the treasure from that place.

لم يسبق لأي روح حية أن نهبت الكنز من هذا المكان.

The dead were dead, and dead men tell no tales.

لقد كان الموتى أمواتًا، والموتى لا يروون حكايات.

So Thornton and his friends headed into the East.

لذا توجه ثورنتون وأصدقاؤه إلى الشرق.

Pete and Hans joined, bringing Buck and six strong dogs.

انضم بيت وهانز، وأحضروا باك وستة كلاب قوية.

They set off down an unknown trail where others had failed.

انطلقوا في طريق غير معروف حيث فشل الآخرون.

They sledded seventy miles up the frozen Yukon River.

لقد تزلجوا على مسافة سبعين ميلاً على نهر يوكون المتجمد.

They turned left and followed the trail into the Stewart.

اتجهوا إلى اليسار وتبعوا المسار إلى ستيوارت.

They passed the Mayo and McQuestion, pressing farther on.

لقد تجاوزوا مايو ومكويستيون، واستمروا في الضغط على بعضهم البعض.

The Stewart shrank into a stream, threading jagged peaks.

انكمش نهر ستيوارت إلى مجرى مائي، يتخلله قمم متعرجة.

These sharp peaks marked the very spine of the continent.

تشكل هذه القمم الحادة العمود الفقري للقارة.

John Thornton demanded little from men or the wild land.

لم يطلب جون ثورنتون الكثير من الرجال أو من الأرض البرية.

He feared nothing in nature and faced the wild with ease.

لم يكن يخاف من أي شيء في الطبيعة وواجه البرية بكل سهولة.

With only salt and a rifle, he could travel where he wished.

باستخدام الملح والبندقية فقط، كان بإمكانه السفر إلى أي مكان يريده.

Like the natives, he hunted food while he journeyed along.

مثل السكان الأصليين، كان يبحث عن الطعام أثناء رحلاته.

If he caught nothing, he kept going, trusting luck ahead.

إذا لم يتمكن من الحصول على شيء، فإنه يستمر في طريقه، معتمدًا على الحظ في المستقبل.

On this long journey, meat was the main thing they ate.

في هذه الرحلة الطويلة، كان اللحم هو الشيء الرئيسي الذي تناولوه.

The sled held tools and ammo, but no strict timetable.

كانت الزلاجة تحمل أدوات وذخيرة، ولكن لم يكن هناك جدول زمني صارم.

Buck loved this wandering; the endless hunt and fishing.

كان باك يحب هذا التجوال؛ والصيد وصيد الأسماك الذي لا ينتهي.

For weeks they were traveling day after steady day.

لمدة أسابيع كانوا يسافرون يومًا بعد يوم.

Other times they made camps and stayed still for weeks.

وفي أوقات أخرى، أقاموا معسكرات وبقوا في أماكنهم لأسابيع.

The dogs rested while the men dug through frozen dirt.

استراحت الكلاب بينما قام الرجال بالحفر في التراب المتجمد.

They warmed pans over fires and searched for hidden gold.

قاموا بتسخين المقالي على النار وبحثوا عن الذهب المخفي.

Some days they starved, and some days they had feasts.

في بعض الأيام كانوا يموتون من الجوع، وفي بعض الأيام كانوا يقيمون وليمة.

Their meals depended on the game and the luck of the hunt.

وكانت وجباتهم تعتمد على اللعبة وحظ الصيد.

When summer came, men and dogs packed loads on their backs.

عندما جاء الصيف، كان الرجال والكلاب يحملون الأحمال على ظهورهم.

They rafted across blue lakes hidden in mountain forests.

لقد قاموا بالتجول عبر البحيرات الزرقاء المخفية في الغابات الجبلية.

They sailed slim boats on rivers no man had ever mapped.

لقد أبحروا بقوارب نحيفة على أنهار لم يسبق لأي إنسان أن رسم خريطة لها.

Those boats were built from trees they sawed in the wild.

تم بناء هذه القوارب من الأشجار التي قطعوها في البرية.

The months passed, and they twisted through the wild unknown lands.

ومرت الأشهر، وتجولوا عبر الأراضي البرية المجهولة.

There were no men there, yet old traces hinted that men had been.

لم يكن هناك رجال هناك، لكن الآثار القديمة كانت تشير إلى وجود رجال هناك.

If the Lost Cabin was real, then others had once come this way.

إذا كانت الكابينة المفقودة حقيقية، فهذا يعني أن آخرين قد أتوا من هنا في وقت ما.

They crossed high passes in blizzards, even during the summer.

لقد عبروا الممرات المرتفعة أثناء العواصف الثلجية، حتى خلال فصل الصيف.

They shivered under the midnight sun on bare mountain slopes.

كانوا يرتجفون تحت شمس منتصف الليل على منحدرات الجبال العارية.

Between the treeline and the snowfields, they climbed slowly.

بين خط الأشجار وحقول الثلوج، تسلقوا ببطء.

In warm valleys, they swatted at clouds of gnats and flies.

في الوديان الدافئة، قاموا بضرب سحب البعوض والذباب.

They picked sweet berries near glaciers in full summer bloom.

قاموا بقطف التوت الحلو بالقرب من الأنهار الجليدية في أوج ازدهارها في الصيف.

The flowers they found were as lovely as those in the Southland.

وكانت الزهور التي وجدوها جميلة مثل تلك الموجودة في ساوثلاند.

That fall they reached a lonely region filled with silent lakes.

وفي ذلك الخريف وصلوا إلى منطقة منعزلة مليئة بالبحيرات الصامتة.

The land was sad and empty, once alive with birds and beasts.

كانت الأرض حزينة وخالية، وكانت مليئة بالطيور والوحوش.

Now there was no life, just the wind and ice forming in pools.

والآن لم تعد هناك حياة، فقط الرياح والجليد يتشكل في البرك.

Waves lapped against empty shores with a soft, mournful sound.

تلاطمت الأمواج على الشواطئ الفارغة بصوت ناعم وحزين.

Another winter came, and they followed faint, old trails again.

ثم جاء شتاء آخر، وتبعوا مسارات قديمة خافتة مرة أخرى.

These were the trails of men who had searched long before them.

كانت هذه هي آثار الرجال الذين بحثوا قبلهم بوقت طويل.

Once they found a path cut deep into the dark forest.

ذات مرة، وجدوا طريقًا مقطوعًا عميقًا في الغابة المظلمة.

It was an old trail, and they felt the lost cabin was close.

لقد كان دربًا قديمًا، وشعروا أن الكابينة المفقودة كانت قريبة.

But the trail led nowhere and faded into the thick woods.

لكن الطريق لم يؤدِ إلى أي مكان وتلاشى في الغابة الكثيفة.

Whoever made the trail, and why they made it, no one knew.

من صنع هذا المسار، ولماذا صنعه، لا أحد يعلم.

Later, they found the wreck of a lodge hidden among the trees.

وفي وقت لاحق، عثروا على حطام نزل مخفي بين الأشجار.

Rotting blankets lay scattered where someone once had slept.

كانت هناك بطانيات متعفنة متناثرة حيث كان شخص ما ينام ذات يوم.

John Thornton found a long-barreled flintlock buried inside.

عثر جون ثورنتون على بندقية ذات ماسورة طويلة مدفونة بالداخل.

He knew this was a Hudson Bay gun from early trading days.

لقد علم أن هذا كان مدفع خليج هدسون من أيام التجارة المبكرة.

In those days such guns were traded for stacks of beaver skins.

في تلك الأيام كان يتم مقايضة هذه الأسلحة بأكوام من جلود القندس.

That was all—no clue remained of the man who built the lodge.

كان هذا كل شيء ـ لم يتبق أي دليل على الرجل الذي بنى النزل.

Spring came again, and they found no sign of the Lost Cabin.

لقد جاء الربيع مرة أخرى، ولم يجدوا أي أثر للكوخ المفقود.

Instead they found a broad valley with a shallow stream.

وبدلاً من ذلك، وجدوا واديًا واسعًا مع مجرى مائي ضحل.

Gold lay across the pan bottoms like smooth, yellow butter.

كان الذهب متوضعًا في قاع المقلاة مثل الزبدة الصفراء الناعمة.

They stopped there and searched no farther for the cabin.

توقفوا هناك ولم يبحثوا عن الكابينة أبعد من ذلك.

Each day they worked and found thousands in gold dust.

كل يوم عملوا ووجدوا الآلاف في غبار الذهب.

They packed the gold in bags of moose-hide, fifty pounds each.

قاموا بتعبئة الذهب في أكياس من جلد الموظ، خمسين رطلاً لكل كيس.

The bags were stacked like firewood outside their small lodge.

كانت الحقائب مكدسة مثل الحطب خارج نزلهم الصغير.

They worked like giants, and the days passed like quick dreams.

لقد عملوا مثل العمالقة، ومرت الأيام مثل الأحلام السريعة.

They heaped up treasure as the endless days rolled swiftly by.

لقد جمعوا الكنز بينما مرت الأيام التي لا نهاية لها بسرعة.

There was little for the dogs to do except haul meat now and then.

لم يكن هناك الكثير مما يمكن للكلاب فعله باستثناء نقل اللحوم من وقت لآخر.

Thornton hunted and killed the game, and Buck lay by the fire.

كان ثورنتون يصطاد ويقتل الطرائد، وكان باك مستلقيًا بجانب النار.

He spent long hours in silence, lost in thought and memory.

أمضى ساعات طويلة في صمت، غارقًا في الفكر والذاكرة.

The image of the hairy man came more often into Buck's mind.

كانت صورة الرجل المشعر تظهر في ذهن باك أكثر من أي وقت مضى.

Now that work was scarce, Buck dreamed while blinking at the fire.

الآن بعد أن أصبح العمل نادرًا، حلم باك بينما كان يرمش أمام النار.

In those dreams, Buck wandered with the man in another world.

في تلك الأحلام، كان باك يتجول مع الرجل في عالم آخر.

Fear seemed the strongest feeling in that distant world.

يبدو أن الخوف هو الشعور الأقوى في ذلك العالم البعيد.

Buck saw the hairy man sleep with his head bowed low.

رأى باك الرجل المشعر نائماً ورأسه منحنياً إلى أسفل.

His hands were clasped, and his sleep was restless and broken.

كانت يداه مشبوكتين، وكان نومه مضطربًا ومتقطعًا.

He used to wake with a start and stare fearfully into the dark.

كان يستيقظ فجأة ويحدق بخوف في الظلام.

Then he'd toss more wood onto the fire to keep the flame bright.

ثم يقوم بإلقاء المزيد من الخشب على النار للحفاظ على اشتعال اللهب.

Sometimes they walked along a beach by a gray, endless sea.

في بعض الأحيان كانوا يسيرون على طول الشاطئ بجانب بحر رمادي لا نهاية له.

The hairy man picked shellfish and ate them as he walked.

كان الرجل المشعر يلتقط المحار ويأكله أثناء سيره.

His eyes searched always for hidden dangers in the shadows.

كانت عيناه تبحث دائمًا عن المخاطر المخفية في الظل.

His legs were always ready to sprint at the first sign of threat.

كانت ساقيه مستعدة دائمًا للركض عند أول علامة تهديد.

They crept through the forest, silent and wary, side by side.

تسللوا عبر الغابة، صامتين وحذرين، جنبًا إلى جنب.

Buck followed at his heels, and both of them stayed alert.

وتبعه باك، وبقي كلاهما في حالة تأهب.

Their ears twitched and moved, their noses sniffed the air.

ارتعشت آذانهم وتحركت، واستنشقت أنوفهم الهواء.

The man could hear and smell the forest as sharply as Buck.

كان الرجل يستطيع سماع الغابة وشم رائحتها بنفس حدة باك.

The hairy man swung through the trees with sudden speed.

تأرجح الرجل المشعر بين الأشجار بسرعة مفاجئة.

He leapt from branch to branch, never missing his grip.

كان يقفز من فرع إلى فرع، دون أن يفقد قبضته أبدًا.

He moved as fast above the ground as he did upon it.

لقد تحرك فوق الأرض بنفس السرعة التي تحرك بها عليها.

Buck remembered long nights beneath the trees, keeping watch.

تذكر باك الليالي الطويلة التي قضاها تحت الأشجار وهو يراقب.

The man slept roosting in the branches, clinging tight.

كان الرجل ينام في الأغصان، متشبثًا بها بقوة.

This vision of the hairy man was tied closely to the deep call.

كانت رؤية الرجل المشعر مرتبطة ارتباطًا وثيقًا بالدعوة العميقة.

The call still sounded through the forest with haunting force.

لا يزال النداء يتردد في الغابة بقوة مخيفة.

The call filled Buck with longing and a restless sense of joy.

لقد ملأت المكالمة باك بالشوق والشعور المضطرب بالفرح.

He felt strange urges and stirrings that he could not name.

كان يشعر برغبات وتحركات غريبة لم يستطع تسميتها.

Sometimes he followed the call deep into the quiet woods.

وفي بعض الأحيان كان يتبع النداء إلى أعماق الغابة الهادئة.

He searched for the calling, barking softly or sharply as he went.

كان يبحث عن النداء، وينبح بهدوء أو بحدة أثناء سيره.

He sniffed the moss and black soil where the grasses grew.

كان يشتم الطحالب والتربة السوداء حيث تنمو الأعشاب.

He snorted with delight at the rich smells of the deep earth.

كان يشخر بسعادة عند سماعه الروائح الغنية للأرض العميقة.

He crouched for hours behind trunks covered in fungus.

اختبئ لساعات خلف جذوع الأشجار المغطاة بالفطريات.

He stayed still, listening wide-eyed to every tiny sound.

لقد بقي ساكنًا، يستمع بعينين واسعتين إلى كل صوت صغير.

He may have hoped to surprise the thing that gave the call.

ربما كان يأمل أن يفاجئ الشيء الذي أعطى المكالمة.

He did not know why he acted this way—he simply did.

لم يكن يعلم لماذا يتصرف بهذه الطريقة، لقد فعل ذلك ببساطة.

The urges came from deep within, beyond thought or reason.

جاءت الرغبات من أعماقنا، بعيدًا عن الفكر والعقل.

Irresistible urges took hold of Buck without warning or reason.

سيطرت رغبات لا تقاوم على باك دون سابق إنذار أو سبب.

At times he was dozing lazily in camp under the midday heat.

في بعض الأحيان كان ينام ببطء في المخيم تحت حرارة منتصف النهار.

Suddenly, his head lifted and his ears shoot up alert.

فجأة، رفع رأسه وارتفعت أذنيه في حالة تأهب.

Then he sprang up and dash into the wild without pause.

ثم قفز وانطلق إلى البرية دون توقف.

He ran for hours through forest paths and open spaces.

ركض لساعات عبر مسارات الغابات والمساحات المفتوحة.

He loved to follow dry creek beds and spy on birds in the trees.

كان يحب متابعة مجاري الأنهار الجافة والتجسس على الطيور في الأشجار.

He could lie hidden all day, watching partridges strut around.

كان بإمكانه البقاء مختبئًا طوال اليوم، وهو يراقب طيور الحجل وهي تتبختر حوله.

They drummed and marched, unaware of Buck's still presence.

لقد طبلوا وساروا، غير مدركين لوجود باك.

But what he loved most was running at twilight in summer.

لكن ما كان يحبه أكثر من أي شيء آخر هو الجري عند الغسق في الصيف.

The dim light and sleepy forest sounds filled him with joy.

كان الضوء الخافت وأصوات الغابة النائمة تملأه بالفرح.

He read the forest signs as clearly as a man reads a book.

كان يقرأ علامات الغابة بوضوح كما يقرأ الرجل كتابًا.

And he searched always for the strange thing that called him.

وكان يبحث دائمًا عن الشيء الغريب الذي يناديه.

That calling never stopped—it reached him waking or sleeping.

لم يتوقف هذا النداء أبدًا ـ فقد وصل إليه وهو مستيقظ أو نائم.

One night, he woke with a start, eyes sharp and ears high.

في إحدى الليالي، استيقظ مذعوراً، وكانت عيناه حادتين وأذناه مرتفعتين.

His nostrils twitched as his mane stood bristling in waves.

ارتعش أنفه بينما وقف شعره منتصبا في الأمواج.

From deep in the forest came the sound again, the old call.

من أعماق الغابة جاء الصوت مرة أخرى، النداء القديم.

This time the sound rang clearly, a long, haunting, familiar howl.

هذه المرة كان الصوت واضحاً، عواء طويل، مخيف، مألوف.

It was like a husky's cry, but strange and wild in tone.

لقد كان مثل صراخ كلب الهاسكي، ولكن غريب ومتوحش في نبرته.

Buck knew the sound at once—he had heard the exact sound long ago.

عرف باك الصوت على الفور ـ لقد سمع الصوت بالضبط منذ زمن طويل.

He leapt through camp and vanished swiftly into the woods.

قفز عبر المخيم واختفى بسرعة في الغابة.

As he neared the sound, he slowed and moved with care.

وعندما اقترب من الصوت، أبطأ وتحرك بحذر.

Soon he reached a clearing between thick pine trees.

وسرعان ما وصل إلى فسحة بين أشجار الصنوبر الكثيفة.

There, upright on its haunches, sat a tall, lean timber wolf.

هناك، جلس ذئب خشبي طويل ونحيف على ركبتيه.

The wolf's nose pointed skyward, still echoing the call.

أشار أنف الذئب نحو السماء، ولا يزال يردد النداء.

Buck had made no sound, yet the wolf stopped and listened.

لم يصدر باك أي صوت، ومع ذلك توقف الذئب واستمع.

Sensing something, the wolf tensed, searching the darkness.

عندما شعر الذئب بشيء ما، توتر، باحثًا في الظلام.

Buck crept into view, body low, feet quiet on the ground.

تسلل باك إلى المشهد، وكان جسده منخفضًا وقدميه هادئتين على الأرض.

His tail was straight, his body coiled tight with tension.

كان ذيله مستقيماً، وجسمه ملتفًا بإحكام بسبب التوتر.

He showed both threat and a kind of rough friendship.

لقد أظهر التهديد ونوعًا من الصداقة القاسية.

It was the wary greeting shared by beasts of the wild.

لقد كانت هذه التحية الحذرة التي يتبادلها الوحوش البرية.

But the wolf turned and fled as soon as it saw Buck.

لكن الذئب استدار وهرب بمجرد أن رأى باك.

Buck gave chase, leaping wildly, eager to overtake it.

طارده باك، وقفز بعنف، راغبًا في تجاوزه.

He followed the wolf into a dry creek blocked by a timber jam.

تبع الذئب إلى جدول جاف مسدود بكتلة من الخشب.

Cornered, the wolf spun around and stood its ground.

عندما حوصر الذئب، استدار ووقف في مكانه.

The wolf snarled and snapped like a trapped husky dog in a fight.

زأر الذئب وانفجر مثل كلب أجش محاصر في قتال.

The wolf's teeth clicked fast, its body bristling with wild fury.

نقرت أسنان الذئب بسرعة، وكان جسده مليئًا بالغضب الجامح.

Buck did not attack but circled the wolf with careful friendliness.

لم يهاجم باك الذئب بل دار حوله بحذر وود.

He tried to block his escape by slow, harmless movements.

حاول منع هروبه بحركات بطيئة وغير ضارة.

The wolf was wary and scared—Buck outweighed him three times.

كان الذئب حذرًا وخائفًا ـ فقد كان وزن باك يفوق وزنه بثلاث مرات.

The wolf's head barely reached up to Buck's massive shoulder.

بالكاد وصل رأس الذئب إلى كتف باك الضخم.

Watching for a gap, the wolf bolted and the chase began again.

وبينما كان الذئب يراقب الفجوة، انطلق مسرعًا وبدأ المطاردة مرة أخرى.

Several times Buck cornered him, and the dance repeated.

عدة مرات حاصره باك، وتكررت الرقصة.

The wolf was thin and weak, or Buck could not have caught him.

كان الذئب نحيفًا وضعيفًا، وإلا لما استطاع باك أن يمسكه.

Each time Buck drew near, the wolf spun and faced him in fear.

في كل مرة يقترب باك، يدور الذئب ويواجهه في خوف.

Then at the first chance, he dashed off into the woods once more.

ثم في أول فرصة، اندفع إلى الغابة مرة أخرى.

But Buck did not give up, and finally the wolf came to trust him.

ولكن باك لم يستسلم، وأخيرًا جاء الذئب ليثق به.

He sniffed Buck's nose, and the two grew playful and alert.

شمّ أنف باك، وأصبح الاثنان مرحين ومتيقظين.

They played like wild animals, fierce yet shy in their joy.

لقد لعبوا مثل الحيوانات البرية، شرسين ولكن خجولين في فرحهم.

After a while, the wolf trotted off with calm purpose.

وبعد فترة من الوقت، هرع الذئب بعيدًا بهدوء.

He clearly showed Buck that he meant to be followed.

لقد أظهر لباك بوضوح أنه يقصد أن يتم اتباعه.

They ran side by side through the twilight gloom.

لقد ركضوا جنبًا إلى جنب في ظلام الشفق.

They followed the creek bed up into the rocky gorge.

ثم تبعوا مجرى النهر حتى وصلوا إلى الوادي الصخري.

They crossed a cold divide where the stream had begun.

لقد عبروا مضيقًا باردًا حيث بدأ التيار.

On the far slope they found wide forest and many streams.

وعلى المنحدر البعيد وجدوا غابة واسعة والعديد من الجداول.

Through this vast land, they ran for hours without stopping.

عبر هذه الأرض الشاسعة، ركضوا لساعات دون توقف.

The sun rose higher, the air grew warm, but they ran on.

ارتفعت الشمس، وأصبح الهواء دافئًا، لكنهم واصلوا الركض.

Buck was filled with joy—he knew he was answering his calling.

كان باك مليئًا بالفرح ـ لقد علم أنه يجيب على نداءه.

He ran beside his forest brother, closer to the call's source.

ركض بجانب أخيه في الغابة، أقرب إلى مصدر المكالمة.

Old feelings returned, powerful and hard to ignore.

عادت المشاعر القديمة، قوية ويصعب تجاهلها.

These were the truths behind the memories from his dreams.

كانت هذه هي الحقائق وراء ذكريات أحلامه.

He had done all this before in a distant and shadowy world.

لقد فعل كل هذا من قبل في عالم بعيد ومظلم.

Now he did this again, running wild with the open sky above.

والآن فعل ذلك مرة أخرى، وهو يركض في جنون مع السماء المفتوحة أعلاه.

They stopped at a stream to drink from the cold flowing water.

توقفوا عند مجرى مائي ليشربوا من الماء البارد المتدفق.

As he drank, Buck suddenly remembered John Thornton.

وبينما كان يشرب، تذكر باك فجأة جون ثورنتون.

He sat down in silence, torn by the pull of loyalty and the calling.

جلس في صمت، ممزقًا بين جاذبية الولاء والدعوة.

The wolf trotted on, but came back to urge Buck forward.

ركض الذئب، لكنه عاد ليحث باك على المضي قدمًا.

He sniffed his nose and tried to coax him with soft gestures.

شمّ أنفه وحاول إقناعه بإيماءات ناعمة.

But Buck turned around and started back the way he came.

لكن باك استدار وبدأ العودة من حيث أتى.

The wolf ran beside him for a long time, whining quietly.

ركض الذئب بجانبه لفترة طويلة، وهو يئن بهدوء.

Then he sat down, raised his nose, and let out a long howl.

ثم جلس ورفع أنفه وأطلق عواءً طويلاً.

It was a mournful cry, softening as Buck walked away.

لقد كانت صرخة حزينة، خففت عندما ابتعد باك.

Buck listened as the sound of the cry faded slowly into the forest silence.

استمع باك إلى صوت الصراخ وهو يتلاشى ببطء في صمت الغابة.

John Thornton was eating dinner when Buck burst into the camp.

كان جون ثورنتون يتناول العشاء عندما اقتحم باك المخيم.

Buck leapt upon him wildly, licking, biting, and tumbling him.

قفز باك عليه بعنف، يلعقه، ويعضه، ويسقطه أرضًا.

He knocked him over, scrambled on top, and kissed his face.

لقد دفعه أرضًا، وتسلق فوقه، وقبل وجهه.

Thornton called this "playing the general tom-fool" with affection.

أطلق ثورنتون على هذا الأمر اسم "اللعب بدور الأحمق العام" بمودة.

All the while, he cursed Buck gently and shook him back and forth.

في هذه الأثناء، كان يلعن باك بلطف ويهزه ذهابًا وإيابًا.

For two whole days and nights, Buck never left the camp once.

لمدة يومين وليلتين كاملتين، لم يغادر باك المخيم مرة واحدة.

He kept close to Thornton and never let him out of his sight.

لقد ظل قريبًا من ثورنتون ولم يتركه بعيدًا عن نظره أبدًا.

He followed him as he worked and watched him while he ate.

كان يتبعه أثناء عمله ويراقبه أثناء تناوله الطعام.

He saw Thornton into his blankets at night and out each morning.

لقد رأى ثورنتون في بطانياته في الليل وخارجه كل صباح.

But soon the forest call returned, louder than ever before.

ولكن سرعان ما عاد نداء الغابة، وكان أعلى من أي وقت مضى.

Buck grew restless again, stirred by thoughts of the wild wolf.

أصبح باك مضطربًا مرة أخرى، وقد تحركت أفكاره حول الذئب البري.

He remembered the open land and running side by side.

تذكر الأرض المفتوحة والجري جنبًا إلى جنب.

He began wandering into the forest once more, alone and alert.

بدأ يتجول في الغابة مرة أخرى، وحيدًا ويقظًا.

But the wild brother did not return, and the howl was not heard.

ولكن الأخ البري لم يعود، ولم يسمع العواء.

Buck started sleeping outside, staying away for days at a time.

بدأ باك في النوم بالخارج، والبقاء بعيدًا لعدة أيام في كل مرة.

Once he crossed the high divide where the creek had begun.

وبمجرد عبوره للتقسيم المرتفع حيث بدأ الخور.

He entered the land of dark timber and wide flowing streams.

دخل إلى أرض الأشجار المظلمة والجداول المتدفقة الواسعة.

For a week he roamed, searching for signs of the wild brother.

تجول لمدة أسبوع، باحثًا عن علامات الأخ البري.

He killed his own meat and travelled with long, tireless strides.

كان يذبح لحمه بنفسه ويسافر بخطوات طويلة لا تعرف الكلل.

He fished for salmon in a wide river that reached the sea.

كان يصطاد سمك السلمون في نهر واسع يصل إلى البحر.

There, he fought and killed a black bear maddened by bugs.

هناك، قاتل وقتل دبًا أسودًا غاضبًا من الحشرات.

The bear had been fishing and ran blindly through the trees.

كان الدب يصطاد السمك ويركض بشكل أعمى بين الأشجار.

The battle was a fierce one, waking Buck's deep fighting spirit up.

كانت المعركة شرسة، مما أيقظ روح القتال العميقة لدى باك.

Two days later, Buck returned to find wolverines at his kill.

بعد يومين، عاد باك ليجد حيوان الوشق في مكان صيده.

A dozen of them quarreled over the meat in noisy fury.

تشاجر نحو عشرة منهم على اللحوم بغضب شديد.

Buck charged and scattered them like leaves in the wind.

هاجمهم باك وشتتهم مثل الأوراق في الريح.

Two wolves remained behind—silent, lifeless, and unmoving forever.

بقي ذئبان خلفنا - صامتين، بلا حياة، ولا حركة إلى الأبد.

The thirst for blood grew stronger than ever.

لقد أصبح التعطش للدماء أقوى من أي وقت مضى.

Buck was a hunter, a killer, feeding off living creatures.

كان باك صيادًا وقاتلًا، يتغذى على الكائنات الحية.

He survived alone, relying on his strength and sharp senses.

لقد نجا وحيدًا، معتمدًا على قوته وحواسه الحادة.

He thrived in the wild, where only the toughest could live.

لقد ازدهر في البرية، حيث لا يمكن أن يعيش إلا الأقوى.

From this, a great pride rose up and filled Buck's whole being.

ومن هنا ارتفع كبرياء عظيم وملأ كيان باك بأكمله.

His pride showed in his every step, in the ripple of every muscle.

كان فخره يظهر في كل خطوة، وفي تموج كل عضلة.

His pride was as clear as speech, seen in how he carried himself.

كان كبرياؤه واضحا مثل الكلام، ويتجلى ذلك في الطريقة التي يحمل بها نفسه.

Even his thick coat looked more majestic and gleamed brighter.

حتى معطفه السميك بدا أكثر روعة وألمع إشراقا.

Buck could have been mistaken for a giant timber wolf.

ربما كان من الممكن الخلط بين باك وذئب الخشب العملاق.

Except for brown on his muzzle and spots above his eyes.

باستثناء اللون البني على وجهه والبقع فوق عينيه.

And the white streak of fur that ran down the middle of his chest.

والخط الأبيض مَن الفراء الذي يمتد على طول منتصف صدره.

He was even larger than the biggest wolf of that fierce breed.

لقد كان أكبر من أكبر ذئب من هذا الصنف الشرس.

His father, a St. Bernard, gave him size and heavy frame.

أعطاه والده، وهو من فصيلة سانت برنارد، حجمًا وجسمًا ثقيلًا.

His mother, a shepherd, shaped that bulk into wolf-like form.

قامت أمه، وهي راعية، بتشكيل هذا الجسم الضخم على شكل ذئب.

He had the long muzzle of a wolf, though heavier and broader.

كان لديه كمامة طويلة مثل كمامة الذئب، على الرغم من أنها أثقل وأوسع.

His head was a wolf's, but built on a massive, majestic scale.

كان رأسه مثل رأس ذئب، لكنه مبني على نطاق ضخم ومهيب.

Buck's cunning was the cunning of the wolf and of the wild.

كان مكر باك بمثابة مكر الذئب والبرية.

His intelligence came from both the German Shepherd and St. Bernard.

لقد جاء ذكاؤه من الراعي الألماني والقديس برنارد.

All this, plus harsh experience, made him a fearsome creature.

كل هذا، بالإضافة إلى التجربة القاسية، جعله مخلوقًا مخيفًا.

He was as formidable as any beast that roamed the northern wild.

لقد كان هائلاً مثل أي وحش يجوب البرية الشمالية.

Living only on meat, Buck reached the full peak of his strength.

بفضل اعتماده على اللحوم فقط، وصل باك إلى ذروة قوته.

He overflowed with power and male force in every fiber of him.

لقد فاض بالقوة والقوة الذكورية في كل أليافه.

When Thornton stroked his back, the hairs sparked with energy.

عندما قام ثورنتون بمداعبة ظهره، كانت الشعرات تتألق بالطاقة.

Each hair crackled, charged with the touch of living magnetism.

كانت كل شعرة تتشقق، مشحونة بلمسة من المغناطيسية الحية.

His body and brain were tuned to the finest possible pitch.

لقد تم ضبط جسده وعقله على أعلى درجة ممكنة.

Every nerve, fiber, and muscle worked in perfect harmony.

كل عصب وليفة وعضلة عملت في تناغم تام.

To any sound or sight needing action, he responded instantly.

لقد استجاب على الفور لأي صوت أو مشهد يحتاج إلى عمل.

If a husky leaped to attack, Buck could leap twice as fast.

إذا قفز الهاسكي للهجوم، يمكن لباك أن يقفز بسرعة مضاعفة.

He reacted quicker than others could even see or hear.

لقد كان رد فعله أسرع مما يمكن للآخرين رؤيته أو سماعه.

Perception, decision, and action all came in one fluid moment.

الإدراك، والقرار، والفعل، كل ذلك جاء في لحظة واحدة سلسة.

In truth, these acts were separate, but too fast to notice.

في الحقيقة، كانت هذه الأفعال منفصلة، ولكنها كانت سريعة جدًا بحيث لم يتم ملاحظتها.

So brief were the gaps between these acts, they seemed as one.

كانت الفجوات بين هذه الأفعال قصيرة جدًا، حتى أنها بدت وكأنها فعل واحد.

His muscles and being was like tightly coiled springs.

كانت عضلاته وكيانه مثل الينابيع الملفوفة بإحكام.

His body surged with life, wild and joyful in its power.

كان جسده مليئا بالحياة، جامحا ومبهجا في قوته.

At times he felt like the force was going to burst out of him entirely.

في بعض الأحيان كان يشعر وكأن القوة ستخرج منه بالكامل.

"Never was there such a dog," Thornton said one quiet day.

"لم يكن هناك قط كلب مثله"، قال ثورنتون في أحد الأيام الهادئة.

The partners watched Buck striding proudly from the camp.

كان الشركاء يراقبون باك وهو يخرج بفخر من المخيم.

"When he was made, he changed what a dog can be," said Pete.

"عندما تم صنعه، غيّر ما يمكن أن يكون عليه الكلب"، قال بيت.

"By Jesus! I think so myself," Hans quickly agreed.

"يا إلهي! أعتقد ذلك بنفسي"، وافق هانز بسرعة.

They saw him march off, but not the change that came after.

لقد رأوه يبتعد، ولكنهم لم يروا التغيير الذي حدث بعد ذلك.

As soon as he entered the woods, Buck transformed completely.

بمجرد دخوله الغابة، تحول باك بشكل كامل.

He no longer marched, but moved like a wild ghost among trees.

لم يعد يسير، بل كان يتحرك مثل شبح بري بين الأشجار.

He became silent, cat-footed, a flicker passing through shadows.

أصبح صامتًا، يتحرك كالقط، وميض يمر عبر الظلال.

He used cover with skill, crawling on his belly like a snake.

لقد استخدم الغطاء بمهارة، وكان يزحف على بطنه مثل الثعبان.

And like a snake, he could leap forward and strike in silence.

ومثل الثعبان، كان بإمكانه أن يقفز إلى الأمام ويضرب في صمت.

He could steal a ptarmigan straight from its hidden nest.

كان بإمكانه سرقة طائر الطيهوج مباشرة من عشه المخفي.

He killed sleeping rabbits without a single sound.

لقد قتل الأرانب النائمة دون أن يصدر صوتًا واحدًا.

He could catch chipmunks midair as they fled too slowly.

كان بإمكانه اصطياد السناجب في الهواء لأنها كانت تهرب ببطء شديد.

Even fish in pools could not escape his sudden strikes.

حتى الأسماك في البرك لم تستطع النجاة من ضرباته المفاجئة.

Not even clever beavers fixing dams were safe from him.

حتى القنادس الذكية التي تعمل على إصلاح السدود لم تكن في مأمن منه.

He killed for food, not for fun—but liked his own kills best.

كان يقتل من أجل الغذاء، وليس من أجل المتعة، لكنه كان يحب أن يقتل بنفسه أكثر.

Still, a sly humor ran through some of his silent hunts.

ومع ذلك، كان هناك روح الدعابة الماكرة في بعض رحلات الصيد الصامتة التي قام بها.

He crept up close to squirrels, only to let them escape.

لقد تسلل إلى جانب السناجب، فقط ليسمح لهم بالهروب.

They were going to flee to the trees, chattering in fearful outrage.

كانوا في طريقهم للفرار إلى الأشجار، وهم يتحادثون بغضب مخيف.

As fall came, moose began to appear in greater numbers.

مع حلول فصل الخريف، بدأ ظهور الموظ بأعداد أكبر.

They moved slowly into the low valleys to meet the winter.

انتقلوا ببطء إلى الوديان المنخفضة لمواجهة الشتاء.

Buck had already brought down one young, stray calf.

كان باك قد أحضر بالفعل عجلًا صغيرًا ضالًا.

But he longed to face larger, more dangerous prey.

ولكنه كان يتوق لمواجهة فريسة أكبر وأكثر خطورة.

One day on the divide, at the creek's head, he found his chance.

ذات يوم، على التقسيم، عند رأس الخور، وجد فرصته.

A herd of twenty moose had crossed from forested lands.

لقد عبر قطيع مكون من عشرين موسًا من الأراضي الحرجية.

Among them was a mighty bull; the leader of the group.

وكان من بينهم ثور عظيم، زعيم المجموعة.

The bull stood over six feet tall and looked fierce and wild.

كان الثور يبلغ طوله أكثر من ستة أقدام ويبدو شرسًا ووحشيًا.

He tossed his wide antlers, fourteen points branching outward.

ألقى بقرونه العريضة، التي تتفرع منها أربعة عشر نقطة نحو الخارج.

The tips of those antlers stretched seven feet across.

امتدت أطراف تلك القرون إلى مسافة سبعة أقدام.

His small eyes burned with rage as he spotted Buck nearby.

اشتعلت عيناه الصغيرة بالغضب عندما رأى باك في مكان قريب.

He let out a furious roar, trembling with fury and pain.

أطلق هديرًا غاضبًا، يرتجف من الغضب والألم.

An arrow-end stuck out near his flank, feathered and sharp.

برزت نهاية السهم بالقرب من جنبه، وكانت ريشية وحادة.

This wound helped explain his savage, bitter mood.

ساعد هذا الجرح في تفسير مزاجه الوحشي والمرير.

Buck, guided by ancient hunting instinct, made his move.

لقد قام باك، مسترشدًا بغريزة الصيد القديمة، بالتحرك.

He aimed to separate the bull from the rest of the herd.

وكان هدفه فصل الثور عن باقي القطيع.

This was no easy task—it took speed and fierce cunning.

لم تكن هذه مهمة سهلة، بل تطلبت السرعة والدهاء الشديد.

He barked and danced near the bull, just out of range.

نبح ورقص بالقرب من الثور، خارج نطاقه.

The moose lunged with huge hooves and deadly antlers.

انقض الموظ بحوافر ضخمة وقرون مميتة.

One blow could have ended Buck's life in a heartbeat.

ضربة واحدة كانت كفيلة بإنهاء حياة باك في لحظة.

Unable to leave the threat behind, the bull grew mad.

لم يتمكن الثور من ترك التهديد خلفه، فغضب بشدة.

He charged in fury, but Buck always slipped away.

لقد هاجم بغضب، لكن باك كان دائمًا يفلت من العقاب.

Buck faked weakness, luring him farther from the herd.

تظاهر باك بالضعف، وأغراه بالابتعاد عن القطيع.

But young bulls were going to charge back to protect the leader.

لكن الثيران الصغيرة كانت على وشك الهجوم لحماية الزعيم.

They forced Buck to retreat and the bull to rejoin the group.

أجبروا باك على التراجع والثور على الانضمام إلى المجموعة.

There is a patience in the wild, deep and unstoppable.

هناك صبر في البرية، عميق ولا يمكن إيقافه.

A spider waits motionless in its web for countless hours.

يظل العنكبوت ينتظر بلا حراك في شبكته لساعات لا حصر لها.

A snake coils without twitching, and waits till it is time.

الثعبان يتلوى دون أن يرتعش، وينتظر حتى يحين الوقت.

A panther lies in ambush, until the moment arrives.

النمر يكمن في الكمين، حتى تأتي اللحظة.

This is the patience of predators who hunt to survive.

هذا هو صبر الحيوانات المفترسة التي تصطاد من أجل البقاء.

That same patience burned inside Buck as he stayed close.

كان نفس الصبر يحترق داخل باك وهو يبقى قريبًا.

He stayed near the herd, slowing its march and stirring fear.

وبقي بالقرب من القطيع، يبطئ مسيرته ويثير الخوف فيه.

He teased the young bulls and harassed the mother cows.

لقد أزعج الثيران الصغيرة وأزعج الأبقار الأمهات.

He drove the wounded bull into a deeper, helpless rage.

لقد دفع الثور الجريح إلى غضب أعمق وعاجز.

For half a day, the fight dragged on with no rest at all.

لمدة نصف يوم، استمر القتال دون أي راحة على الإطلاق.

Buck attacked from every angle, fast and fierce as wind.

هاجم باك من كل زاوية، بسرعة وعنيفة مثل الريح.

He kept the bull from resting or hiding with its herd.

لقد منع الثور من الراحة أو الاختباء مع قطيعه.

Buck wore down the moose's will faster than its body.

لقد أنهك باك إرادة الموظ أسرع من جسده.

The day passed and the sun sank low in the northwest sky.

مر اليوم وغابت الشمس في السماء الشمالية الغربية.

The young bulls returned more slowly to help their leader.

عاد الثيران الصغار ببطء أكثر لمساعدة زعيمهم.

Fall nights had returned, and darkness now lasted six hours.

عادت ليالي الخريف، واستمر الظلام الآن لمدة ست ساعات.

Winter was pressing them downhill into safer, warmer valleys.

كان الشتاء يدفعهم إلى أسفل التل نحو وديان أكثر أمانًا ودفئًا.

But still they couldn't escape the hunter that held them back.

لكنهم لم يتمكنوا من الهروب من الصياد الذي كان يحتجزهم.

Only one life was at stake—not the herd's, just their leader's.

كانت حياة واحدة فقط على المحك ـ ليست حياة القطيع، بل حياة زعيمهم فقط.

That made the threat distant and not their urgent concern.

وهذا ما جعل التهديد بعيدًا وليس مصدر قلقهم العاجل.

In time, they accepted this cost and let Buck take the old bull.

وبمرور الوقت، تقبلوا هذه التكلفة وسمحوا لباك بأخذ الثور القديم.

As twilight settled in, the old bull stood with his head down.

وعندما حل الشفق، وقف الثور العجوز ورأسه إلى أسفل.

He watched the herd he had led vanish into the fading light.

لقد شاهد القطيع الذي قاده يختفي في الضوء الخافت.

There were cows he had known, calves he had once fathered.

كانت هناك أبقار كان يعرفها، وعجول كان والده في السابق.

There were younger bulls he had fought and ruled in past seasons.

كان هناك ثيران أصغر سناً حاربها وحكمها في المواسم الماضية.

He could not follow them—for before him crouched Buck again.

لم يكن بوسعه أن يتبعهم، لأن باك كان يجلس القرفصاء أمامه مرة أخرى.

The merciless fanged terror blocked every path he might take.

لقد سدت أنياب الرعب التي لا ترحم كل طريق قد يسلكه.

The bull weighed more than three hundredweight of dense power.

كان وزن الثور أكثر من ثلاثمائة رطل من القوة الكثيفة.

He had lived long and fought hard in a world of struggle.

لقد عاش طويلاً وقاتل بشدة في عالم من النضال.

Yet now, at the end, death came from a beast far beneath him.

ولكن الآن، في النهاية، جاء الموت من وحش بعيد تحته.

Buck's head did not even rise to the bull's huge knuckled knees.

لم يرتفع رأس باك حتى إلى ركبتي الثور الضخمتين.

From that moment on, Buck stayed with the bull night and day.

منذ تلك اللحظة، بقي باك مع الثور ليلًا ونهارًا.

He never gave him rest, never allowed him to graze or drink.

لم يمنحه الراحة أبدًا، ولم يسمح له بالرعي أو الشرب.

The bull tried to eat young birch shoots and willow leaves.

حاول الثور أن يأكل براعم البتولا الصغيرة وأوراق الصفصاف.

But Buck drove him off, always alert and always attacking.

لكن باك أبعده بعيدًا، وكان دائمًا متيقظًا ومهاجمًا.

Even at trickling streams, Buck blocked every thirsty attempt.

حتى في الجداول المتساقطة، حجب باك كل محاولة عطشى.

Sometimes, in desperation, the bull fled at full speed.

في بعض الأحيان، في حالة اليأس، كان الثور يهرب بأقصى سرعة.

Buck let him run, loping calmly just behind, never far away.

تركه باك يركض، وكان يركض بهدوء خلفه مباشرة، ولم يكن بعيدًا عنه أبدًا.

When the moose paused, Buck lay down, but stayed ready.
عندما توقف الموظ، استلقى باك، لكنه بقي مستعدًا.

If the bull tried to eat or drink, Buck struck with full fury.
إذا حاول الثور أن يأكل أو يشرب، كان باك يضربه بكل غضبه.

The bull's great head sagged lower under its vast antlers.
انحنى رأس الثور الكبير إلى أسفل تحت قرونه الضخمة.

His pace slowed, the trot became a heavy; a stumbling walk.
تباطأت خطواته، وأصبح الهرولة ثقيلة، ومشية متعثرة.

He often stood still with drooped ears and nose to the ground.
كان يقف في كثير من الأحيان ساكنًا، وأذنيه متدليتان وأنفه على الأرض.

During those moments, Buck took time to drink and rest.
خلال تلك اللحظات، أخذ باك بعض الوقت للشرب والراحة.

Tongue out, eyes fixed, Buck sensed the land was changing.
أخرج لسانه، وثبت عينيه، وشعر باك أن الأرض كانت تتغير.

He felt something new moving through the forest and sky.
شعر بشيء جديد يتحرك عبر الغابة والسماء.

As moose returned, so did other creatures of the wild.
مع عودة الموظ، عادت معه بقية المخلوقات البرية.

The land felt alive with presence, unseen but strongly known.
كانت الأرض مليئة بالحياة والحضور، غير مرئي ولكن معروف بقوة.

It was not by sound, sight, nor by scent that Buck knew this.
لم يكن باك يعرف ذلك عن طريق الصوت أو البصر أو الرائحة.

A deeper sense told him that new forces were on the move.
أخبره إحساس أعمق أن قوى جديدة كانت تتحرك.

Strange life stirred through the woods and along the streams.
كانت هناك حياة غريبة تتحرك في الغابات وعلى طول الجداول.

He resolved to explore this spirit, after the hunt was complete.
قرر استكشاف هذه الروح، بعد انتهاء الصيد.

On the fourth day, Buck brought down the moose at last.
في اليوم الرابع، تمكن باك أخيرًا من اصطياد الموظ.

He stayed by the kill for a full day and night, feeding and resting.

بقي بالقرب من الفريسة لمدة يوم كامل وليلة كاملة، يتغذى ويستريح.

He ate, then slept, then ate again, until he was strong and full.

أكل ثم نام ثم أكل مرة أخرى حتى شبع وقوي.

When he was ready, he turned back toward camp and Thornton.

عندما أصبح مستعدًا، عاد إلى المخيم وثورنتون.

With steady pace, he began the long return journey home.

بخطى ثابتة، بدأ رحلة العودة الطويلة إلى المنزل.

He ran in his tireless lope, hour after hour, never once straying.

كان يركض بلا كلل، ساعة بعد ساعة، دون أن يضل طريقه ولو مرة واحدة.

Through unknown lands, he moved straight as a compass needle.

عبر الأراضي المجهولة، تحرك بشكل مستقيم مثل إبرة البوصلة.

His sense of direction made man and map seem weak by comparison.

إن إحساسه بالاتجاهات جعل الإنسان والخريطة يبدوان ضعيفين بالمقارنة.

As Buck ran, he felt more strongly the stir in the wild land.

وبينما كان باك يركض، شعر بقوة أكبر بالضجة في الأرض البرية.

It was a new kind of life, unlike that of the calm summer months.

لقد كانت حياة جديدة، مختلفة عن حياة أشهر الصيف الهادئة.

This feeling no longer came as a subtle or distant message.

لم يعد هذا الشعور يأتي كرسالة خفية أو بعيدة.

Now the birds spoke of this life, and squirrels chattered about it.

والآن تحدثت الطيور عن هذه الحياة، وتحدثت السناجب عنها.

Even the breeze whispered warnings through the silent trees.

حتى النسيم كان يهمس بالتحذيرات من خلال الأشجار الصامتة.

Several times he stopped and sniffed the fresh morning air.

توقف عدة مرات واستنشق هواء الصباح النقي.

He read a message there that made him leap forward faster.

قرأ هناك رسالة جعلته يقفز للأمام بشكل أسرع.

A heavy sense of danger filled him, as if something had gone wrong.

كان يشعر بخطر شديد، وكأن شيئًا ما قد حدث خطأ.

He feared calamity was coming—or had already come.

كان يخشى أن تكون الكارثة قادمة ـ أو أنها جاءت بالفعل.

He crossed the last ridge and entered the valley below.

عبر التلال الأخيرة ودخل الوادي أدناه.

He moved more slowly, alert and cautious with every step.

كان يتحرك ببطء أكثر، ويقظًا وحذرًا مع كل خطوة.

Three miles out he found a fresh trail that made him stiffen.

على بعد ثلاثة أميال وجد مسارًا جديدًا جعله متيبسًا.

The hair along his neck rippled and bristled in alarm.

كان شعر رقبته يتجعد ويشعر بالانزعاج.

The trail led straight toward the camp where Thornton waited.

كان الطريق يؤدي مباشرة إلى المخيم حيث كان ثورنتون ينتظر.

Buck moved faster now, his stride both silent and swift.

تحرك باك بشكل أسرع الآن، وكانت خطواته صامتة وسريعة.

His nerves tightened as he read signs others were going to miss.

توترت أعصابه عندما قرأ العلامات التي كان من الممكن أن يغفلها الآخرون.

Each detail in the trail told a story—except the final piece.

كل تفصيل في المسار كان يحكي قصة، باستثناء القطعة الأخيرة.

His nose told him about the life that had passed this way.

أخبره أنفه عن الحياة التي مرت بهذه الطريقة.

The scent gave him a changing picture as he followed close behind.

أعطته الرائحة صورة متغيرة عندما تبعه عن كثب.

But the forest itself had gone quiet; unnaturally still.

لكن الغابة نفسها أصبحت هادئة، ساكنة بشكل غير طبيعي.

Birds had vanished, squirrels were hidden, silent and still.

اختفت الطيور، واختفت السناجب، صامتة وساكنة.

He saw only one gray squirrel, flat on a dead tree.

لقد رأى سنجابًا رماديًا واحدًا فقط، مستلقيًا على شجرة ميتة.

The squirrel blended in, stiff and motionless like a part of the forest.

اندمج السنجاب، جامدًا وثابتًا مثل جزء من الغابة.

Buck moved like a shadow, silent and sure through the trees.

تحرك باك مثل الظل، صامتًا ومتأكدًا من خلال الأشجار.

His nose jerked sideways as if pulled by an unseen hand.

تحرك أنفه إلى الجانب كما لو كان يتم سحبه بواسطة يد غير مرئية.

He turned and followed the new scent deep into a thicket.

استدار وتبع الرائحة الجديدة في أعماق الغابة.

There he found Nig, lying dead, pierced through by an arrow.

وهناك وجد نيج ملقىً ميتًا، وقد اخترق سهمٌ جسده.

The shaft passed clear through his body, feathers still showing.

لقد مر من العمود من خلال جسده، والريش لا يزال يظهر.

Nig had dragged himself there, but died before reaching help.

سحب نيج نفسه إلى هناك، لكنه مات قبل أن يصل إلى المساعدة.

A hundred yards farther on, Buck found another sled dog.

على بعد مائة ياردة، وجد باك كلب زلاجة آخر.

It was a dog that Thornton had bought back in Dawson City.

كان هذا كلبًا اشتراه ثورنتون في داوسون سيتي.

The dog was in a death struggle, thrashing hard on the trail.

كان الكلب في صراع مميت، يضرب بقوة على الطريق.

Buck passed around him, not stopping, eyes fixed ahead.

مر باك حوله، دون توقف، وكانت عيناه مثبتتين للأمام.

From the direction of the camp came a distant, rhythmic chant.

ومن جهة المخيم جاءت ترنيمة بعيدة إيقاعية.

Voices rose and fell in a strange, eerie, sing-song tone.

ارتفعت الأصوات وانخفضت بنبرة غريبة ومرعبة وغنائية.

Buck crawled forward to the edge of the clearing in silence.

زحف باك إلى الأمام نحو حافة المقاصة في صمت.

There he saw Hans lying face-down, pierced with many arrows.

هناك رأى هانز ملقى على وجهه، وقد اخترقته العديد من السهام.

His body looked like a porcupine, bristling with feathered shafts.

كان جسده يبدو مثل القنفذ، ممتلئًا بالريش.

At the same moment, Buck looked toward the ruined lodge.

وفي نفس اللحظة، نظر باك نحو النزل المدمر.

The sight made the hair rise stiff on his neck and shoulders.

أدى هذا المنظر إلى تصلب شعر رقبته وكتفيه.

A storm of wild rage swept through Buck's whole body.

اجتاحت عاصفة من الغضب الجامح جسد باك بأكمله.

He growled aloud, though he did not know that he had.

لقد هدر بصوت عالٍ، على الرغم من أنه لم يكن يعلم أنه فعل ذلك.

The sound was raw, filled with terrifying, savage fury.

كان الصوت خامًا، مليئًا بالغضب المرعب والوحشي.

For the last time in his life, Buck lost reason to emotion.

للمرة الأخيرة في حياته، فقد باك عقله أمام العاطفة.

It was love for John Thornton that broke his careful control.

لقد كان حب جون ثورنتون هو الذي كسر سيطرته الدقيقة.

The Yeehats were dancing around the wrecked spruce lodge.

كان أفراد عائلة ييهات يرقصون حول كوخ التنوب المدمر.

Then came a roar—and an unknown beast charged toward them.

ثم جاء هدير - وهاجمهم وحش مجهول.

It was Buck; a fury in motion; a living storm of vengeance.

لقد كان باك؛ غضبًا في الحركة؛ عاصفة حية من الانتقام.

He flung himself into their midst, mad with the need to kill.

ألقى بنفسه في وسطهم، مجنونًا بالحاجة إلى القتل.

He leapt at the first man, the Yeehat chief, and struck true.

قفز على الرجل الأول، رئيس الييهات، وضربه في مكانه.

His throat was ripped open, and blood spouted in a stream.

لقد تمزق حلقه، وتدفق الدم على شكل جدول.

Buck did not stop, but tore the next man's throat with one leap.

لم يتوقف باك، بل مزق حلق الرجل التالي بقفزة واحدة.

He was unstoppable—ripping, slashing, never pausing to rest.

لقد كان لا يمكن إيقافه - يمزق، ويقطع، ولا يتوقف أبدًا للراحة.

He darted and sprang so fast their arrows could not touch him.

لقد انطلق بسرعة كبيرة لدرجة أن سهامهم لم تستطع أن تلمسه.

The Yeehats were caught in their own panic and confusion.

لقد وقع آل ييهات في حالة من الذعر والارتباك.

Their arrows missed Buck and struck one another instead.

لقد أخطأت سهامهم باك وضربت بعضها البعض بدلا من ذلك.

One youth threw a spear at Buck and hit another man.

ألقى أحد الشباب رمحًا على باك وأصاب رجلاً آخر.

The spear drove through his chest, the point punching out his back.

انطلق الرمح عبر صدره، وضربت النقطة ظهره.

Terror swept over the Yeehats, and they broke into full retreat.

سيطر الرعب على أهل ييهات، مما دفعهم إلى التراجع الكامل.

They screamed of the Evil Spirit and fled into the forest shadows.

صرخوا من الروح الشريرة وهربوا إلى ظلال الغابة.

Truly, Buck was like a demon as he chased the Yeehats down.

في الحقيقة، كان باك مثل الشيطان عندما طارد عائلة ييهات.

He tore after them through the forest, bringing them down like deer.

انطلق وراءهم عبر الغابة، وأسقطهم مثل الغزلان.

It became a day of fate and terror for the frightened Yeehats.

لقد أصبح يومًا من القدر والرعب لليهات الخائفين.

They scattered across the land, fleeing far in every direction.

وتفرقوا في جميع أنحاء الأرض، وهربوا في كل اتجاه.

A full week passed before the last survivors met in a valley.

لقد مر أسبوع كامل قبل أن يلتقي آخر الناجين في الوادي.

Only then did they count their losses and speak of what happened.

حينها فقط بدأوا يحسبون خسائرهم ويتحدثون عما حدث.

Buck, after tiring of the chase, returned to the ruined camp.

بعد أن سئم باك من المطاردة، عاد إلى المخيم المدمر.

He found Pete, still in his blankets, killed in the first attack.

ووجد بيت، وهو لا يزال في بطانيته، مقتولاً في الهجوم الأول.

Signs of Thornton's last struggle were marked in the dirt nearby.

كانت علامات كفاح ثورنتون الأخير واضحة على التراب القريب.

Buck followed every trace, sniffing each mark to a final point.

تبع باك كل أثر، واستنشق كل علامة حتى وصل إلى النقطة النهائية.

At the edge of a deep pool, he found faithful Skeet, lying still.

وعلى حافة بركة عميقة، وجد سكيت المؤمن مستلقياً في صمت.

Skeet's head and front paws were in the water, unmoving in death.

كان رأس سكيت ومخالبه الأمامية في الماء، بلا حراك في الموت.

The pool was muddy and tainted with runoff from the sluice boxes.

كان المسبح موحلًا وملوثًا بالمياه المتدفقة من صناديق الصرف.

Its cloudy surface hid what lay beneath, but Buck knew the truth.

لقد أخفى سطحها الغائم ما كان تحته، لكن باك عرف الحقيقة.

He tracked Thornton's scent into the pool—but the scent led nowhere else.

لقد تتبع رائحة ثورنتون إلى المسبح ـ لكن الرائحة لم تقود إلى أي مكان آخر.

There was no scent leading out—only the silence of deep water.

لم تكن هناك رائحة تؤدي إلى الخارج ـ فقط صمت المياه العميقة.

All day Buck stayed near the pool, pacing the camp in grief.

بقي باك طوال اليوم بالقرب من المسبح، يتجول في المخيم في حزن.

He wandered restlessly or sat in stillness, lost in heavy thought.

كان يتجول بلا راحة أو يجلس في صمت، غارقًا في أفكار ثقيلة.

He knew death; the ending of life; the vanishing of all motion.

لقد عرف الموت، ونهاية الحياة، واختفاء كل حركة.

He understood that John Thornton was gone, never to return.

لقد فهم أن جون ثورنتون قد رحل ولن يعود أبدًا.

The loss left an empty space in him that throbbed like hunger.

لقد تركت الخسارة فراغًا في داخله ينبض مثل الجوع.

But this was a hunger food could not ease, no matter how much he ate.

لكن هذا الجوع كان طعامًا لا يستطيع إشباعه، بغض النظر عن كمية الطعام التي تناولها.

At times, as he looked at the dead Yeehats, the pain faded.

في بعض الأحيان، عندما كان ينظر إلى ييهات الميتة، كان الألم يتلاشى.

And then a strange pride rose inside him, fierce and complete.

ثم ارتفع في داخله كبرياء غريب، شرس وكامل.

He had killed man, the highest and most dangerous game of all.

لقد قتل الإنسان، اللعبة الأعلى والأخطر على الإطلاق.

He had killed in defiance of the ancient law of club and fang.

لقد قتل متحديًا القانون القديم للهراوة والأنياب.

Buck sniffed their lifeless bodies, curious and thoughtful.

استنشق باك أجسادهم الخالية من الحياة، فضوليًا ومدروسًا.

They had died so easily—much easier than a husky in a fight.

لقد ماتوا بسهولة ـ أسهل بكثير من موت كلب الهاسكي في قتال.

Without their weapons, they had no true strength or threat.

بدون أسلحتهم، لم تكن لديهم أي قوة أو تهديد حقيقي.

Buck was never going to fear them again, unless they were armed.

لن يخاف باك منهم مرة أخرى، إلا إذا كانوا مسلحين.

Only when they carried clubs, spears, or arrows he'd beware.

فقط عندما يحملون الهراوات أو الرماح أو السهام كان يحذر.

Night fell, and a full moon rose high above the tops of the trees.

حل الليل، وارتفع القمر عالياً فوق قمم الأشجار.

The moon's pale light bathed the land in a soft, ghostly glow like day.

غمر ضوء القمر الخافت الأرض بوهج ناعم يشبه النهار.

As the night deepened, Buck still mourned by the silent pool.

ومع تعمق الليل، كان باك لا يزال حزينًا بجانب المسبح الصامت.

Then he became aware of a different stirring in the forest.

ثم أدرك أن هناك تحركًا مختلفًا في الغابة.

The stirring was not from the Yeehats, but from something older and deeper.

لم يكن التحريك من ييهات، ولكن من شيء أقدم وأعمق.

He stood up, ears lifted, nose testing the breeze with care.

وقف، وأذنيه مرفوعتين، وأنفه يختبر النسيم بعناية.

From far away came a faint, sharp yelp that pierced the silence.

من بعيد جاء صوت خافت حاد يخترق الصمت.

Then a chorus of similar cries followed close behind the first.

ثم تبعتها جوقة من الصيحات المشابهة مباشرة خلف الصيحة الأولى.

The sound drew nearer, growing louder with each passing moment.

كان الصوت يقترب أكثر فأكثر، ويزداد قوة مع كل لحظة تمر.

Buck knew this cry—it came from that other world in his memory.

عرف باك هذه الصرخة ـ لقد جاءت من ذلك العالم الآخر في ذاكرته.

He walked to the center of the open space and listened closely.

توجه إلى وسط المساحة المفتوحة واستمع باهتمام.

The call rang out, many-noted and more powerful than ever.

لقد دوى النداء، وكان كثير الأصوات وأقوى من أي وقت مضى.

And now, more than ever before, Buck was ready to answer his calling.

والآن، أكثر من أي وقت مضى، أصبح باك مستعدًا للإجابة على نداءه.

John Thornton was dead, and no tie to man remained within him.

لقد مات جون ثورنتون، ولم يبق في داخله أي رابط إنساني.

Man and all human claims were gone—he was free at last.

لقد ذهب الإنسان وكل المطالبات الإنسانية ـ لقد أصبح حرا في النهاية.

The wolf pack were chasing meat like the Yeehats once had.

كانت مجموعة الذئاب تطارد اللحوم مثلما كان يفعل ييهات ذات يوم.

They had followed moose down from the timbered lands.

لقد تبعوا الموظ من الأراضي المشجرة.

Now, wild and hungry for prey, they crossed into his valley.

والآن، وهم متوحشون وجائعون للفريسة، عبروا إلى الوادي.

Into the moonlit clearing they came, flowing like silver water.

لقد جاءوا إلى المقاصة المضاءة بالقمر، يتدفقون مثل الماء الفضي.

Buck stood still in the center, motionless and waiting for them.

كان باك واقفا في الوسط، بلا حراك، وينتظرهم.

His calm, large presence stunned the pack into a brief silence.

لقد أذهل حضوره الهادئ والكبير المجموعة في صمت قصير.

Then the boldest wolf leapt straight at him without hesitation.

ثم قفز الذئب الأكثر جرأة نحوه مباشرة دون تردد.

Buck struck fast and broke the wolf's neck in a single blow.

ضرب باك بسرعة وكسر رقبة الذئب بضربة واحدة.

He stood motionless again as the dying wolf twisted behind him.

لقد وقف بلا حراك مرة أخرى بينما كان الذئب المحتضر يتلوى خلفه.

Three more wolves attacked quickly, one after the other.

هاجمت ثلاثة ذئاب أخرى بسرعة، واحدًا تلو الآخر.

Each retreated bleeding, their throats or shoulders slashed.

تراجع كل منهم ينزف، وكان حنجرته أو كتفه مقطوعة.

That was enough to trigger the whole pack into a wild charge.

كان ذلك كافيا لتحريك العبوة بأكملها إلى هجوم بري.

They rushed in together, too eager and crowded to strike well.

لقد اندفعوا معًا، وكانوا متلهفين للغاية ومزدحمين لدرجة أنهم لم يتمكنوا من الضرب بشكل جيد.

Buck's speed and skill allowed him to stay ahead of the attack.

سمحت سرعة باك ومهارته له بالبقاء في صدارة الهجوم.

He spun on his hind legs, snapping and striking in all directions.

لقد دار على رجليه الخلفيتين، وكان يلتقط ويضرب في جميع الاتجاهات.

To the wolves, this seemed like his defense never opened or faltered.

بالنسبة للذئاب، بدا الأمر كما لو أن دفاعه لم يفتح أو يتعثر أبدًا.

He turned and slashed so quickly they could not get behind him.

استدار وضرب بسرعة كبيرة حتى أنهم لم يتمكنوا من الوصول خلفه.

Nonetheless, their numbers forced him to give ground and fall back.

ومع ذلك، فإن أعدادهم أجبرته على التراجع والتراجع.

He moved past the pool and down into the rocky creek bed.

انتقل عبر المسبح إلى أسفل مجرى النهر الصخري.

There he came up against a steep bank of gravel and dirt.

وهناك واجه ضفة شديدة الانحدار من الحصى والأوساخ.

He edged into a corner cut during the miners' old digging.

لقد اصطدم بقطع الزاوية أثناء الحفر القديم الذي قام به عمال المناجم.

Now, protected on three sides, Buck faced only the front wolf.

الآن، أصبح باك محميًا من ثلاث جهات، ولم يواجه سوى الذئب الأمامي.

There, he stood at bay, ready for the next wave of assault.

هناك، وقف في مكانه، مستعدًا للموجة التالية من الهجوم.

Buck held his ground so fiercely that the wolves drew back.

لقد تمسك باك بموقفه بشراسة لدرجة أن الذئاب تراجعت.

After half an hour, they were worn out and visibly defeated.

وبعد مرور نصف ساعة، كانوا مرهقين وواضح عليهم الهزيمة.

Their tongues hung out, their white fangs gleamed in moonlight.

كانت ألسنتهم معلقة، وأنيابهم البيضاء تلمع في ضوء القمر.

Some wolves lay down, heads raised, ears pricked toward Buck.

استلقى بعض الذئاب، ورؤوسهم مرفوعة، وآذانهم منتصبة تجاه باك.

Others stood still, alert and watching his every move.

وكان الآخرون واقفين في مكانهم، متيقظين ويراقبون كل تحركاته.

A few wandered to the pool and lapped up cold water.

توجه عدد قليل منهم إلى المسبح وشربوا الماء البارد.

Then one long, lean gray wolf crept forward in a gentle way.

ثم زحف ذئب رمادي طويل ونحيف إلى الأمام بطريقة لطيفة.

Buck recognized him—it was the wild brother from before.

تعرف عليه باك ـ لقد كان الأخ البري من قبل.

The gray wolf whined softly, and Buck replied with a whine.

أطلق الذئب الرمادي أنينًا خفيفًا، ورد باك بأنين.

They touched noses, quietly and without threat or fear.

لقد تلامسوا أنوفهم بهدوء ومن دون تهديد أو خوف.

Next came an older wolf, gaunt and scarred from many battles.

وبعد ذلك جاء ذئب أكبر سنًا، نحيفًا ومُصابًا بندوب نتيجة معارك عديدة.

Buck started to snarl, but paused and sniffed the old wolf's nose.

بدأ باك في الهدير، لكنه توقف واستنشق أنف الذئب العجوز.

The old one sat down, raised his nose, and howled at the moon.

جلس الرجل العجوز، ورفع أنفه، وعوى على القمر.

The rest of the pack sat down and joined in the long howl.

جلس بقية القطيع وانضموا إلى العواء الطويل.

And now the call came to Buck, unmistakable and strong.

والآن جاء النداء إلى باك، لا لبس فيه وقوية.

He sat down, lifted his head, and howled with the others.

جلس ورفع رأسه وعوى مع الآخرين.

When the howling ended, Buck stepped out of his rocky shelter.

عندما انتهى العواء، خرج باك من ملجأه الصخري.

The pack closed in around him, sniffing both kindly and warily.

أحاطت به المجموعة، وهي تشم رائحته بلطف وحذر.

Then the leaders gave the yelp and dashed off into the forest.

ثم أطلق القادة صرخة عالية وانطلقوا إلى الغابة.

The other wolves followed, yelping in chorus, wild and fast in the night.

وتبعه الذئاب الأخرى، وهم ينبحون في جوقة، وحشيين وسريعين في الليل.

Buck ran with them, beside his wild brother, howling as he ran.

ركض باك معهم، بجانب أخيه البري، وهو يعوي أثناء ركضه.

Here, the story of Buck does well to come to its end.

وهنا تصل قصة باك إلى نهايتها.

In the years that followed, the Yeehats noticed strange wolves.

وفي السنوات التي تلت ذلك، لاحظ البيهات ذئابًا غريبة.

Some had brown on their heads and muzzles, white on the chest.

وكان بعضهم بني اللون على رؤوسهم وخطمهم، وأبيض اللون على صدورهم.

But even more, they feared a ghostly figure among the wolves.

ولكن أكثر من ذلك، كانوا يخافون من وجود شخصية شبحية بين الذئاب.

They spoke in whispers of the Ghost Dog, leader of the pack.

لقد تحدثوا همسًا عن الكلب الشبح، زعيم المجموعة.

This Ghost Dog had more cunning than the boldest Yeehat hunter.

كان هذا الكلب الشبح أكثر دهاءً من صياد بيهات الأكثر جرأة.

The ghost dog stole from camps in deep winter and tore their traps apart.

سرق الكلب الشبح من المخيمات في الشتاء القارس ومزق مصائدهم.

The ghost dog killed their dogs and escaped their arrows without a trace.

قتل الكلب الشبح كلابهم ونجا من سهامهم دون أن يترك أثرا.

Even their bravest warriors feared to face this wild spirit.

حتى محاربيهم الأكثر شجاعة كانوا يخافون من مواجهة هذه الروح البرية.

No, the tale grows darker still, as the years pass in the wild.

لا، فالقصة تصبح أكثر ظلمة مع مرور السنين في البرية.

Some hunters vanish and never return to their distant camps.

يختفي بعض الصيادين ولا يعودون أبدًا إلى معسكراتهم البعيدة.

Others are found with their throats torn open, slain in the snow.

وقد تم العثور على آخرين وقد تمزقت حناجرهم، مقتولين في الثلج.

Around their bodies are tracks—larger than any wolf could make.

حول أجسادهم آثار أقدام أكبر من تلك التي يمكن لأي ذئب أن يتركها.

Each autumn, Yeehats follow the trail of the moose.

في كل خريف، يتبع بيهات أثر الموظ.

But they avoid one valley with fear carved deep into their hearts.

لكنهم يتجنبون واديًا واحدًا بسبب الخوف المحفور عميقًا في قلوبهم.

They say the valley is chosen by the Evil Spirit for his home.

يقال أن الروح الشريرة اختارت الوادي ليكون موطنها.

And when the tale is told, some women weep beside the fire.

وعندما تُحكى الحكاية، تبكي بعض النساء بجانب النار.

But in summer, one visitor comes to that quiet, sacred valley.

ولكن في الصيف، يأتي زائر واحد إلى هذا الوادي الهادئ المقدس.

The Yeehats do not know of him, nor could they understand.

لا يعرفه أهل بيهات، ولا يستطيعون أن يفهموه.

The wolf is a great one, coated in glory, like no other of his kind.

الذئب عظيم، مغطى بالمجد، لا يشبه أي شخص آخر من نوعه.

He alone crosses from green timber and enters the forest glade.

يعبر وحده من الغابة الخضراء ويدخل إلى فسحات الغابة.

There, golden dust from moose-hide sacks seeps into the soil.

هناك، يتسرب الغبار الذهبي من أكياس جلد الموظ إلى التربة.

Grass and old leaves have hidden the yellow from the sun.

لقد أخفى العشب والأوراق القديمة اللون الأصفر من الشمس.

Here, the wolf stands in silence, thinking and remembering.

وهنا يقف الذئب في صمت، يفكر ويتذكر.

He howls once—long and mournful—before he turns to go.

يصرخ مرة واحدة - طويلًا وحزينًا - قبل أن يستدير ليذهب.

Yet he is not always alone in the land of cold and snow.

ولكنه ليس وحيدًا دائمًا في أرض البرد والثلوج.

When long winter nights descend on the lower valleys.

عندما تهبط ليالي الشتاء الطويلة على الوديان السفلية.

When the wolves follow game through moonlight and frost.

عندما تتبع الذئاب الطرائد عبر ضوء القمر والصقيع.

Then he runs at the head of the pack, leaping high and wild.

ثم يركض نحو رأس المجموعة، ويقفز عالياً وبجنون.

His shape towers over the others, his throat alive with song.

شكله يرتفع فوق الآخرين، وحلقه ينبض بالحياة مع الأغنية.

It is the song of the younger world, the voice of the pack.

إنها أغنية العالم الأصغر، صوت القطيع.

He sings as he runs—strong, free, and forever wild.

إنه يغني أثناء ركضه ـ قويًا، حرًا، ومتوحشًا إلى الأبد.

www.tranzlaty.com

www.ingramcontent.com/pod-product-compliance
Lightning Source LLC
Chambersburg PA
CBHW011734020426
42333CB00024B/2887